# Praise for HOLD ON TO YOUR KIDS

## NATIONAL BESTSELLER

"A must-read for anyone with children."
— *Ottawa Citizen*

"Thoughtful, gentle, adaptive parenting."
— *Calgary Herald*

"Though this is Neufeld's personal theory, Maté (*Scattered Minds, When the Body Says No*) has expressed his colleague's ideas in precise and hard-hitting prose that makes complex ideas accessible without dumbing them down. The result is a book that grabs hard, with the potential to hit many parents where they live."
— *Edmonton Journal*

"A wonderful book and a powerful wake-up call to parents. The authors' description of how peer orientation gets in the way of healthy emotional maturation is both striking and sobering. But the book is also upbeat, as it emphasizes the extreme importance of attachment in child raising and how it can get implemented day to day. I found the book both thoughtful and thought provoking. It is a wise and important book."
—Anthony Wolf, clinical psychologist and author of *Get Out of My Life, but First Could You Drive Me & Cheryl to the Mall?: A Parent's Guide to the New Teenager*

"*Hold On to Your Kids* is a visionary book that goes beyond the usual explanations to illuminate a crisis of unrecognized proportions. The authors show us how we are losing contact with our children and how this loss undermines their development and threatens the very fabric of society. Most importantly they offer, through concrete examples and clear suggestions, practical help for parents to fulfill their instinctual roles. A brilliant and well-written book, one to be taken seriously, very seriously."
—Peter A. Levine Ph.D., international teacher and author of the bestselling books *Waking the Tiger, Healing Trauma* and *It Won't Hurt Forever: Guiding Your Child through Trauma*

"With the benefit of thirty years of research and experience, Neufeld has crafted a coherent, compelling theory of child development that will cause an immediate frisson of recognition and acceptance in its readers. His approach has the power to change, if not save, the lives of our children."
—*National Post*

"This important book boldly states the problem and maps out plans for its solution. Let us take its suggestions seriously now so that together we can improve the future for our children and their children as well."
—Daniel J. Siegel, M.D., author of *The Developing Mind* and *Parenting from the Inside Out;* founding member of UCLA's Center for Culture, Brain and Development; and Associate Clinical Professor of Psychiatry, UCLA

"This book represents a great step forward in grasping the sorrow and suffering that our kids are experiencing. Gordon Neufeld locates this suffering in the child's loss of attachment to parents and a deepening attachment to his peers. Neufeld's mind is powerful, capable of understanding where our culture is going. This is a brilliant book on the level of Paul Goodman's *Growing Up Absurd.* Give a copy of this book to every parent you know."
—Robert Bly, poet and author of *The Sibling Society* and *Iron John*

"The thoughts and perspectives presented by the authors are informative— even inspirational—for those who choose to dedicate their lives and energy to students."
—*National Association of Secondary School Principals Bulletin*

"Here is an important new book on parenting. . . . The concepts, principles and practical advice will empower parents."
—*Life Learning Magazine*

"The authors present doable strategies to help parents help their kids. If their advice is taken to heart, there's hope there will be more warmth and security all round."
—*The Georgia Straight*

# HOLD ON TO YOUR KIDS

## WHY PARENTS NEED TO MATTER
## MORE THAN PEERS

### GORDON NEUFELD, PH.D.,
### AND GABOR MATÉ, M.D.

VINTAGE CANADA

Published in Canada by Vintage Canada, a division of Random House of Canada
Limited, Toronto, and simultaneously by Ballantine Books, a division of
Random House, Inc., New York. Originally published in hardcover in 2004 by Alfred
A. Knopf Canada, a division of Random House of Canada Limited. Distributed in
Canada by Random House of Canada Limited, Toronto.

Vintage Canada and colophon are registered trademarks of
Random House of Canada Limited.

www.randomhouse.ca

National Library of Canada Cataloguing in Publication

Neufeld, Gordon, 1946–
Hold on to your kids : why parents need to matter more than peers / Gordon Neufeld
and Gabor Maté.

ISBN 978-0-676-97472-0

1. Parenting. 2. Peer pressure in children. I. Maté, Gabor II. Title.

HQ755.8.N477 2005      649'.1      C2004-902709-3

Text design by Jo Anne Metsch

Printed and bound in the United States of America

11  13  15  17  18  16  14  12

*We dedicate this book*
*to our children*
*as well as the present and future*
*children of our children.*

⁓

*They have inspired these insights*
*and have given us good reason to articulate them.*

⁓

*Tamara, Natasha, Bria, Shay, and Braden*
*&*
*Daniel, Aaron, and Hannah*
*&*
*Kiara, Julian, and Sinead*

Action has meaning only in relationship and without understanding relationship, action on any level will only breed conflict. The understanding of relationship is infinitely more important than the search for any plan of action.

J. KRISHNAMURTI

# NOTE TO THE READER

GORDON NEUFELD and I have known each other for many years, having first met when my wife, Rae, and I turned to him for advice with our oldest child. Our son was then eight years old. We thought we had a problem kid on our hands. Gordon showed us, in short order, that there was no problem with the child or with ourselves, only with our approach to our relationship with him. A few years later we became concerned when our second son, as a young adolescent, no longer seemed to accept our authority or even want our company. Again, we consulted Gordon, whose response was that we had to woo this son back into a relationship with us, away from his peers. That is when I first learned of Dr. Neufeld's concept of peer orientation, of peers having replaced parents as the primary influence on children and of the many negative consequences of this shift, endemic in modern society. I have had many reasons to be grateful ever since for the insights Rae and I then acquired.

Gordon and I have written *Hold On to Your Kids* with the radical intent of reawakening people's natural parenting instincts. If our book succeeds in that purpose, it will stand on its head much of what is currently perceived as wisdom about how children ought to be reared and educated. Our focus is not on what parents should do but on who they need to be for their children. We offer here an understanding of the child, of child development, and, also, of the impediments that today stand in the way of the healthy development of our children. From that understanding and from the heartfelt commitment parents bring to the task of child-rearing will arise the spontaneous and compassionate wisdom that is the source of successful parenting.

The modern obsession with parenting as a set of skills to be followed along lines recommended by experts is, really, the result of lost intuitions and of a lost relationship with children previous generations could take for granted. That is what parenthood is, a relationship. Biology or marriage or adoption may appoint us to take on that relationship, but only a two-way connection with our child can secure it. When our parenthood is secure, natural instincts are activated that dictate far more astutely than any expert how to nurture and teach the young ones under our care. The secret is to honor our relationship with our children in all of our interactions with them.

In today's world, for reasons we will make clear, parenthood is being undermined. We face much insidious competition that would draw our children away from us while, simultaneously, we are drawn away from parenthood. We no longer have the economic and social basis for a culture that would support parenthood and hold its mission sacred. If previous cultures could assume that the attachment of children to their parents was firm and lasting, we do not have that luxury. As modern parents, we have to become conscious of what is missing, of why and how things are not working in the parenting and education of our children and adolescents. That awareness will prepare us for the challenge of creating a relationship with our children in which we, the caregiving adults, are back in the lead, free from relying on coercion and artificial consequences to gain our children's cooperation, compliance, and respect. It is in their relationship with us that our children will reach their developmental destiny of becoming independent, self-motivated, and mature beings valuing their own self-worth and mindful of the feelings, rights, and human dignity of others.

*Hold On to Your Kids* is divided into five parts. The first explains what peer orientation is and how it has come to be such a pervasive dynamic in our culture. The second and third parts detail the many negative impacts of peer orientation, respectively, on our ability to parent and on our children's development. Also in these first three parts, the outlines of healthy child development are etched, in contrast to the perverse development fostered by the peer culture. The fourth part offers a program for building a lasting bond with our children, a relationship that will serve as a safe cocoon for their maturation. The fifth and final part explains how to prevent the seduction of our children by the peer world.

Dr. Neufeld's background and experience as a psychologist and his brilliantly original work are the source of the central thesis we present and the advice we offer. In that sense he is the sole author. Many of the thousands of parents and educators attending Gordon's seminars over the decades have asked him, with some impatience, "When is your book coming out?" That the preparation and publication of *Hold On to Your Kids* no longer has to be deferred to some future time is my contribution. The planning, writing, and shaping of the book have been our joint labor.

I am proud to help bring Gordon Neufeld's transformative ideas to a much broader public. That is long overdue and we both feel grateful to have established a friendship and working partnership that has made the creation of this book possible. We hope—and more, we have the confidence to believe—that the reader will also find ours to have been a fortunate collaboration.

We wish also to acknowledge our two editors, Diane Martin in Toronto and Susanna Porter in New York. Diane saw the possibilities in this work from its inception and has supported it warmly throughout. Susanna patiently and expertly worked her way through a somewhat turgid and lumbering manuscript and, with her deft suggestions, helped ease our way to preparing a lighter and better organized version in which our message comes across with greater clarity. The result is a book that readers will find more congenial and certainly the authors are happier with.

Gabor Maté, M.D.

# ACKNOWLEDGMENTS

SEVEN PEOPLE provided indispensable, practical, hands-on assistance in the formation and preparation of this book: Gail Carney, Christine Dearing, Sheldon Klein, Joy Neufeld, Kate Taschereau, Suzanne Walker, and Elaine Wynne. Collectively, they became known as the Tuesday Evening Group. They met with us weekly, from the earliest writing to the final submission of the manuscript. They deliberated, debated, and critiqued first the concepts to be presented and then, chapter by chapter, the work-in-progress that became *Hold On to Your Kids*. The group was committed to bringing our message into print in a way that respected the intent of the book and, at the same time, the needs and sensibilities of the reader. We, the two authors, came to look forward to these spirited and fruitful meetings and experienced a sense of loss and regret when the completion of the manuscript also brought our regular gatherings to an end. We gratefully acknowledge our debt to the Tuesday Evening Group: without their dedicated support our task would have been heavier and our result less satisfying.

# CONTENTS

# PART ONE

# THE PHENOMENON OF PEER ORIENTATION

# WHY PARENTS MATTER
# MORE THAN EVER

TWELVE-YEAR-OLD Jeremy is hunched over the keyboard, his eyes intent on the computer monitor. It's eight o'clock in the evening and tomorrow's homework is far from complete but his father's repeated admonishments to "get on with it" fall on deaf ears. Jeremy is on MSN Messenger, exchanging notes with his friends: gossip about who likes whom, sorting out who is a buddy and who an enemy, disputes over who said what to whom at school that day, the latest on who is hot and who is not. "Stop bugging me," he snaps at his father who, one more time, comes to remind him about schoolwork. "If you were doing what you're supposed to," the father shoots back, his tone shaking with frustration, "I wouldn't be bugging you." The verbal battle escalates, the voices grow strident, and in a few moments Jeremy yells "You don't understand anything," as he slams the door.

The father is upset, angry with Jeremy but, above all, with himself. "I blew it again," he thinks. "I don't know how to communicate with my son." He and his wife are both concerned about Jeremy: once a cooperative child, he is now impossible to control or even to advise. His attention seems focused exclusively on contact with his friends. This same scenario of conflict is acted out in the home several times a week and neither the child nor the parents are able to respond with any new thoughts or actions to break the deadlock. The parents feel helpless and powerless. They have never relied much on punishment, but now they are more and more inclined to "lower the boom." When they do, their son becomes ever more embittered and defiant.

Should parenting be this difficult? Was it always so? Older generations have often in the past complained about the young being less respectful and less disciplined than they used to be, but today many parents intuitively know that something is amiss. Children are not quite the same as we remember being. They are less likely to take their cues from adults, less afraid of getting into trouble. They also seem less innocent and naive — lacking, it seems, the wide-eyed wonder that leads a child to have excitement for the world, for exploring the wonders of nature or of human creativity. Many children seem inappropriately sophisticated, even jaded in some ways, pseudo-mature before their time. They appear to be easily bored when away from each other or when not engaged with technology. Creative, solitary play seems a vestige of the past. "As a child I was endlessly fascinated by the clay I would dig out of a ditch near our home," one forty-four-year-old mother recalls. "I loved the feel of it; I loved molding it into shapes or just kneading it in my hands. And yet, I can't get my six-year-old son to play on his own, unless it's with the computer or Nintendo or video games."

Parenting, too, seems to have changed. Our parents were more confident, more certain of themselves, and had more impact on us, for better or for worse. For many today, parenting does not feel natural.

Today's parents love their children as much as parents ever have, but the love doesn't always get through. We have just as much to teach, but our capacity to get our knowledge across has, somehow, diminished. We do not feel empowered to guide our children toward fulfilling their potential. Sometimes they live and act as if they have been seduced away from us by some siren song we do not hear. We fear, if only vaguely, that the world has become less safe for them and that we are powerless to protect them. The gap opening up between children and adults can seem unbridgeable at times.

We struggle to live up to our image of what parenting ought to be like. Not achieving the results we want, we plead with our children, we cajole, bribe, reward, or punish. We hear ourselves address them in tones that seem harsh even to us and foreign to our true nature. We sense ourselves grow cold in moments of crisis, precisely when we would wish to summon our unconditional love. We feel hurt as parents, and rejected. We blame ourselves for failing at the parenting task, or our children for being recalcitrant, or television for distracting them, or the school system for not being strict enough. When our impotence becomes unbearable we reach for simplistic, authoritarian formulas consistent with the do-it-yourself/quick-fix ethos of our era.

The very importance of parenting to the development and maturation of young human beings has come under question. "Do Parents Matter?" was the title of a cover article in *Newsweek* magazine in 1998. "Parenting has been oversold," argued a book that received international attention that year. "You have been led to believe that you have more of an influence on your child's personality than you really do."[1]

The question of parental influence might not be quite so crucial if things were going well with our young. That our children do not seem to listen to us, or embrace our values as their own, would perhaps be acceptable in itself if they were truly self-sufficient, self-directed, and grounded in themselves, if they had a positive sense of who they are, and if they possessed a clear sense of direction and purpose in life. We see that for so many children and young adults those qualities are lacking. In homes, in schools, in community after community, developing young people have lost their moorings. Many lack self-control and are increasingly prone to alienation, drug use, violence, or just a general aimlessness. They are less teachable and more difficult to manage than their counterparts of even a few decades ago. Many have lost their ability to adapt, to learn from negative experience and to mature. Unprecedented numbers of children and adolescents are now being prescribed medications for depression, anxiety, or a host of other diagnoses. The crisis of the young has manifested itself ominously in the growing problem of bullying in the schools and, at its very extreme, in the murder of children by children. Such tragedies, though rare, are only the most visible eruptions of a widespread malaise, an aggressive streak rife in today's youth culture.

Committed and responsible parents are frustrated. Despite our loving care, kids seem highly stressed. Parents and other elders no longer appear to be the natural mentors for the young, as always used to be the case with human beings and is still the case with all other species living in their natural habitats. Senior generations, parents and grandparents of the baby-boomer group, look at us with incomprehension. "We didn't need how-to manuals on parenting in our days, we just did it," they say, with some mixture of truth and misunderstanding.

This state of affairs is ironic, given that more is known about child development than ever before and that we have more access to courses and books on childrearing than any previous generation of parents.

## THE MISSING CONTEXT FOR PARENTING

So what has changed? The problem, in a word, is *context*. No matter how well intentioned, skilled, or compassionate we may be, parenting is not something we can engage in with just any child. Parenting requires a context to be effective. A child must be receptive if we are to succeed in nurturing, comforting, guiding, and directing her. Children do not automatically grant us the authority to parent them just because we are adults, or just because we love them or think we know what is good for them or have their best interests at heart. Stepparents are often confronted by this fact, as are others who have to look after children not their own, be they foster parents, babysitters, nannies, day-care providers, or teachers. Even with one's own children the natural parenting authority can become lost if the context for it becomes eroded.

If parenting skills or even loving the child are not enough, what then is needed? There is an indispensable special kind of relationship without which parenting lacks a firm foundation. Developmentalists — psychologists or other scientists who study human development — call it an *attachment* relationship. For a child to be open to being parented by an adult, he must be actively attaching to that adult, be wanting contact and closeness with him. At the beginning of life this drive to attach is quite physical — the infant literally clings to the parent and needs to be held. If everything unfolds according to design, the attachment will evolve into an emotional closeness and finally a sense of psychological intimacy. Children who lack this kind of connection with those responsible for them are very difficult to parent or, often, even to teach. Only the attachment relationship can provide the proper context for child-rearing.

The secret of parenting is not in what a parent *does* but rather who the parent *is* to a child. When a child seeks contact and closeness with us, we become empowered as a nurturer, a comforter, a guide, a model, a teacher, or a coach. For a child well attached to us, we are her home base from which to venture into the world, her retreat to fall back to, her fountainhead of inspiration. All the parenting skills in the world cannot compensate for a lack of attachment relationship. All the love in the world cannot get through without the psychological umbilical cord created by the child's attachment.

The attachment relationship of child to parent needs to last at least as long as a child needs to be parented. That is what is becoming more difficult in today's world. Parents haven't changed — they haven't become less competent or less devoted. The fundamental nature of children has also not changed—they haven't become less dependent or more resistant. What has changed is the culture in which we are rearing our children. Children's attachments to parents are no longer getting the support required from culture and society. Even parent-child relationships that at the beginning are powerful and fully nurturing can become undermined as our children move out into a world that no longer appreciates or reinforces the attachment bond. Children are increasingly forming attachments that compete with their parents, with the result that the proper context for parenting is less and less available to us. It is not a lack of love or of parenting know-how but the erosion of the attachment context that makes our parenting ineffective.

## THE IMPACT OF THE PEER CULTURE

The chief and most damaging of the competing attachments that undermine parenting authority and parental love is the increasing bonding of our children with their peers. It is the thesis of this book that the disorder affecting the generations of young children and adolescents now heading toward adulthood is rooted in the lost orientation of children toward the nurturing adults in their lives. Far from seeking to establish yet one more medical-psychological disorder here—the last thing today's bewildered parents need—we are using the word *disorder* in its most basic sense: a disruption of the natural order of things. For the first time in history young people are turning for instruction, modeling, and guidance not to mothers, fathers, teachers, and other responsible adults but to people whom nature never intended to place in a parenting role—their own peers. They are not manageable, teachable, or maturing because they no longer take their cues from adults. Instead, children are being brought up by immature persons who cannot possibly guide them to maturity. They are being brought up by each other.

The term that seems to fit more than any other for this phenomenon is *peer orientation*. It is peer orientation that has muted our parenting instincts, eroded our natural authority, and caused us to parent not from the heart but from the head—from manuals, the advice of "experts," and the confused expectations of society.

What is peer orientation?

Orientation, the drive to get one's bearings and become acquainted with one's surroundings, is a fundamental human instinct and need. Disorientation is one of the least bearable of all psychological experiences. Attachment and orientation are inextricably intertwined. Humans and other creatures automatically orient themselves by seeking cues from those to whom they are attached.

Children, like the young of any warm-blooded species, have an innate orienting instinct: they need to get their sense of direction from somebody. Just as a magnet turns automatically toward the North Pole, so children have an inborn need to find their bearings by turning toward a source of authority, contact, and warmth. Children cannot endure the lack of such a figure in their lives: they become disoriented. They cannot endure what I call an *orientation void.** The parent, or any adult acting as parent substitute, is the nature-intended pole of orientation for the child, just as adults are the orienting influences in the lives of all animals that rear their young.

It so happens that this orienting instinct of humans is much like the imprinting instinct of a duckling. Hatched from the egg, the duckling immediately imprints on the mother duck—he will follow her around, heeding her example and her directions until he grows into mature independence. That is how nature would prefer it, of course. In the absence of the mother duck, however, the duckling will begin to follow the nearest moving object—a human being, a dog, or even a mechanical toy. Needless to say, neither the human, the dog, nor the toy are as well suited as the mother duck to raise that duckling to successful adult duckhood. Likewise, if no parenting adult is available, the human child will orient to whomever is near. Social, economic, and cultural trends in the past five or six decades have displaced the parent from his intended position as the orienting influence on the child. The peer group has moved into this orienting void, with deplorable results.

As we will show, children cannot be oriented to both adults and other children simultaneously. One cannot follow two sets of conflicting directions at the same time. The child's brain must automatically choose between parental values and peer values, parental guidance and peer guidance, parental culture and peer culture whenever the two would appear to be in conflict.

Are we saying that children should have no friends their own age or form connections with other children? On the contrary, such ties are natural and can serve a healthy purpose. In adult-oriented cultures, where the guiding principles and values are those of the more mature genera-

*Unless otherwise noted, the first person singular in this book refers to Gordon Neufeld.

tions, kids attach to each other without losing their bearings or rejecting the guidance of their parents. In our society that is no longer the case. Peer bonds have come to replace relationships with adults as children's primary sources of orientation. What is unnatural is not peer contact, but that children should have become the dominant influence on one another's development.

## NORMAL BUT NOT NATURAL OR HEALTHY

So ubiquitous is peer orientation these days that it has become the norm. Many psychologists and educators, as well as the lay public, have come to see it as natural—or, more commonly, do not even recognize it as a specific phenomenon to be distinguished. It is simply taken for granted as the way things are. But what is "normal," in the sense of conforming to a norm, is not necessarily the same as "natural" or "healthy." There is nothing either healthy or natural about peer orientation. Only recently has this counterrevolution against the natural order triumphed in the most industrially advanced countries, for reasons we will explore (see Chapter 3). Peer orientation is still foreign to indigenous societies and even in many places in the Western world outside the "globalized" urban centers. Throughout human evolution and until about the Second World War, adult orientation was the norm in human development. We, the adults who should be in charge—parents and teachers—have only recently lost our influence without even being aware that we have done so.

Peer orientation masquerades as natural or goes undetected because we have become divorced from our intuitions and because we have unwittingly become peer-oriented ourselves. For members of the postwar generations born in England, North America, and many other parts of the industrialized world, our own preoccupation with peers is blinding us to the seriousness of the problem.

Culture, until recently, was always handed down vertically, from generation to generation. For millennia, wrote Joseph Campbell, "the youth have been educated and the aged rendered wise" through the study, experience, and understanding of traditional cultural forms. Adults played a critical role in the transmission of culture, taking what they received from their own parents and passing it down to their children. However, the culture *our* children are being introduced to is much more likely to be the culture of their peers than that of their parents. Children are generating their own culture, very distinct from that of their parents and, in some ways, also very alien. Instead of culture being passed down vertically, it is being transmitted horizontally within the younger generation.

Essential to any culture are its customs, its music, its dress, its celebrations, its stories. The music children listen to bears very little resemblance to the music of their grandparents. The way they look is dictated by the way other children look rather than by the parents' cultural heritage. Their birthday parties and rites of passage are influenced by the practices of other children around them, not by the customs of their parents before them. If all that seems normal to us, it's only due to our own peer orientation. The existence of a youth culture, separate and distinct from that of adults, dates back only fifty years or so. Although half a century is a relatively short time in the history of humankind, in the life of an individual person it constitutes a whole era. Most readers of this book will already have been raised in a society where the transmission of culture is horizontal rather than vertical. In each new generation this process, potentially corrosive to civilized society, gains new power and velocity. Even in the twenty-two years between my first and my fifth child, it seems that parents have lost ground.

According to a large international study headed by the British child psychiatrist Sir Michael Rutter and criminologist David Smith, a children's culture first emerged after the Second World War and is one of the most dramatic and ominous social phenomena of the twentieth century.[2] This study, which included leading scholars from sixteen countries, linked the escalation of antisocial behavior to the breakdown of the vertical transmission of mainstream culture. Accompanying the rise in a children's culture, distinct and separate from the mainstream culture, were increases in youth crime, violence, bullying, and delinquency.

Such broad cultural trends are paralleled by similar patterns in the development of our children as individuals. Who we want to be and what we want to be like is defined by our orientation, by who we appoint as our model of how to be and how to act—by who we identify with. Current psychological literature emphasizes the role of peers in creating a child's sense of identity.[3] When asked to define themselves, children often do not even refer to their parents but rather to the values and expectations of other children and of the peer groups they belong to. Something significantly systemic has shifted. For far too many children today, peers have replaced parents in creating the core of their personalities.

A few generations ago, all indications were that parents mattered the most. Carl Jung suggested that it is not even so much what happens in the parent-child relationship that has the greatest impact on the child. What is missing in that relationship leaves the greatest scar on the child's personality—or "nothing happening when something might profitably have happened," in the words of the great British child psychiatrist D. W. Winnicott. Scary thought. An even scarier thought is that if peers have replaced adults as the ones who matter most, what is missing in those peer relationships is going to have the most profound impact. Absolutely missing in peer relationships are unconditional love and acceptance, the desire to nurture, the ability to extend oneself for the sake of the other, the willingness to sacrifice for the growth and development of the other. When we compare peer relationships with parent relationships for what is missing, parents come out looking like saints. The results spell disaster for many children.

Paralleling the increase of peer orientation in our society is a startling and dramatic increase in the suicide rate among children, fourfold in the last fifty years for the ten-to-fourteen age range in North America. Suicide rates among that group are the fastest growing with a 120 percent increase from 1980 to 1992 alone. In inner cities, where peers are the most likely to replace parents, these suicide rates have increased even more.[4] What is behind these suicides is highly revealing. Like many students of human development, I had always assumed that parental rejection would be the most significant precipitating factor. That is no longer the case. I worked for a time with young offenders. Part of my job was to investigate the psychological dynamics in children and adolescents who attempted suicide, successfully or not. To my absolute shock and surprise, the key trigger for the great majority was how they were being treated by their peers, not their parents. My experience was not isolated, as is confirmed by the increasing numbers of reports of childhood suicides triggered by peer rejection and bullying. The more peers matter, the more children are devastated by the insensitive relating of their peers, by failing to fit in, by perceived rejection or ostracization.

No society, no culture, is immune. In Japan, for instance, traditional values passed on by elders have succumbed to Westernization and the rise of a youth culture. That country was almost free of delinquency and school problems among its children until very recently but now experiences the most undesirable products of peer orientation, including lawlessness, childhood suicide, and an increasing school drop-out rate. *Harper's* magazine recently published a selection of suicide notes left by Japanese children: most of them gave intolerable bullying by peers as the reason for their decision to take their own lives.[5]

The effects of peer orientation are most obvious in the teenager, but its early signs are visible by the second or third grade. Its origins go back to even before kindergarten and need to be understood by all parents, especially the parents of young children who want to avoid the problem or to reverse it as soon as it appears.

## A WAKE-UP CALL

The first warning came as long as four decades ago. The textbooks I used for teaching my courses in developmental psychology and parent-child relations contained references to an American researcher in the early 1960s who had sounded an alarm that parents were being replaced by peers as the primary source of cues for behavior and of values. In a study of seven thousand young people, Dr. James Coleman discovered that relationships with friends took priority over those with parents. He was concerned that a fundamental shift had occurred in American society.[6] Scholars remained skeptical, however, pointing out that this was Chicago and not mainstream North America. They were optimistic that this finding was probably due to the disruption in society caused by the Second World War and would go away as soon as things got back to normal. The idea of peers becoming the dominant influence on a child came from untypical cases on the fringe of society, maintained his critics. James Coleman's concerns were dismissed as alarmist.

I, too, buried my head in the sand until my own children abruptly disrupted my denial. I had never expected to lose my kids to their peers. To my dismay, I noticed that on reaching adolescence both my older daughters began to orbit around their friends, following their lead, imitating their language, internalizing their values. It became more and more difficult to bring them into line. Everything I did to impose my wishes and expectations only made things worse. It's as if the parental influence my wife and I had taken for granted had all of a sudden evaporated. Sharing our children is one thing, being replaced is quite another. I thought my children were immune: they showed no interest in gangs or delinquency, were brought up in the context of relative stability with an extended family that dearly loved them, lived in a solid family-oriented community, and had not had their childhood disrupted by a major world war. Coleman's findings just did not seem relevant to my family's life. Yet when I started putting the pieces together, I found that what was happening with my children was more typical than exceptional.

"But aren't we meant to let go?" many parents ask. "Aren't our children meant to become independent of us?" Absolutely, but only when our job is done and only in order for them to be themselves. Fitting in with the immature expectations of the peer group is not how the young grow to be independent, self-respecting adults. By weakening the natural lines of attachment and responsibility, peer orientation undermines healthy development.

Children may know what they want, but it is dangerous to assume that they know what they need. To the peer-oriented child it seems only natural to prefer contact with friends to closeness with family, to be with them as much as possible, to be as much like them as possible. A child does not know best. Parenting that takes its cues from the child's preferences can get you retired long before the job is done. To nurture our children, we must reclaim them and take charge of providing for their attachment needs.

Extreme manifestations of peer orientation catch the attention of the media: violent bullying, peer murders, childhood suicides. Although we are all shocked by such dreadful events, most of us do not feel that they concern us directly. And they are not the focus of this book. But such childhood tragedies are only the most dramatic signs of peer orientation, a phenomenon no longer limited to the concrete jungles and cultural chaos of large urbanized centers like Chicago, New York, Toronto, Los Angeles. It has hit the family neighborhoods—the communities characterized by middle-class homes and good schools. The focus of this book is not what is happening out there, one step removed from us, but what's happening in our very own backyard.

For the two authors, our personal wake-up call came with the increasing peer orientation of our own children. We hope *Hold On to Your Kids* can serve as a wake-up call to parents everywhere and to society at large.

## THE GOOD NEWS

We may not be able to reverse the social, cultural, and economic forces driving peer orientation, but there is much we can do in our homes and in our classrooms to keep ourselves from being prematurely replaced. Because culture no longer leads our children in the right direction—toward genuine independence and maturity—parents and other child-rearing adults matter more than ever before.

Nothing less will do than to place the parent-child (and adult-child) relationship back onto its natural foundation. Just as relationship is at the heart of our current parenting and teaching difficulties, it is also at the heart of the solution. Adults who ground their parenting in a solid relationship with the child parent intuitively. They do not have to resort to techniques or manuals but act from understanding and empathy. If we know how to be with our children and who to be for them, we need much less advice on what to do. Practical approaches emerge spontaneously from our own experience once the relationship has been restored.

The good news is that nature is on our side. Our children want to belong to us, even if they don't feel that way, and even if their words or actions seem to signal the opposite. We can reclaim our proper role as their nurturers and mentors. In Part 4 of this book we present a detailed program for keeping our kids close to us until they mature, and for reestablishing the relationship if it has been weakened or lost. There are always things we can do. Although no approach can be guaranteed to work in all circumstances, in my experience there are many, many more successes than failures once parents understand where to focus their efforts. But the cure, as always, depends on the diagnosis. We look first at what is missing and how things have gone awry.

# SKEWED ATTACHMENTS,
# SUBVERTED INSTINCTS

THE PARENTS OF fourteen-year-old Cynthia were confused and distraught. For reasons they could not discern, their daughter's behavior had changed in the past year. She had become rude, secretive, and sometimes hostile. Sullen when around them, she seemed happy and charming when relating to her friends. She was obsessive about her privacy and insistent that her life was none of her parents' business. Her mother and father found it difficult to speak with her without being made to feel intrusive. Their previously loving daughter appeared to be less and less comfortable in their company. Cynthia no longer seemed to enjoy family meals and would excuse herself from the table at the earliest opportunity. It was impossible to sustain any conversation with her. The only time the mother could get her daughter to join her in some shared activity was if she offered to go shopping for clothes. The girl they thought they knew was now an enigma.

In her father's eyes Cynthia's disturbing new stance was purely a behavior problem. He wanted some tips on bringing her into line, having failed with the usual methods of discipline—sanctions, groundings, time-outs. They only led to greater difficulties. For her part, the mother felt exploited by her daughter, even abused. She was at a loss to understand Cynthia's behavior. Did it represent normal teenage rebellion? Were the hormones of adolescence responsible? Should the parents be concerned? How should they react?

The cause of Cynthia's puzzling behavior becomes self-evident only if we picture the same scenario in the adult realm. Imagine that your spouse or lover suddenly begins to act strangely: won't look you in the eye, rejects physical contact, speaks to you irritably in monosyllables, shuns your approaches, and avoids your company. Then imagine that you go to your friends for advice. Would they say to you, "Have you tried a time-out? Have you imposed limits and made clear what your expectations are?" It would be obvious to everyone that, in the context of adult interaction, you're dealing not with a *behavior* problem but a *relationship* problem. And probably the first suspicion to arise would be that your partner was having an affair.

What would seem so clear to us in the adult arena has us befuddled when it occurs between child and parent. Cynthia was entirely preoccupied with her peers. Her single-minded pursuit of contact with them competed with her attachment to her family. It was as if she were having an affair.

The analogy of an affair fits in a number of ways, not the least of them being the feelings of frustration, hurt, rejection, and betrayal experienced by Cynthia's parents. Humans can have many attachments—to work, to family, to friends, to a sports team, a cultural icon, a religion—but we cannot abide competing attachments. In the case of a marriage, when an attachment—any attachment—interferes with and threatens one's closeness and connectedness with a spouse, it will be experienced by that spouse as an affair, in the emotional sense of that word. A man who avoids his wife and obsessively spends time on the Internet will evoke in her emotions of abandonment and jealousy. In our culture, peer relationships have come to compete with children's attachments to adults. Quite innocently but with devastating effects, children are involved in *attachment affairs* with each other.

## WHY WE MUST BECOME
## CONSCIOUS OF ATTACHMENT

What is attachment? Most simply stated, it is a force of attraction pulling two bodies toward each other. Whether in physical, electrical, or chemical form, it is the most powerful force in the universe. We take it for granted every day of our lives. It holds us to the earth and keeps our bodies in one piece. It holds the particles of the atom together and binds the planets in orbit around the sun. It gives the universe its shape.

In the psychological realm, attachment is at the heart of relationships and of social functioning. In the human domain, attachment is the pursuit and preservation of proximity, of closeness and connection: physically, behaviorally, emotionally, and psychologically. As in the material world, it is invisible and yet fundamental to our existence. A family cannot be a family without it. When we ignore its inexorable laws we court trouble.

We are creatures of attachment, whether or not we are aware of it. Ideally, we should not have to become conscious of attachment. We ought to be able to take its forces for granted: like gravity keeping our feet on the ground, like the planets staying in orbit, like our compasses pointing to the magnetic North Pole. One doesn't have to understand attachment or even know that it exists to benefit from its work and its power, just as one doesn't have to understand computers to use them or to know about engines to drive a car. Only when things break down is such knowledge required. It is primarily attachment that orchestrates the instincts of a child as well as of a parent. As long as attachments are working, we can afford to simply follow our instincts—automatically and without thought. When attachments are out of order, our instincts will be, too. Fortunately, we humans can compensate for skewed instincts by increasing our awareness of what has gone awry.

Why must we become conscious of attachment now? Because we no longer live in a world where we can take its work for granted. Economics and culture today no longer provide the context for the natural attachment of children to their nurturing adults. From the point of view of attachment we may truly say that as a society we are living in historically unprecedented times—and in the next chapter we will discuss how the social, economic, and cultural bases for healthy child-parent attachments have become eroded. To find our way back to natural parenting that best serves healthy child development, we need to become fully aware of the attachment dynamic. In a world of increasing cultural turbulence, a consciousness of attachment is probably the most important knowledge a parent could possess. But it is not enough to understand attachment from the outside. We must know it from within. The two ways of knowing—*to know about* and *to experience intimately*—must come together. We must feel attachment in our bones.

Attachment is at the core of our being, but as such it is also far removed from consciousness. In this sense, it is like the brain itself: the deeper into it one goes, the less consciousness one finds. We like to see ourselves as creatures with intellect: *Homo sapiens* we call our species, "man who knows." And yet the thinking part of our brain is only a thin layer, while a much larger part of our cerebral circuitry is devoted to the psychological dynamics that serve attachment. This apparatus, which has been aptly called the "attachment brain," is where our unconscious emotions and instincts reside. We humans share this part of our brain with many other creatures, but we alone have the capacity to become conscious of the attachment process.

In the psychological life of the developing young human being—and for many grown-ups, too, if we're honest about it—attachment is what matters most. For children, it's an absolute need. Unable to function on their own, they must attach to an adult. Physical attachment in the womb is necessary until our offspring are viable enough to be born. Likewise, our children must be attached to us emotionally until they are capable of standing on their own two feet, able to think for themselves and to determine their own direction.

## ATTACHMENT AND ORIENTATION

Closely related to the orienting instinct introduced in the previous chapter, attachment is crucial to parenting, to education, and to the transmission of culture. Like attachment, the orienting instinct is basic to our nature, even if we rarely become conscious of it. In its most concrete and physical form, orienting involves locating oneself in space and time. When we have difficulty doing this, we become anxious. If on waking we are not sure where we are or whether we are still dreaming, locating ourselves in space and time gets top priority. If we get lost while on a hike, we will not pause to admire the flora and fauna, or to assess our life goals, or even to think about supper. Getting our bearings will command all of our attention and consume most of our energy.

Our orienting needs are not just physical. Psychological orientation is just as important in human development. As children grow, they have an increasing need to orient: to have a sense of who they are, of what is real, why things happen, what is good, what things mean. To fail to orient is to suffer disorientation, to be lost psychologically—a state our brains are programmed to do almost anything to avoid. Children are utterly incapable of orienting by themselves. They need help.

Attachment provides that help. The first business of attachment is to create a *compass point* out of the person attached to. As long as the child can find himself in relation to this compass point, he will not feel lost. Instincts activated in the child impel him to keep that working compass point ever close. Attachment enables children to hitch a ride with adults who are, at least in the mind of a child, assumed to be more capable of orienting themselves and finding their way.

What children fear more that anything, including physical harm, is getting lost. To them, being lost means losing contact with their compass point. *Orienting voids*, situations where we find nothing or no one to orient by, are absolutely intolerable to the human brain. Even adults who are relatively self-orienting can feel a bit lost when not in contact with the person in their lives who functions as their working compass point.

If we as adults can experience disorientation when apart from those we are attached to, how much more will children. I still remember how bereft I felt when Mrs. Ackerberg, the first-grade teacher to whom I was very attached, was absent: like a lost soul, cut adrift, aimless.

A parent is by far a child's best compass point — or another adult, like a teacher, who acts as a parent substitute. But who becomes the compass point is a function of attachment. And attachment, as we all know, can be fickle. The crucially important orienting function can be bestowed on someone ill-suited for the task — a child's peers, for example. When a child becomes so attached to her peers that she would rather be with them and be like them, those peers, whether singly or as a group, become that child's working compass point. It will be her peers with whom she will seek closeness. She will look to her peers for cues on how to act, what to wear, how to look, what to say, and what to do. Her peers will become the arbiters of what is good, what is happening, what is important, and even of how she defines herself. That is precisely what had occurred in Cynthia's case: in her emotional universe, her peers had replaced her parents as the center of gravity. She revolved around them — a complete subversion of the natural order of things.

Only recently have the psychological attachment patterns of children been well charted and understood. Absolutely clear is that children were meant to revolve around their parents and the other adults responsible for them, just as the planets revolve around the sun. And yet more and more children are now orbiting around each other.

Far from being qualified to orient anyone else, children are not even capable of self-orienting in any realistic sense of that word. Our children's peers are not the ones we want them to depend on. They are not the ones to give our children a sense of themselves, to point out right from wrong, to distinguish fact from fantasy, to identify what works and what doesn't, and to direct them as to where to go and how to get there.

What do children get from orienting to each other? Let us imagine ourselves, once more, on a dark and entangled wilderness trail completely unfamiliar to us. On our own, we may feel intense fear or even panic. If led by a guide who seems to know where he is going, or if we believe that he does, we would proceed with confidence. There would be nothing to trigger an alarm unless, of course, our guide betrayed his own anxiety.

In the same way, by using each other as compass points, children defend themselves against the nightmarish anxiety of experiencing an orientation void. On the conscious level, they are able to prevent feeling lost, muddled, or confused. Peer-oriented children are remarkably devoid of these feelings. That is the irony: they look like the blind leading the blind, like a school of fish revolving around each other, but they *feel* just fine. It does not seem to matter that their operational compass points are inadequate, inconsistent, and unreliable. These children are lost and truly disoriented without consciously feeling bewildered.

For children who have replaced adults with their peers, it is enough to just be with each other, even if they are completely off the map. They do not accept direction from adults or ask for guidance. They frustrate us with their apparent certainty that they are all right, no matter how clearly we see that they're heading in the wrong direction or in no direction at all. Many parents have had the vexing experience of trying to point out reality to a teenager whose world may be in shambles but who is blithely and adamantly insisting that absolutely nothing is amiss.

Superficially, one could argue that their attachment with peers is serving them well if it keeps them from being lost and bewildered. In reality, it does not save them from getting lost, only from *feeling* lost.

## THE SIX WAYS OF ATTACHING

If we are to nurture our kids successfully, or if we are to reorient them to us once they've been seduced by the peer culture, we must come to terms with attachment. The following discussion is intended to help parents gain a working knowledge of this crucial dynamic. "If you don't understand your kid," said one mother interviewed for this book, "you can't stand your kid." Understanding attachment is the single most important factor in making sense of kids from the inside out. It also enables us to identify the warning signs when a child is becoming peer-oriented.

We can identify six ways of attaching, each of them providing a clue to the behavior of our children—and, often, to our own behavior as well. These six ways ascend from the simple to the more complex. Notice that peer-oriented kids tend to employ only the most basic modes when attaching to each other.

## Senses

Physical proximity is the goal of the first way of attaching. The child needs to sense the person he is attached to, whether through smell, sight, sound, or touch. He will do whatever he can to maintain contact with that person. When closeness is threatened or disrupted, he will express alarm and bitter protest.

Although it begins in infancy, the hunger for physical proximity never goes away. The less mature a person is, the more he will rely on this basic mode of attaching. Peer-oriented kids like Cynthia are preoccupied with being together, occupying the same space, hanging out, and staying in touch. When attachment is this primitive, the talking can be gibberish and nonsense. "My friends and I talk for hours without saying anything," says Peter, a fifteen-year-old. "It's all 'what's happening' and 'whazzup, man' and 'you got a smoke' and 'where we going' or 'where is so-and-so.' " The talking is not about communication; it is an attachment ritual for the simple purpose of making auditory contact. Peer-oriented kids have no idea what drives them so intensely; for them it feels absolutely natural and even urgent to want always to be close to each other. They are just following their skewed instincts.

## Sameness

The second way of attaching is usually well in evidence by toddlerhood. The child seeks to be like those she feels closest to. She attempts to assume the same form of existence or expression by imitation and emulation. This form of attachment figures prominently in learning language and in the transmission of culture. It has been noted that since the Second World War the vocabulary of the average child has diminished significantly. Why? Because children now acquire language from each other. Peer-oriented children model one another's walk and talk, preferences and gestures, appearance and demeanor.

Another means of attaching through sameness is *identification*. To identify with someone or something is to be one with that person or thing. One's sense of self merges with the object of identification. This entity may be a parent, a hero, a group, a role, a country, a sports team, a rock star, an idea, or even one's work. Extreme nationalism and racism are based on identifying one's sense of self with one's country or ethnic group.

The more dependent a child or person is, the more intense these identifications are likely to be. In our society, peers—or the pop icons of the peer world—have become the focus of identification in place of parents or the outstanding figures of history and culture.

### Belonging and Loyalty

The third way of attaching also makes its debut in toddlerhood—if all is unfolding as it should. To be close to someone is to consider that person as one's own. The attaching toddler will lay claim to whomever or whatever he is attached to—be it mommy or daddy or teddy bear or baby sister. In the same way, peer-oriented kids jealously seek to possess one another and to protect against loss. Conflicts generated by possessiveness can become vicious and intense. Who is whose best friend occurs as a life-or-death question to many adolescents. This immature mode of attaching predominates much of the interaction of peer-oriented children, especially between peer-oriented girls.

On the heels of belonging comes loyalty—being faithful and obedient to one's chosen attachment figures. Peer-oriented kids are just following their natural attachment instincts when they keep each other's secrets, take each other's side, and do the other's bidding. Loyalty can be intense, but it merely follows attachment. If a child's attachment changes, so will the sense of belonging and loyalty.

Highly peer-oriented kids are notoriously loyal to one another and to their group. The death of Reena Virk, a teenager in Victoria, British Columbia, killed by her peers, was known by many adolescents but no adult was told about it for several days—an incident that became notorious internationally.

### Significance

The fourth way of pursuing closeness and connection is to seek *significance*, which means that we feel we matter to somebody. It is human nature to hold close what we value. To be dear to someone is to ensure closeness and connection. The attaching preschooler seeks ardently to please and to win approval. He is extremely sensitive to looks of displeasure and disapproval. Such children live for the happy face of those they are attached to. Peer-oriented children do the same, but the countenance they want to shine is that of their peers. Those they call "nice" are usually the ones who like and approve of them, even if the same "nice" person is nasty to others.

The problem with this way of attaching is that it makes a child vulnerable to being hurt. To want to be significant to someone is to suffer when we feel we don't matter to that special person. Seeking someone's favor leads to feeling wounded by signs of disfavor. A sensitive child can be easily crushed when the eyes he is scanning for signs of warmth and pleasure do not light up in his presence, be they the eyes of parent or peer. Most parents, though imperfect, are far less likely than peers to keep on hurting children this way.

### Feeling

A fifth way of finding closeness is through *feeling*: warm feelings, loving feelings, affectionate feelings. Emotion is always involved in attachment, but in a preschooler who can feel deeply and vulnerably, the pursuit of *emotional intimacy* becomes intense. Children who pursue connection in this way often fall in love with those they attach to. A child who experiences emotional intimacy with the parent can tolerate much more physical separation and yet hold the parent close. If attaching via the senses—the first and most primitive way—is the short arm of attachment, love would be the long arm. The child carries the image of the loving and beloved parent in his mind, and finds support and comfort in it.

But now we are getting into dangerous territory. To give one's heart away is to risk it being broken. Some people never develop the capacity to be emotionally open and vulnerable, usually due to early perceptions of rejection or abandonment. Those who have loved and suffered hurt may retreat to less vulnerable modes of attaching. As we will show, vulnerability is something peer-oriented children seek to escape. When deeper forms of attachment appear too risky, the less vulnerable modes will predominate. Emotional intimacy is much less common among peer-oriented kids than in parent-oriented kids.

### Being Known

The sixth way of attaching is through *being known*. The first signs of this final way of attaching are usually observable by the time a child enters school. To feel close to someone is to be known by them. In some ways, this is a recapitulation of attaching by way of the senses, except that being seen and heard are now experienced psychologically instead of strictly physically. In the pursuit of closeness, a child will share his secrets. In fact, closeness will often be defined by the secrets shared. Parent-oriented children do not like to keep secrets from their parents because of the resulting loss of closeness. For a peer-oriented child, his best friend is the one he has no secrets from. One cannot get much more vulnerable than to expose oneself psychologically. To share oneself with another and then be misunderstood or rejected is, for many, a risk not worth taking. As a result, this is the rarest of intimacies and the reason so many of us are reluctant to share even with loved ones our deepest concerns and insecurities about ourselves. Yet there is no closeness that can surpass the sense of feeling known and still being liked, accepted, welcomed, invited to exist.

As we observe our children busily and furtively exchanging secrets, it is easy to assume that they are sharing themselves vulnerably with each other. In fact, the secrets they do share are most commonly in the form of gossip about other people. True psychological intimacy is the exception among peer-oriented children, most likely because the risks are too great. Children who do share their secrets with their parents are often seen as a little weird by their more peer-oriented friends. "My friends can't believe I tell you so much," one fourteen-year-old said to her father on one of their walks together. "They say it's crazy."

Six ways of attaching but only one underlying drive for connection. If development is healthy, these six strands become interwoven into a strong rope of connection that can preserve closeness even under the most adverse circumstances. A fully attached child has many ways of staying close and holding on, even when physically apart. The less mature the child, the more primitive—the more like an infant's or a toddler's—will be his style of attaching. Not all children come to realize their attachment potential, the peer-oriented least of all. For reasons we will make clear, peer-oriented children are likely to stay immature and their emotional relating is designed to avoid any conscious sense of their vulnerability (discussed further in Chapters 8 and 9). Peer-oriented children live in a universe of severely limited and superficial attachments. The quest for sameness being the least vulnerable way of attaching, it is the one usually chosen by kids impelled to seek contact with their peers. Hence their drive to be as much like one another as possible: to resemble one another in look, demeanor, thought, tastes, and values.

Compared with children whose attachments to parents are healthy, peer-oriented kids are often limited to only two or three ways of establishing connection and holding on. Children who are limited in their ways of attaching are heavily dependent on these modes, just as people devoid of sight are more dependent on the other senses to take in their world. If there is only one way of holding on, the clinging is likely to be intense and desperate. And that is how peer-oriented children attach to each other, intensely and desperately.

## WHEN IMPORTANT ATTACHMENTS COMPETE

Given the central importance of attachment in the child's psyche, whomever the child is most attached to will have the greatest impact on her life.

Shouldn't it be possible for children to be connected with their parents and teachers and, at the same time, with their peers? That is not only possible but desirable, as long as those several attachments are not in competition with one another. What does not work, and cannot work, is the coexistence of competing *primary* attachments, competing orienting relationships—in other words, orienting relationships with conflicting values, conflicting messages. When primary attachments compete, one will lose out. And it is easy to see why. A sailor relying on a compass could not find his way if there were two magnetic North Poles. No more successfully could a child simultaneously use both peers and adults as working compass points. The child will orient either by the values of the peer world or the values of the parents, but not both. Either the peer culture dominates or the culture of the parents takes the lead. The attachment brain of immature beings cannot tolerate two orienting influences of equal force, two sets of messages dissonant with each other. It must select one over the other; otherwise, emotions would be confused, motivation paralyzed, and action impaired. The child wouldn't know which way to turn. In the same way, when an infant's eyes diverge so that he has double vision, the brain automatically suppresses visual information from one of the eyes. The ignored eye will go blind.

Compared with adults—mature adults, that is—children are much more intensely driven by their attachment needs. Adults may also have powerful attachment needs, as many of us have experienced, but with true maturity comes some ability to keep those needs in perspective. Children have no such capacity. When the child's energies are invested in a relationship that competes with his parental attachment, the effects on his personality and behavior are dramatic. The powerful gravity pull of peer relationships was what Cynthia's parents were witnessing with their daughter, to their chagrin.

Beneath many parents' anger and frustration is a sense of hurt consistent with feeling betrayed. Yet we typically ignore or discount this internal warning. We attempt to soothe our unease by reducing the matter to behavior problems or to hormones or to "normal teenage rebellion." Such pseudo-biological explanations or psychological assumptions distract us from the real issue of incompatible, competing attachments. Hormones have always been part of the normal physiological makeup of human beings, but they haven't always led to the massive alienation of parents we are experiencing today. Irritating and rude behaviors are, always, only surface manifestations of deeper issues. Trying to punish or control behaviors without addressing the underlying dynamics is like a doctor prescribing something for symptoms while ignoring their causes. A deeper understanding of their children will empower parents to deal with "bad behavior" in truly effective ways, as we will show throughout this book. As to "normal" teenage rebellion: our children's compulsive drive to belong to the peer group, to fit in and conform at the expense of their own true individuality, has nothing to do with healthy maturation and development, as we will see in later chapters.

The fundamental issue we as parents need to face is that of the competing attachments that have seduced our children away from our loving care.

## WHEN ATTACHMENT TURNS AGAINST US

Now that we understand how Cynthia's peers replaced her parents, we are still left with a troubling question: How do we account for her hostile behavior toward her mother and father? Many parents of adolescents and even younger children these days are similarly shocked by the rude and aggressive language their kids direct toward them. Why is it that the ascendancy of peer relationships leads to the child's alienation from the parents?

The answer lies in the bipolar nature of attachment. Human attachment resembles its physical counterparts in the material world, such as magnetism. Magnetism is polarized — one pole attracts the needle in a compass, the other repels it. So the term *bipolar* means existing in two polarities, having two poles at the same time. There is nothing abnormal about this bipolarity; it is the intrinsic nature of attachment.

The closer you get to the earth's North Pole, the farther you are from the South Pole. The parallel is true in the human personality, especially for children and other immature creatures of attachment. A child pursuing closeness with one person will likely resist anyone he perceives as competing with that person, just as an adult who falls in love with someone new may, suddenly, find her former lover unbearable. Yet he, the old beau, hasn't changed, only her attachments have. The very same people can be desired or repudiated, depending on which way the attachment compass is pointing. When the primary attachment shifts, people hitherto close to us can suddenly become objects of disdain, to be repelled. Such shifts can occur with bewildering rapidity—as many parents have witnessed when their child comes home in tears, embittered and disheartened at some unexpected rejection by his "best friend."

Most of us have an intuitive sense of the bipolar nature of attachment. We know how quickly pursuing can turn to distancing, liking to revulsion, affection to contempt, loving to hatred. But few appreciate that such strong emotions and impulses are really the flip sides of the same coin.

The bipolarity of attachment is critical for today's parents to understand. With peer orientation on the rise, so is the corresponding parent alienation and all the problems that come with it. Today's children are not only turning to their peers but, like Cynthia, are actively and energetically turning away from their parents. Nothing is neutral in attachment. To the degree that attachment governs the child, relationships will be highly charged. Attachment divides the child's world into those the child likes and those the child is indifferent to, those who attract and those who repel, those to approach and those to avoid. All too commonly in today's world parents and peers have become attachments that compete—like lovers who compete for the same beloved. As many parents have experienced to their great sorrow, children cannot be both peer-oriented and parent-oriented at the same time.

A child's alienated stance toward his parents does not represent a character flaw, ingrained rudeness, or behavior problems. It is what we see when attachment instincts have become misdirected.

Under normal circumstances the bipolar nature of attachment serves the benign purpose of keeping the child close to the nurturing adults. Its first expression occurs in infancy and is often termed *stranger protest*. The more strongly the infant bonds to specific adults, the more he will resist contact with those he is not attached to. When an infant wants closeness with you and someone he is not connected to approaches, he will shy away from the intruder and lean into you. It's pure instinct. Nothing could be more natural than distancing from strangers who come too close for comfort. Yet we have all witnessed parents already chastising their infants for this alienating gesture and apologizing to other adults for their child's "rudeness."

Adults find these reactions even less palatable in toddlers and completely intolerable in older children. Peer orientation turns the natural, instinctual responses of stranger protest against the child's own parents. The adolescent's expression of reversed attachment may not be as graphic as a toddler's sticking out the tongue, but there are other gestures of alienation equally effective—the eyes that hold you at a distance, the stone-faced look, the refusal to smile, the rolling of the eyes, the refusal to look at you, the foiling of contact, the resistance to connection.

Sometimes we can actually sense the polarity shifting. Imagine that you are the mother of Rachel, a girl in the third grade. You have had the wonderful experience of walking her to school, hand in hand, ever since kindergarten. Before you leave her, you always hug and kiss and whisper an endearment or two. But Rachel has become preoccupied with peers recently, wanting to be with them without pause. When she comes home, she brings things that belong to them, like their gestures, language, preferences in clothes, even their laughs. One day you set out as usual, hand in hand, with a mutual desire for closeness and connection. On the way, some of her classmates cross your path. Something shifts. You are still holding her hand, but her grip is not quite reciprocal. She seems to be half a step ahead or behind, not aligned. As more children appear, the gulf widens. Suddenly she drops your hand and runs ahead. When you reach your destination, you bend toward her for the customary hug, and she pulls away, as if embarrassed. Instead of being cuddled affectionately, you are held at arm's length and she barely looks at you as she waves good-bye. It is as if you have violated some basic instincts. What you have actually experienced is the dark, reverse side of attachment—the rejection of what was formerly held close, upon the appearance of a new, more highly valued relationship. In plain language, our children are rudely jilting us for their peers.

This negative pole of attachment manifests itself in several ways. The rejection of sameness is one. The quest for sameness plays a huge role in shaping the personality and behavior of the child. Children well attached to their parents are eager to be like them. Until adolescence, at least, they take great pleasure when similarities and likenesses are noticed by others, whether it is the same sense of humor, the same preferences in food, the same ideas on a topic, the same reactions to a movie, the same taste in music. (Some readers may greet this assertion with disbelief, as hopelessly idealistic and behind the times. If so, it's only a sign of how peer-oriented the adult generations have become over the past several decades, to what degree peer orientation has become accepted as the norm.)

Peer-oriented kids are repelled by similarity to their parents and want to be as different as possible from them. Since sameness means closeness, pursuing difference is a way of distancing. Such children will often go out of their way to take the opposite point of view and form opposite kinds of preferences. They are filled with contrary opinions and judgments.

We may confuse this obsessive need for difference from the parents with the child's quest for individuality. That would be a misreading of the situation. Genuine individuation would be manifested in all of the child's relationships, not just with adults. A child truly seeking to be her own person asserts her selfhood in the face of all pressures to conform. Quite the reverse, many of these "strongly individualistic" children are completely consumed with melding with their peer group, appalled by anything that may make them seem different. What adults see as the child's individualism masks an intense drive to conform to peers.

One of our more alienating behaviors as humans is to mock and mimic those we wish to distance ourselves from. This behavior appears to be cross-cultural, attesting to its deep instinctive roots. The instinct to mock is the polar opposite of our attempt to achieve closeness through imitating and emulating. To be imitated may be the greatest compliment, but to be mocked and mimicked is one of the most offensive put-downs.

The more a child seeks closeness with his peers through sameness, the more likely his mocking behavior will be aimed at adults. To be mocked by one's students or one's child cuts to the quick; it pushes all the buttons. It is a powerful sign of peer orientation when such alienating behavior is directed at those responsible for the child. In the same way, the polar opposites of liking and finding favor are disdain and contempt. When children become peer-oriented, parents often become the objects of scorn and ridicule, insults and put-downs. The badmouthing first starts behind the parent's back, often as a way of winning points with peers, but as peer orientation intensifies, so may the openness of the attack. Such a hostile stance should be reserved for enemies, where burning bridges is exactly what is desired. To have our children treat us like enemies makes no sense whatsoever, for us, for them, or for our relationship. It can do children no good at all to bite the hand that feeds them. Yet the peer-oriented child is just doing what seems quite natural and in keeping with his instincts. Again, it is the instincts that are out of order; the behavior is simply following suit. That is what happens when attachments compete and become polarized.

Sometimes the disowning is passive. Peer-oriented kids often act, especially around one another, as if they don't have parents. Parents are neither acknowledged nor discussed. At school functions the parents often get ignored.

Jesus captured the incompatibility of competing attachments and, too, the bipolar nature of attachment when he said, "No man can serve two masters: for either he will hate the one, and love the other; or else he will hold to the one, and despise the other" (Matthew 6:24). When the loyalty is to the peers, it will not feel right for the child to be on our side or to do our bidding. Children are not disloyal to us on purpose; they are simply following their instincts—instincts that have become subverted for reasons far beyond their control.

# WHY WE'VE COME UNDONE

Hᴏᴡ ɪꜱ ɪᴛ that, in today's world, children so readily transfer their attachments from nurturing adults to each other? The cause is not individual parental failure but an unprecedented cultural breakdown for which our instincts cannot adequately compensate.

Our society does not serve the developmental needs of our children. Just as researchers in the twentieth century were discovering the key role of attachments in healthy psychological growth, subtle shifts in society were leaving the adult orientation of young people unprotected. Economic forces and cultural trends dominant in the past several decades have dismantled the social context for the natural functioning of both the parenting instincts of adults and the attachment drives of children.

Although the young human is driven by a powerful genetic drive to attach, there is no archetype of parent or teacher embedded somewhere in a child's brain. That brain is programmed only to orient, to attach, and finally to preserve contact with whomever becomes the working compass point. Nothing induces the child to seek only someone who looks like mom or dad or who seems nurturing, capable, and mature. There is no inherent preference for choosing the adult in charge, no respect in the primitive attachment brain for a person who has been certified by the government or trained for child-rearing. No inborn circuitry recognizes socially appointed roles or cares that the teacher, the day-care provider, or ultimately even the parent is "supposed" to be heeded, respected, and kept close.

Historically, no such programming was needed. As with all mammals and many other animals, it was simply the natural order of things that the innate attachment drive itself bonded the young with caregivers—adults of the same species—until maturity. That is nature's way of ensuring the survival of the young into healthy adulthood. It is the context in which the young are fully enabled to realize their genetic potential and in which their instincts are best given full and vigorous expression.

In our society, that natural order has been subverted. From an early age, we thrust our children into many situations and interactions that encourage peer orientation. Unwittingly, we promote the very phenomenon that, in the long term, erodes the only sound basis of healthy development: children's attachment to the adults responsible for their nurturing. Placing our young in a position where their attachment and orienting instincts are directed toward peers is an aberration. We are not prepared for it; our brains are not organized to adapt successfully to the natural agenda being so distorted.

John Bowlby, British psychiatrist and a great pioneer of attachment research, wrote that "the behavioral equipment of a species may be beautifully suited to life within one environment and lead only to sterility and death in another." Each species has what Bowlby called its "environment of adaptedness," the circumstances to which its anatomy, physiology, and psychological capacities are best suited. In any other environment the organism or species cannot be expected to do so well, and may even exhibit behavior "that is at best unusual and at worst positively unfavorable to survival."[1] In postindustrial society the environment no longer encourages our children to develop along natural lines of attachment.

## A CULTURE OF MISSING ATTACHMENTS

The contrasts between traditional multigenerational cultures and today's North American society are striking. In modern urbanized North America—and in other industrialized countries where the American way of life has become the norm—children find themselves in attachment voids everywhere, situations in which they lack consistent and deep connection with nurturing adults. There are many factors promoting this trend.

One result of economic changes since the Second World War is that children are placed early, sometimes soon after birth, in situations where they spend much of the day in one another's company. Most of their contact is with other children, not with the significant adults in their lives. They spend much less time bonding with parents and adults. As they grow older, the process only accelerates.

Society has generated economic pressure for both parents to work outside the home when children are very young, but it has made little provision for the satisfaction of children's needs for emotional nourishment. Surprising though it may seem, early childhood educators, teachers, and psychologists—to say nothing of physicians and psychiatrists—are seldom taught about attachment. In our institutions of child care and education there exists no collective consciousness regarding the pivotal importance of attachment relationships. Although many individual caregivers and teachers intuitively grasp the need to form a connection with children, it is not rare for such persons to find themselves at odds with a system that does not support their approach.

Because caring for the young is undervalued in our society, day care is not well funded. It is difficult for a nonrelative to meet an individual child's attachment and orienting needs fully, especially if several other infants and toddlers are vying for that caregiver's attention. Although many day-care facilities are well run and staffed by dedicated albeit poorly paid workers, standards are far from uniformly satisfactory. For example, the State of New York demands that no more than seven toddlers be under the care of any one worker—a hopelessly unwieldy ratio. The importance of adult connection is not appreciated. Children in such situations have little option but to form attachment relationships with one another.

It is not both parents working that is so damaging. The key problem is the lack of consideration we give attachment in making our child-care arrangements. There are no cultural customs in mainstream society that make it the first item of business for day-care workers and preschool teachers to form connections with the parents and then, through friendly introductions, to cultivate a working attachment with the child. Both parents and professionals are left to their own intuition—or more often the lack of it. Due to a lack of collective consciousness, most adults simply follow current practices that were not designed with attachment in mind. An attachment custom that used to be followed in many places—that of preschool and kindergarten teachers visiting the homes of future students—has largely been scrapped, except perhaps in well-funded private schools. Up against the fiscal scissors, no one could adequately explain the vital function this custom served. Economics are much easier to grasp than attachment.

The crux of the issue is not societal change by itself but the lack of compensation for that change. If we are going to share the task of raising our children with others, we need to build the context for it by creating what I call a village of attachment—a set of nurturing adult relationships to replace what we have lost. There are many ways to do this, as I will show in Chapter 18.

After day care and kindergarten, our children enter school. They will now live most of each day in the company of peers, in an environment where adults have less and less primacy. If there were a deliberate intention to create peer orientation, schools as currently run would surely be our best instrument. Assigned to large classes with overwhelmed teachers in charge, children find connection with one another. Rules and regulations tend to keep them out of the classroom before classes begin, ensuring that they are on their own without much adult contact. They spend recess and lunchtime in one another's company. Teacher training completely ignores attachment; thus educators learn about teaching *subjects* but not about the essential importance of connected *relationships* to the learning process of young human beings. Unlike a few decades ago, today's teachers do not mingle with their students in the halls or on the playground and are discouraged from interacting with them in a more personal manner. In contrast to more traditional societies, the vast majority of students in North America do not go home to spend lunchtime with their parents.

"There are five hundred students in the school my kids go to," says Christina, the mother of two children—in the third and seventh grades, respectively. "I pick them up for lunch every day, but they are two of only ten in that five hundred who go home for lunch. And there is even pressure from the teachers to let them stay. They seem to think I'm somehow weird, too much of a fussy mother hen. Yet I find that time essential. My kids have so much to tell me, so much to debrief about what happened in school, what they found difficult, what they are excited about." "My daughter would run into my car," says another parent who used to bring her child home for lunch. "She would just explode with information— anything that happened, how she felt about it, what she felt when she did something 'wrong' or did something very well." One wonders, hearing these two moms, what a multitude of experiences and feelings remain unspoken and unprocessed for many of the other children.

In general, we focus more on getting our children fed than on the eating rituals meant to keep us connected. In his groundbreaking book *The Sibling Society*, the American poet Robert Bly describes many manifestations of peer orientation, and hints at its causes. Although Bly doesn't fully analyze the phenomenon, his insights should have received more attention. "Family meals, talks, reading together no longer take place," writes Bly. "What the young need—stability, presence, attention, advice, good psychic food, unpolluted stories—is exactly what the sibling society won't give them."[2]

In today's society, attachment voids abound. A gaping attachment void has been created by the loss of the extended family. Children often lack close relationships with older generations—the people who, for much of human history, were often better able than parents themselves to offer the unconditional loving acceptance that is the bedrock of emotional security. The reassuring, consistent presence of grandparents and aunts and uncles, the protective embrace of the multigenerational family, is something few children nowadays are able to enjoy.

A powerful influence favoring peer orientation is our increased mobility, because it interrupts cultural continuity. Culture develops over generations living in the same community. We no longer live in villages and are therefore no longer connected to those we live next to. Incessant transplanting has rendered us anonymous, creating the antithesis to the attachment village. Our children cannot be coparented by people whose names we hardly even know.

Owing to geographic dislocations and frequent moves, and to the increasing peer orientation of adults themselves, today's children are much less likely to enjoy the company of elders committed to their welfare and development. That lack goes beyond the family and characterizes virtually all social relationships. Generally missing are attachments with adults who assume some responsibility for the child. One example of an endangered species is the family physician, a person who knew generations of a family and who was a stable and emotionally present figure in its members' lives, whether in times of crisis or times of celebration. The faceless and inconstantly available doctor at the walk-in clinic is hardly a substitute. In the same way, the neighborhood shopkeeper, tradesman, and artisan have long been replaced by generic businesses with no local ties and no personal connections with the communities in which they function. The beloved Mr. Hooper of TV's "Sesame Street" is, nowadays, only a benign fiction. These are far more than economic matters; they go to the very heart of what an attachment village is all about. Where are the surrogate grandparents, the surrogate uncles and aunts who supplemented and substituted the nuclear and extended family in the past? Where is the adult attachment safety net should parents become inaccessible? Where are the adult mentors to help guide our adolescents? Our children are growing up peer rich and adult poor.

Another attachment void has been created by the secularization of society. Quite apart from religion, the church, temple, mosque, or synagogue community functioned as an important supporting cast for parents and an attachment village for children. Secularization has meant more than the loss of faith or spiritual rootedness; it has brought the loss of this attachment community. Beyond that, peer interaction has become a priority for many churches. For example, many churches divide the family as they enter the door, grouping the members by age rather than by family. There are nurseries and teen groups, junior churches, and even senior classes. To those unaware of the importance of attachment and the dangers posed by peer orientation, it seems only self-evident that people belong with those their own age. Large religious organizations have evolved to deal with only the youth or the young adult, inadvertently promoting the loss of multigenerational connections.

## FAMILY TIES TORN ASUNDER

The nuclear family is said to be the basic unit of society but is itself under extreme pressure. Divorce rates have soared. Divorce is a double whammy for kids because it creates competing attachments as well as attachment voids. Children naturally like all their working attachments to be under one roof. The togetherness of the parents enables them to satisfy their desire of closeness and contact with both simultaneously. Furthermore, many children are attached to their parents as a *couple*. When parents divorce, it becomes impossible to be close to both simultaneously, at least physically. Children who are more mature and have more fully developed attachments with their parents are better equipped to keep close to both even when they, the parents, are apart—to belong to both simultaneously, to love both simultaneously, and to be known by both simultaneously. But many children, even older ones, cannot manage this. Parents who compete with the other parent or treat the other parent as persona non grata place the child (or, more precisely, the child's attachment brain) in an impossible situation: to be close to one, the child must separate from the other, both physically and psychologically.

The problem of competing attachments may be exacerbated when parents take new partners. Again, children will often instinctually shun contact with a stepparent in order to preserve closeness with the original parent. The challenge, for both biological parents and stepparents, is to facilitate a new attachment that doesn't compete and, better yet, supports the existing relationship. Only when the relationships are complementary can the child's attachment brain relax its guard and become receptive to overtures of connection from both sides.

Owing to the marital conflict that precedes divorce, attachment voids may develop long before the divorce happens. When parents lose each other's emotional support or become preoccupied with their relationship to each other, they become less accessible to their children. Deprived of emotional contact with adults, children turn to their peers. Also, under stressed circumstances, it is tempting for parents themselves to seek some relief from caregiving responsibility. One of the easiest ways of doing so is to encourage peer interaction. When children are with each other, they make fewer demands on us.

Studies on children of divorce find them, as a group, more susceptible to school problems and aggression. They are also more likely to exhibit behavioral problems.[3] The studies, however, have not been able to pinpoint why this happens. With an understanding of attachment, we see that these symptoms turn out to be the direct result of their loss of parental emotional connection and overreliance on peer relationships.

None of this is to suggest that for parents to stay in conflict-ridden marriages would be any better for the children involved.[4] But, again, we need to become more conscious of the impact of parental strife on our children's attachments. Whether we are less accessible because of marital strain or because of divorce, we would do well to engage other adults to take on the caretaking role. Instead of using our children's peers to provide some relief from parental duties, we should be calling upon our relatives and our friends to step into the void and create an attachment safety net.

Even nuclear families still intact are vulnerable to attachment voids. Nowadays it often takes two parents working full-time to secure the same standard of living one wage earner could provide thirty or forty years ago. Deepening social stresses and the growing sense of economic insecurity even in the midst of relative wealth have all combined to create a milieu in which calm, connected parenting is increasingly difficult. Precisely when parents and other adults need to form stronger attachment bonds with their children than ever before, they have less time and energy to do so.

Robert Bly notes that "in 1935 the average working man had forty hours a week free, including Saturday. By 1990, it was down to seventeen hours.

The twenty-three lost hours of free time a week since 1935 are the very hours in which the father could be a nurturing father, and find some center in himself, and the very hours in which the mother could feel she actually has a husband."[5] These patterns characterize not only the early years of parenting but entire childhoods. Although many fathers today are more conscientious in taking a share of parenting responsibility, the stresses of modern life and the chronic lack of time subvert their best intentions.

Our society puts a higher value on consumerism than the healthy development of children. For economic reasons, the natural attachments of children to their parents are actively discouraged. As a family physician, my cowriter often found himself in the ludicrous position of having to write letters to employers justifying on "health" grounds a woman's decision to stay home an extra few months following her baby's birth so that she could breast-feed—an essential physiological need of the infant, but also a potent natural attachment function in all mammalian species, especially in human beings. It is for economic reasons that parenting does not get the respect it should. That we live where we do rather than where our natural supporting cast is—friends, the extended family, our communities of origin—has come about for economic reasons, often beyond the control of individual parents, as, for example, when whole industries are shut down or relocated. It is for economic reasons that we build schools too large for connection to happen and that we have classes too large for children to receive individual attention.

As we will see in Part 3, peer orientation exacts immense costs on society by fueling aggression and delinquency, by making students less teachable, and by fomenting unhealthy lifestyle choices. If we were to assess the true economic loss to society of peer orientation in the areas of the justice system, education, and health, there would not be a shadow of doubt about our current shortsightedness. Some countries have recognized this. They provide tax relief and even direct support for parents to stay at home longer after the birth or adoption of children, before returning to work.

### RAPID CHANGE, TECHNOLOGY GONE HAYWIRE

More than anything, we have lost the cultural customs and traditions that bring extended families together, linking adults and children in caring relationships, that give the adult friends of parents a place in their children's lives. It is the role of culture to cultivate connections between the dependent and the dependable and to prevent attachment voids from occurring. Among the many reasons that culture is failing us, two bear mentioning.

The first is the jarringly rapid rate of change in twentieth-century industrial societies. It requires time to develop customs and traditions that serve attachment needs, hundreds of years to create a working culture that serves a particular social and geographical environment. Our society has been changing much too rapidly for culture to evolve accordingly. The psychoanalyst Erik H. Erikson devoted a chapter in his Pulitzer Prize–winning *Childhood and Society* to his reflections on the American identity. "This dynamic country," he wrote, "subjects its inhabitants to more extreme contrasts and abrupt changes during a generation than is normally the case with other great nations."[6] Such trends have only accelerated since Erikson made that observation in 1950. There is now more change in a decade than previously in a century. When circumstances change more quickly than our culture can adapt to, customs and traditions disintegrate. It is not surprising that today's culture is failing its traditional function of supporting adult-child attachments.

Part of the rapid change has been the electronic transmission of culture, allowing commercially blended and packaged culture to be broadcast into our homes and into the very minds of our children. Instant culture has replaced what used to be passed down through custom and tradition and from one generation to another. "Almost every day I find myself fighting the bubble-gum culture my children are exposed to," said a frustrated father interviewed for this book. Not only is the content often alien to the culture of the parents but the process of transmission has taken grandparents out of the loop and made them seem sadly out of touch. Games, too, have become electronic. They have always been an instrument of culture to connect people to people, especially children to adults. Now games have become a solitary activity, watched in parallel on television sportscasts or engaged in in isolation on the computer.

The most significant change in recent times has been the technology of communication—first the phone and then the Internet through e-mail and instant messaging. We are enamored of communication technology without being aware that one of its primary functions is to facilitate attachments. We have unwittingly put it into the hands of children who, of course, are using it to connect with their peers. Because of their strong attachment needs, the contact is highly addictive, often becoming a major preoccupation. Our culture has not been able to evolve the customs and traditions to contain this development, and so again we are all left to our own devices. This wonderful new technology would be a powerfully positive instrument if used to facilitate child-adult connections—as it does, for example, when it enables easy communication between students living away from home, and their parents. Left unchecked, it promotes peer orientation.

## AN ATTACHMENT CULTURE AT WORK

The deficiency of our North American culture is readily driven home to us when we observe a society that still honors traditional attachments. I had the opportunity to do so when I, along with my wife, Joy, and our children, recently spent time in the village of Rognes, Provence.

Provence immediately brings to mind images of a timeless culture. The sunny clime, the grapes, the old-world charm, the food evoke a sense of nostalgia. It is instructive to look at Provencal society from another point of view, for what it could teach us about attachment. As we will see in our final chapter, even in the vastly different environment of postindustrial North America, it is not beyond us to apply some of the lessons as we re-create our own attachment village, as I like to call it.

When we first went to Provence, I assumed I would be observing a different culture. With attachment in mind, it became obvious to me that it is much more than a different culture—I was witnessing a culture at work and a culture that worked. Children greeted adults and adults greeted children. Socializing involved whole families, not adults with adults and children with children. There was only one village activity at a time, so families were not pulled in several directions. Sunday afternoon was for family walks in the countryside. Even at the village fountain, the local hangout, teens mixed with seniors. Festivals and celebrations, of which there were many, were all family affairs. The music and dancing brought the generations together instead of separating them. Culture took precedence over materialism. One could not even buy a baguette without first engaging in the appropriate greeting rituals. Village stores were closed for three hours at midday while schools emptied and families reconvened. Lunch was eaten in a congenial manner as multigenerational groupings sat around tables, sharing conversation and a meal.

The attachment customs around the village primary school were equally impressive. Children were personally escorted to school and picked up by their parents or grandparents. The school was gated and the grounds could be entered only by a single entrance. At the gate were the teachers, waiting for their students to be handed over to them. Again, culture dictated that connection be established with appropriate greetings between the adult escorts and the teachers as well as the teachers and the students. Sometimes when the class had been collected but the school bell had not yet rung, the teacher would lead the class through the playground, like a mother goose followed by her goslings. While to North American eyes this may appear to be a preschool ritual, even absurd, in Provence it was self-evidently part of the natural order of things. When children were released from school, it was always one class at a time, the teacher in the lead. The teacher would wait with the students at the gate until all had been collected by their adult escort. Their teachers were their teachers whether on the grounds or in the village market or at the village festival. There weren't many cracks to fall through. Provençal culture was keeping attachment voids to a minimum.

I ventured to ask questions about why they did this or why they did that. I never got an answer. The sense I got was that my questions were out of order, as if there was some kind of taboo around analyzing customs and traditions. The culture was to be followed, not questioned. The attachment wisdom was obviously in the culture itself, not in people's consciousness. How did Provençal society retain the traditional power of older generations to transmit to their children their culture and values? Why were the young in the French countryside able to form peer attachments that did not seem to compete with their attachments to adults? The answer has to do with how a peer attachment is formed.

## THE NATURAL WAY OF FORMING ATTACHMENTS

Attachments generally come into being in one of two ways. They are either the natural offspring of existing attachments or they are called into being when an attachment void becomes intolerable. The first of these is evidenced already in infancy. By six months of age, most children show a resistance to contact and closeness with those they are not attached to. Overcoming this requires a certain kind of interaction between the child's working attachment and the "stranger." For example, if the mother engages in a period of friendly contact with the stranger, taking care not to push the infant into contact but simply allowing the infant to observe, the resistance usually softens and the child becomes receptive to connection with the newcomer. There must be a friendly introduction, a "blessing," so to speak. Once the attachment instincts of the infant have become engaged and a time of nearness is enjoyed, the child will usually move toward contact with the new person and allow himself to be taken care of by him. The previously "strange" adult—a friend of the family, for example, or a babysitter—will now have earned the child's "permission" to become a caregiver.

This design is ingenious. When a new attachment is born out of the child's existing working relationships, there is much less likelihood of it becoming a competing force. The attachment with the parent is more likely to be honored. The parent is upheld as the ultimate compass point, and the relationship with the parent will continue to have the priority. Contacts with siblings, grandparents, extended family, and family friends are much less likely to take the child away from the parents, even if peers are involved.

The capacity of working attachments to generate new relationships allows for the creation of what I've called a natural attachment village, originating essentially from the parents. The parents' attachments ultimately become the child's and provide a context within which the child can be raised. This is why the peer attachments of the children in Rognes did not seem to compete with the attachments to their parents, and why the children in Rognes were receptive to being parented by almost any adult in the village.

## ATTACHMENTS BORN OF A VOID

In American society—and in other societies that function along the American model—most attachments to peers do not arise naturally. They spring from the young's inability to endure an attachment void—the voids that occur when traditional bonds are eroded and the child finds himself bereft of a natural compass point. In such a situation, the brain is programmed to seek a substitute, someone to function as a working attachment. For a needy child, this agenda has the highest priority.

As story and legend tell us, attachments formed out of necessity are basically indiscriminate and accidental—the offspring of coincidence and chaos. The twins Romulus and Remus, the mythical founders of Rome, were thrown into a human attachment abyss and then raised by a she-wolf. Tarzan suffered the same fate but was adopted by some apes. In the Majorie Kinnan Rawlings children's classic *The Yearling* an orphaned fawn is reared by a young boy. A gazelle can attach to a lion. A cat can attach to a dog. My pet bantam rooster imprinted on my brother's Harley-Davidson.

Attachment voids, situations when the child's natural attachments are missing, are dangerous precisely because their results are so indiscriminate. As pointed out earlier, if the mother duck is not on hand when the duckling hatches, the young creature will form an attachment to the nearest moving object. For children, the imprinting process is far more complex, but the compass point is most likely to be the first person who appears to offer relief from the attachment void. Human attachment programming is blind to such factors as dependability, responsibility, security, maturity, and nurturance. There is no intelligence applied to the question of replacement. Many of our attachments, even as adults, are a sad testimony to this fact. For the child, no interview process takes place, not even any internal questioning. Never do the important issues of attachment enter into a child's consciousness: Is the compass point aligned with my parents? Will I be able to be close to both simultaneously? Can I depend on this person? Can this relationship offer me unconditional, loving acceptance? Can I trust in this person's direction and guidance? Am I invited to exist as I am and to express myself authentically? All too often the nurturing adults are displaced in favor of the peer group. What begins as a temporary replacement in specific situations where there is an orientation void ultimately becomes a permanent replacement.

The likelihood of an attachment becoming an "affair" that competes with attachment to parents is much greater when it is born of a void instead of an existing working relationship. Peer relationships are safest when they are the natural offspring of attachments with the parents. Unfortunately, instead of arising from connection, most of the time they are born of disconnection.

The more children form attachments to peers who are not connected to us, the greater the likelihood of incompatibility. The result is an ever-growing spiral of peer orientation. Our parents were less peer-oriented than we have become, and our children are likely to be more peer-oriented than we were, unless we are able to do something about it.

The current immigration experience in North America provides a dramatic illustration of peer orientation undermining time-honored cultural connections. The attachment voids experienced by immigrant children are profound. The hardworking parents are focused on supporting their families economically and, unfamiliar with the language and customs of their new society, they are not able to orient their children with authority or confidence. Peers are often the only people available for such children to latch on to. Thrust into a peer-oriented culture, immigrant families may quickly disintegrate. The gulf between child and parent can widen to the point that becomes unbridgeable. Parents of these children lose their dignity, their power, and their lead. Peers ultimately replace parents and gangs increasingly replace families. Again, immigration or the necessary relocation of people displaced by war or economic misery is not the problem. Transplanted to peer-driven North American society, traditional cultures succumb. We fail our immigrants because of our own societal failure to preserve the child-parent relationship.

In some parts of the country one still sees families, often from Asia, join together in multigenerational groups for outings. Parents, grandparents, and even frail great-grandparents mingle, laugh, and socialize with their children and their children's offspring. Sadly, one sees this only among relatively recent immigrants. As youth become incorporated into North American society, their connections with their elders fade. They distance themselves from their families. Their icons become the artificially created and hypersexualized figures mass-marketed by Hollywood and the U.S. music industry. They rapidly become alienated from the cultures that have sustained their ancestors for generation after generation. As we observe the rapid dissolution of immigrant families under the influence of the peer-oriented society, we witness, as if on fast-forward video, the cultural meltdown we ourselves have suffered in the past half century.

It would be encouraging to believe that other parts of the world will successfully resist the trend toward peer orientation. The opposite is likely to be the case as the global economy exerts its corrosive influences on traditional cultures on other continents. Problems of teenage alienation are now widely encountered in countries that have most closely followed upon the American model—Britain, Australia, and Japan. We may predict similar patterns elsewhere to result from economic changes and massive population shifts. For example, stress-related disorders are proliferating among Russian children. According to a report in the *New York Times,* since the collapse of the Soviet Union a little over a decade ago, nearly a third of Russia's estimated 143 million people—about 45 million—have changed residences. Peer orientation threatens to become one of the least welcome of all American cultural exports.

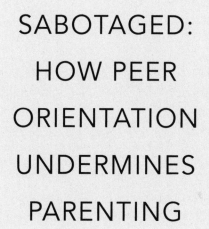

# PART TWO

# SABOTAGED:
# HOW PEER
# ORIENTATION
# UNDERMINES
# PARENTING

# 4

# THE POWER TO PARENT
# IS SLIPPING AWAY

K IRSTEN WAS SEVEN years old when her mother and father first consulted me, upset and worried over a sudden change in their daughter. She tended to do the opposite of what was expected and could be very rude to her parents, especially when her friends were around. The parents were perplexed. Before she entered second grade, Kirsten, the eldest of three sisters, had been loving and affectionate and eager to please. "Parenting Kirsten used to be a wonderful experience," the mother recalled. Now the child was resistant and very difficult to manage. She rolled her eyes to the most innocuous of requests, and everything ended up in a battle. The mother discovered a side of herself she never knew existed, finding herself angry and even enraged. She heard herself yelling and was shocked to hear words coming out of her mouth that frightened her. The father found the atmosphere so tense and the friction so wearing that he increasingly withdrew into his work. Like many parents in their situation, they resorted more and more to scolding, threats, and punishments—all to no avail.

It may be surprising to hear that parenting should be relatively easy. Getting our child to take our cues, follow directions, or respect our values should not require strain and struggle or coercion, nor even the extra leverage of rewards. If pressure tactics are required, something is amiss. Kirsten's mother and father had come to rely on force because, unawares, they had lost the *power to parent*.

Parenting was designed to be power-assisted. In this way, it is much like the luxury vehicles of today, with power-assisted steering, brakes, and windows. If the power fails, many of the cars would be too much to handle. To manage children when our parenting power has been cut is likewise next to impossible, yet millions of parents are trying to do just that. But whereas it is relatively easy to find a good technician to help with your car, the experts to whom parents bring their child-rearing difficulties seldom assess the problem correctly. Too often the children are blamed for being difficult or the parents for being inept or their parenting techniques for being inadequate. It is generally unrecognized by parents and professionals that the root of the problem is not parental ineptitude but parental impotence in the strictest meaning of that word: lacking sufficient power.

The absent quality is power, not love or knowledge or commitment or skill. Our predecessors had much more power than parents today. In getting children to heed, our grandparents wielded more power than our parents could exercise over us or we seem to have over our children. If the trend continues, our children will be in great difficulty when their turn comes at parenting. The power to parent is slipping away.

## THE SPONTANEOUS AUTHORITY TO PARENT

Parental impotence is difficult to recognize and distressing to admit. Our minds seize on more acceptable explanations: our children don't need us anymore, or our children are particularly difficult, or our parenting skill is deficient.

These days many people resist the concept of power. As children, some of us knew all too well the power of parents and became painfully aware of its potential for abuse. We are mindful that power leads to temptation and have experienced that those who seek power over others cannot be trusted. In some ways power has become a dirty word, as in power-seeking and power-hungry. It is not surprising that many have come to eschew it, an attitude I encounter frequently among parents and educators.

Many also confuse power with force. That is not the sense in which we employ the word *power* in this book. In our present discussion of parenting and attachment, power means the *spontaneous authority to parent*. That spontaneous authority flows not from coercion or force but from an appropriately aligned relationship with the child. The power to parent arises when things are in their natural order, and it arises without effort, without posturing, and without pushing. It is when we lack that power that we are likely to resort to force. The more power a parent commands, the less force is required in day-to-day parenting. On the other hand, the less power we possess, the more impelled we are to raise our voices, harshen our demeanor, utter threats, and seek some leverage to make our children comply with our demands. The loss of power experienced by today's parents has led to a preoccupation in the parenting literature with techniques that would be perceived as bribes and threats in almost any other setting. We have camouflaged such signs of impotence with euphemisms like rewards and "natural consequences."

Power is absolutely necessary for the task of parenting. Why do we need power? Because we have responsibilities. Parenting was never meant to exist without the power to fulfill the responsibilities it brings. There is no way of understanding the dynamics of parenting without addressing the question of power.

The power we have lost is the power to command our children's attention, to solicit their good intentions, to evoke their deference and secure their cooperation. Without these four abilities, all we have left is coercion or bribery. This was the problem faced by Kirsten's mother and father when they consulted me, anxious about their daughter's newly developed recalcitrance. I will use Kirsten's relationship with her parents as an example of the loss of natural parenting authority, along with two other cases I'll describe that also help demonstrate the meaning of parental power. There are nine people in this cast of characters—six parents and three children. Their stories typify the dilemma faced by many families today.

The parents of nine-year-old Sean were divorced. Neither had remarried, and the working relationship between the two of them was good enough that they could seek help together. Their difficulties in parenting Sean had contributed to their split. The early years with Sean had been relatively easy, but the past two had been horrendous. He was verbally abusive to his parents and physically aggressive toward his younger sister. Although he was very intelligent, no amount of reasoning could induce him to do as he was told. The parents had consulted several experts and had read many books that recommended various approaches and techniques. Nothing seemed to work with Sean. The usual sanctions only made things worse. Sending him to his room had no apparent impact. Although the mother did not believe in spanking, out of desperation she found herself employing physical punishment. The parents had given up trying to gain Sean's compliance in such simple matters as sitting at the family table during supper. They had no success in getting him to do his homework. Before the marriage broke up, Sean's sullen resistance blighted the atmosphere in the home. So worn down emotionally had they become that neither parent could any longer conjure up feelings of warmth or affection toward their son.

Melanie was thirteen years old. Her father could barely contain his anger when he talked about his daughter. Life with her changed after Melanie's grandmother had died when the child was in the sixth grade. Until that time, Melanie had been cooperative at home, a good student at school, and a loving sister to her brother, who was three years older. Now she was missing classes and couldn't care less about homework. She was sneaking out of the house on a regular basis. She refused to talk to her parents, declaring that she hated them and that she just wanted to be left alone. She, too, refused to eat with her parents, consuming her meals by herself in her room. The mother felt traumatized. She spent much of her time pleading with her daughter to be "nice," to be home on time, and to stop sneaking out. The father could not abide Melanie's insolent attitude. He believed that the solution was somehow to lay down the law, to teach the adolescent "a lesson she would never forget." As far as he was concerned, anything less than a hard-line approach was only indulging Melanie's unacceptable behavior and made matters worse. He was all the more enraged since, until this abrupt change in her personality, Melanie had been "daddy's girl," sweet and compliant.

Three individual scenarios, three separate sets of circumstances, and three very different kids—yet none of them unique. The child-rearing frustrations these parents experienced are shared by many fathers and mothers. The manifestations of difficulty differ from child to child, but the chorus is remarkably the same: parenting is much harder than anticipated. The litany of parental laments is by now a common one: "The children of today don't seem to have the respect for authority that we had when we were kids; I cannot get my child to do his homework, make his bed, do his chores, clean his room." Or the often heard mock complaint, "If parenting is so important, kids should come with a manual!"

## THE SECRET OF PARENTAL POWER

Many people have concluded that parents cannot be expected to know what to do without formal training. There are all kinds of parenting courses now, and even classes teaching parents how to read nursery rhymes to their toddlers. Yet experts cannot teach what is most fundamental to effective parenting. The power to parent does not arise from techniques, no matter how well meant, but from the attachment relationship. In all three of our examples that power was missing.

The secret of a parent's power is in the dependence of the child. Children are born completely dependent, unable to make their own way in this world. Their lack of viability as separate beings makes them utterly reliant on others for being taken care of, for guidance and direction, for support and approval, for a sense of home and belonging. It is the child's state of dependence that makes parenting necessary in the first place. If our children didn't need us, we would not need the power to parent.

At first glance, the dependence of children seems straightforward enough. But here is the glitch: being dependent does not guarantee dependence on the appropriate caregivers. Every child is born in need of nurturing, but after infancy and toddlerhood not all children necessarily look to the parent to provide it. Our power to parent rests not in how dependent our child is, but in how much our child depends specifically on us. The power to execute our parental responsibilities lies not in the neediness of our children but in their looking to us to be the answer to their needs.

We cannot truly take care of a child who does not count on us to be taken care of, or who depends on us only for food, clothing, shelter, and other material concerns. We cannot emotionally support a child who is not leaning on us for his psychological needs. It is frustrating to direct a child who does not welcome our guidance, irksome and self-defeating to assist one who is not seeking our help.

That was the situation faced by the parents of Kirsten, Sean, and Melanie. Kirsten no longer relied on her parents for her attachment needs or for her cues on how to be and what to do. At the tender age of seven, she no longer turned to them for comfort and nurturance. Sean's stance went beyond that: he had developed a deep-seated resistance to being dependent on his father and mother. Sean's resistance, and Melanie's, extended even to being fed—or, more exactly, to the ritual of feeding that takes place at the family table. Melanie, as she entered adolescence, no longer looked to her parents for a sense of home or connection. She had no wish to be understood by them or to be intimately known by them. Not one of these three children felt dependent on their parents, and that was at the root of the frustrations, difficulties, and failures experienced by all these mothers and fathers.

Of course, all children begin life depending on their parents. Something changed along the way for these three kids, as it does for many children today. It is not that they no longer needed to be taken care of. As long as a child is unable to function independently, he will need to depend on someone. No matter what these children may have thought or felt, they were not anywhere close to being ready to stand on their own two feet. They were still dependent—only they no longer experienced themselves as depending on their parents. Their dependency needs had not vanished; what had changed was only on whom they were depending. The power to parent will be transferred to whomever the child depends on, whether or not that person is truly dependable, appropriate, responsible, or compassionate—whether or not, in fact, that person is even an adult.

In the lives of these three children, peers had replaced parents as the objects of emotional dependence. Kirsten had a tight-knit group of three friends who served as her compass point and her home base. For Sean, the peer group in general became his working attachment, the entity to which he became connected in place of his parents. His values, interests, and motivations were invested in his peers and the peer culture. For Melanie, the attachment void created by the death of her grandmother was filled by a girlfriend. In all three cases the peer relationships competed with attachments to the parents, and in each case the peer connection came to dominate.

Such a power shift spells double trouble for us parents. Not only are we left without the power to manage our child, but the innocent and incompetent usurpers acquire the power to lead our children astray. Our children's peers did not actively seek this power—it goes with the territory of dependence. This sinister cut in parenting power often comes when we least expect it and at a time when we are most in need of natural authority. The seeds of peer dependence have usually taken root by the primary grades, but it is in the intermediate years that the growing incompatibility of peer and parent attachments plays havoc with our power to parent. Precisely during our children's adolescence, just when there is more to manage than ever before, and just when our physical superiority over them begins to wane, the power to parent slips from our hands.

What to us looks like independence is really just dependence transferred. We are in such a hurry for our children to be able to do things themselves that we do not see just how dependent they really are. Like power, dependence has become a dirty word. We want our children to be self-directing, self-motivated, self-controlled, self-orienting, self-reliant, and self-assured. We have put such a premium on independence that we lose sight of what childhood is about. Parents will complain of their child's oppositional and off-putting behaviors, but rarely do they note that their children have stopped looking to them for nurturing, comfort, and assistance. They are disturbed by their child's failure to comply with their reasonable expectations but seem unaware that the child no longer seeks their affection, approval, or appreciation. They do not notice that the child is turning to peers for support, love, connection, and belonging. When attachment is displaced, dependence is displaced. So is, along with it, the power to parent.

The ultimate challenge for the parents of Kirsten, Sean, and Melanie was not to enforce rules, induce compliance, or put an end to this or that behavior. It was to reclaim their children, to realign the forces of attachment on the side of parenting. They had to foster in their children the dependence that is the source of the power to parent. To regain their natural authority, they had to displace and usurp the illegitimate jurisdiction of their unsuspecting and unwitting usurpers — their children's friends. While reattaching our children may be easier to conceptualize than to do in practice, it is the only way to regain parental authority. Much of my work with families, and much of the advice I will give in this book, is intended to help parents reassume their natural position of authority.

What enables peers to displace parents in the first place, given that such displacement seems contrary to what is needed? As always, there is logic to the natural order of things. A child's ability to attach to people who are not her biological parents serves an important function, because in life the presence of the birth parents is by no means assured. They could die or disappear. Our attachment programming required the flexibility to find substitutes to attach to and depend on. Humans· are not unique in this transferability of attachments. What makes some creatures such great pets is that they can reattach from their parents to humans, enabling us to both care for them and manage them.

Since humans have a lengthy period of dependence, attachments must be transferable from one person to another, from parents to relatives and neighbors and tribal or village elders. All of these, in turn, are meant to play their role in bringing the child to full maturity. This remarkable adaptability, which has served parents and children for thousands of years, has come to haunt us in recent times. Under today's conditions, that adaptability now enables peers to replace parents.

Most parents are able to sense the loss of power when their child becomes peer-oriented, even if they don't recognize it for what it is. Such a child's attention is harder to command, his deference decreases, the parent's authority is eroded. When specifically asked, the parents of each of the three children in our case examples were able to identify when their power to parent began to wane. That erosion of natural authority is first noted by parents as simply a niggling feeling that something has gone wrong.

## WHAT ENABLES US TO PARENT?

It takes three ingredients to make parenting work: a dependent being in need of being taken care of, an adult willing to assume responsibility, and a good working attachment from the child to the adult. The most critical of these is also the one most commonly overlooked and neglected: the child's attachment to the adult. Many parents and would-be parents still labor under the misconception that one can simply step into the role of parenting, whether as an adoptive parent, a foster parent, a stepparent, or the biological parent. We expect that the child's need to be taken care of and our willingness to parent will suffice. We are surprised and offended when children seem resistant to our parenting.

Recognizing that parental responsibility is insufficient for successful child-rearing, but still not conscious of the role of attachment, many experts assume the problem must be in the parenting know-how. If parenting is not going well, it is because parents are not doing things right. According to this way of thinking, it is not enough to don the role; a parent needs some skill to be effective. The parental role has to be supplemented with all kinds of parenting techniques—or so many experts seem to believe.

Many parents, too, reason something like this: if others can get their children to do what they want them to do but I can't, it must be because I lack the requisite skills. Their questions all presume a simple lack of knowledge, to be corrected by "how to" types of advice for every conceivable problem situation: How do I get my child to listen? How can I get my child to do his homework? What do I need to do to get my child to clean his room? What is the secret to getting a child to do her chores? How do I get my child to sit at the table? Our predecessors would probably have been embarrassed to ask such questions or, for that matter, to show their face in a parenting course. It seems much easier for parents today to confess incompetence rather than impotence, especially when our lack of skill can be conveniently blamed on a lack of training or a lack of appropriate models in our own childhood. The result has been a multibillion-dollar industry of parental advice-giving, from experts advocating time-outs or reward points on the fridge to all the how-to books on effective parenting.

Child-rearing experts and the publishing industry give parents what they ask for instead of the insight they so desperately need. The sheer volume of the advice offered tends to reinforce the feelings of inadequacy and the sense of being unprepared for the job. The fact that these methodologies fail to work has not slowed the torrent of skill teaching.

Once we perceive parenting as a set of skills to be learned, it is difficult for us to see the process any other way. Whenever trouble is encountered the assumption is that there must be another book to be read, another course to be taken, another skill to be mastered. Meanwhile, our supporting cast continues to assume that we have the power to do the job. Teachers act as if we can still get our children to do homework. Neighbors expect us to keep our children in line. Our own parents chide us to take a firmer stand. The experts assume that compliance is just another skill away. The courts hold us responsible for our child's behavior. Nobody seems to get the fact that our hold on our children is slipping.

The reasoning behind parenting as a set of skills seemed logical enough, but in hindsight has been a dreadful mistake. It has led to an artificial reliance on experts, robbed parents of their natural confidence, and often leaves them feeling dumb and inadequate. We are quick to assume that our children don't listen because we don't know how to make them listen, that our children are not compliant because we have not yet learned the right tricks, that children are not respectful enough of authority because we, the parents, have not taught them to be respectful. We miss the essential point that what matters is not the skill of the parents but the relationship of the child to the adult who is assuming responsibility.

When we focus narrowly on what we should be doing, we become blind to our attachment relationship with our children and its inadequacies. Parenthood is above all a relationship, not a skill to be acquired. Attachment is not a behavior to be learned but a connection to be sought.

Parenting impotence is hard to see because the power that parents used to possess was not conscious of itself. It was automatic, invisible, a built-in component of family life and of tradition-based cultures. By and large, the parents of yesteryear could take their power for granted because it was usually sufficient for the task at hand. For reasons we have begun to explore, this is no longer the case. If one does not understand the source of one's ease, one cannot appreciate the root of one's difficulty. Owing to our collective ignorance of attachment, our difficulty recognizing parental impotence, and our aversion to power itself, the most common affliction in parenting is left begging for an explanation.

## THE SEARCH FOR LABELS

The obvious alternative to blaming the parent is to conclude that there is something amiss or lacking in the child. If we are not given to doubt our parenting, we assume the source of our trouble must be the child. We take refuge in the child-blaming thought that we have not failed, but our children have failed to live up to the expected standards. Our attitude is expressed in questions or demands such as Why don't you pay attention? Stop being so difficult! Or, Why can't you do as you're told?

Difficulty in parenting often leads to a hunt to find out what is wrong with the child. We may witness today a frantic search for labels to explain our children's problems. Parents seek the formal diagnoses of a professional or grasp at informal labels—there are, for examples, books on raising the "difficult" or the "spirited" child. The more frustrating parenting becomes, the more likely children will be perceived as difficult and the more labels will be sought for verification. It is no coincidence that the preoccupation with diagnoses has paralleled the rise in peer orientation in our society. Increasingly, children's behavioral problems are ascribed to various medical syndromes such as oppositional defiant disorder or attention deficit disorder. These diagnoses at least have the benefit of absolving the child and of removing the onus of blame from the parents, but they camouflage the reversible dynamics that cause children to misbehave in the first place. Medical explanations help by removing guilt but they hinder by reducing the issues to oversimplified concepts. They assume that the complex behavior problems of many children can be explained by genetics or by miswired brain circuits. They ignore scientific evidence that the human brain is shaped by the environment from birth throughout the lifetime and that attachment relationships are the most important aspect of the child's environment. They also dictate narrow solutions, such as medications, without regard to the child's relationships with peers and with the adult world. In practice, they serve to further disempower parents.

We are not saying that brain physiology is not implicated in some childhood disorders or that medications never have value. My cowriter, for example, sees many children and adults with ADD, a condition in which the brain's functioning is physiologically different from what is the norm, and he does prescribe medications when they seem justifiably needed. What we do object to is reducing childhood problems to medical diagnoses and treatments to the exclusion of the many psychological, emotional, and social factors that contribute to how these problems arise. Even in ADD and other childhood conditions where medical diagnoses and treatments can have value, the attachment relationship with parents must remain the primary concern and the best path toward healing.*

Sean's parents had already gone the route of seeking labels, collecting three different diagnoses from three different experts—two psychologists and a psychiatrist. One professional assessed him as obsessive compulsive, another as oppositionally defiant, and still another as suffering from attention deficit disorder. Finding out that something was indeed wrong with Sean was a great relief to his parents. Their difficulty in parenting was not their fault. Furthermore, the doctors' diagnoses also took Sean off the hook. He couldn't help it. The labels stopped the blaming, which was a good thing.

I had no quarrel with any of these labels; they actually described his behavior rather well. He was highly compulsive, resistant, and inattentive. Furthermore, what these three syndromes have in common is that the children so labeled are also impulsive and nonadaptive. Impulsive children (or adults) are unable to separate impulses from actions. They act out whatever impulse arises in their minds. To be nonadaptive is to fail to adapt when things go wrong and to fail to benefit from adversity, to learn from negative consequences. These failures give parents more inappropriate behavior to handle while at the same time limiting their tools for managing the child's conduct. For example, negative techniques such as admonishment, shaming, sanctions, consequences, and punishment are useless with a youngster who cannot learn from them. So, in one sense, one could accurately say that Sean's parents were having so much difficulty because of what was wrong with Sean. There is some truth in this, but sometimes one truth can mask an even greater truth—in this case, a problem in the relationship.

The medicalized labels made Sean's parents depend on experts. Instead of trusting in their own intuition, learning from their own mistakes and finding their own way, they started to look to others for cues on how to parent. They were mechanically following the advice of others, employing contrived methods of behavior control that ran roughshod over the attachment relationship. Sometimes, they said, it felt as if they were relating to a syndrome rather than to a person. Instead of finding answers, they found as many opinions as there were experts to propound them.

A yet more worrying problem with labels—even ones as informal as

*For a full discussion of these issues, see *Scattered Minds: A New Look at the Origins of Attention Deficit Disorder*, by Gabor Maté (Toronto: Vintage Canada, 1999).

"the difficult child" or as innocuous as "the sensitive child"—is that they create an impression that the root of the problem has been found. They cover up the true source of the difficulty. When an assessment of a problem ignores the underlying relationship factors, it retards the search for genuine solutions.

That Sean was a handful was not in question. His impulsiveness made him harder to manage, to be sure. Most impulses, however, are triggered by attachment, and it was Sean's attachments that had gone astray. It wasn't his impulsiveness but the fact that these impulses were working against the parents that made things so impossible. It went against Sean's natural instincts to depend on his parents, to be close to them or to take his cues from them. This was due to his peer orientation, not some medical disorder. His skewed attachment instincts also explained his oppositional behavior and pointed the way for a cure. The peer-orientation problem did not explain all his attention problems, but restoring healthy attachment with his parents was the way to establish a basis to deal with them. The most salient issue the parents needed to come to terms with was not what was wrong with Sean but what was missing in Sean's relationship to them.

Although neither Kirsten's parents nor Melanie's parents had gone the route of seeking a formal diagnosis, they also wondered whether their children were normal or whether the problem lay in their techniques. On closer examination I did find that Melanie was significantly immature for her age, but this again did not explain the difficulty in parenting. The critical issue was that she was peer dependent, which, given her psychological immaturity, delivered a devastating blow to parenting.

Fortunately, peer orientation is not only preventable but, in most cases, also reversible—Parts 4 and 5 of this book are dedicated to those tasks. We must, however, thoroughly understand what the problem is. Parenting was meant to be natural and intuitive but can be so only when the child is attaching to us. To regain the power to parent we must bring our children back into full dependence on us—not just physical dependence but psychological and emotional, too, as nature has ever intended.

# 5

# FROM HELP TO HINDRANCE:
# WHEN ATTACHMENT WORKS AGAINST US

THE COMEDIAN JERRY Seinfeld, a new father at the age of forty-seven, has commented on how unnerving it is to have a fellow human being look you blithely in the eye and poop his pants at the same time. "Imagine," said Seinfeld, "he is doing this while he is staring directly at you!" What keeps parents in the game is attachment. Commitment and values can go a long way but if it was only that, parenting would be sheer work. If it wasn't for attachment, many parents would not be able to stomach the changing of diapers, forgive the interrupted sleep, put up with the noise and the crying, carry out all the tasks that go unappreciated. Nor, later, could they tolerate the challenges of dealing with the irritating and even obnoxious behaviors of their offspring.

Attachment, we have noted, does its work invisibly. People who out of pure instinct have created a good attachment relationship with their child will be successful and competent parents even if they have never formally learned a single parenting "skill."

There are seven significant ways in which attachment supports effective parenting. It does so by securing the child's dependence on the parent, which is the true source of parental power. Unfortunately, when the child's attachments are out of line these same seven ways work to undermine parenting authority. Readers will find it useful to refer back to this list as they take on the task of reaffirming their connection with their children.

To parents eager for advice on what to do, I say again that patient and heartfelt understanding of attachment is the first requirement. My experience helping thousands of parents and children has convinced me that unless we completely get how and why things don't work—and also how things are meant to work—our attempted solutions, no matter how well-intentioned, will only compound the problem.

## ATTACHMENT ARRANGES THE PARENT AND CHILD HIERARCHICALLY

The first business of attachment is to arrange adults and children in a hierarchical order. When humans enter a relationship, their attachment brain automatically ranks the participants in order of dominance. Embedded in our inborn brain apparatus are archetypal positions that divide roughly into dominant and dependent, caregiving and care-seeking, the one who provides and the one who receives. This is even true for adult attachments, as in marriage, although in healthy, reciprocal relationships there will be a good deal of shifting back and forth between the giving and care-seeking modes, depending on circumstances and depending, too, on how the marriage partners have chosen to divide their responsibilities. With adults, children are meant to be in the dependent, care-seeking mode.

A child is receptive to being taken care of or to being directed as long as he experiences himself in a dependent mode. Children properly placed in the hierarchy of attachment instinctively want to be taken care of. They spontaneously look up to their parents, turn to them for answers, and defer to them. This dynamic is in the very nature of attachment. It's what enables us to do our job. Without that sense of dependence, behavior is difficult to manage.

Peer orientation activates this same programming, but now with negative results. It subverts the instinctual workings of the attachment brain, designed for child-adult attachments. Instead of keeping a child in a healthy relationship with her caregivers, the dominance/dependence dynamic sets up unhealthy situations of dominance and submission among immature peers.

A child whose attachment brain selects a more dominant mode will take charge of, and boss around, his peers. If this dominating child is compassionate and assumes responsibility for others, he will also be nurturing and caregiving. If the child is frustrated, aggressive, and self-centered, we have the making of a bully—as we will explore in later chapters on aggression and bullying. But the chief havoc caused by peer orientation is that it flattens the natural parent-child hierarchy. Parents lose the respect and authority that, in the natural order of things, properly belong to their dominant role.

A peer-oriented child has no inner sense of order or rank, no desire for the parent to be bigger than one or above one. On the contrary, any such posturing in the parent strikes the peer-oriented child as contrived and unnatural, as if the parent is trying to lord it over the child or trying to put him down.

The three children in the previous chapter were all seduced away from their parental attachments by peer orientation. Although Kirsten was only seven years old, her parents had lost their dominant position in the attachment order. That accounted for her rudeness and lack of respect, especially when peers were around. Likewise with Sean and Melanie. As the attachment with parents had weakened, the hierarchical arrangement meant to facilitate parenting had collapsed, which is what Melanie's father felt so acutely and was reacting to so vehemently. Melanie was treating her parents as if they were equals who had no business bossing her around and trying to run her life. Instinctively, Melanie's father was trying to put her in her place. Unfortunately, that's not something a parent can do without the assistance of attachment. Without attachment, the parent succeeds at most in cowing a child into obedience, at the price of grave damage to the relationship and to the child's long-term development.

Peer orientation is not the only way the attachment order can become inverted. It may happen, for example, because the parents have unresolved needs they project onto the child. In our respective practices as psychologist and physician, we have both seen parents who would rely on their children as confidants, complaining to their children about problems with their spouse. The child becomes a listening post for the parent's emotional distress. Instead of being able to confide to her parents her own difficulties, she learns to suppress her needs and to serve the emotional needs of others. Such an inversion of the attachment hierarchy is also harmful to healthy development. In *Attachment*, the first volume of his classic trilogy exploring the influence of parent-child relationships on personality development, the psychiatrist John Bowlby writes that "The reversal of roles between child, or adolescent, and parent, unless very temporary, is almost always not only a sign of pathology in the parent but a cause of it in the child."[1] Role reversal with a parent skews the child's relationship with the whole world. It is a potent source of later psychological and physical stress.

In short, the attachment brain of the adult-oriented child renders her receptive to a parent who takes charge and assumes responsibility for her. To such a child, it feels right for the parent to be in the dominant position. If the arrangement is inverted or if it falls flat due to peer orientation, to be parented will run counter to the child's instincts, no matter how great the need.

## ATTACHMENT EVOKES THE PARENTING INSTINCTS, MAKES THE CHILD MORE ENDEARING, AND INCREASES PARENTAL TOLERANCE

As Jerry Seinfeld's quip illustrates, attachment not only prepares a child to be taken care of, but also evokes the caregiving instincts in an adult. Training or education cannot do what attachment can do: trigger the instincts to take care of. Attachment also renders children more endearing than they otherwise would be. It increases our tolerance of the hardships involved in parenting and the unintentional abuse we may suffer in the process.

There is nothing more appealing than the attachment behavior of an infant—the eyes that engage, the smile that pulls at the heartstrings, the outstretched arms, the melting into you when you pick him up. A person would have to be completely hardened for his attachment buttons not to be pushed. The attachment behavior serves the purpose of awakening the parent within us. It is designed not by the infant but by attachment reflexes that are automatic and spontaneous. If it touches the parent inside us, we will find ourselves drawing near, wanting to hold, primed for assuming responsibility. We are experiencing attachment at work: the impulsive attachment behavior of the infant evoking the attachment instincts of a potential parent.

Such charming and engaging behaviors may fade as children become older, but the impact of the child's attachment behavior on parents remains powerful for the duration of childhood. When our children express by actions or words a desire to attach to us, it makes them sweeter and easier to take. There are hundreds of little gestures and expressions, all unconscious, that serve to soften us up and draw us near. We are not being manipulated by the child, we are being worked on by the forces of attachment, and for very good reason. Parenting involves hardship and we need something to make the burden a little bit easier to bear.

Peer orientation changes all that. The body language of attachment that creates the magnetic pull is no longer directed toward us. The eyes no longer engage us. The face does not endear. The smiles that used to warm our hearts have somehow frozen and now leave us cold or create an ache. Our child no longer responds to our touch. Embraces become perfunctory and one-sided. It becomes difficult to like our child. When not primed by our children's attachment to us, we are left to rely on our love and commitment alone and on our sense of responsibility as a parent. For some that is sufficient; for many it is not.

For Melanie's father it was not enough. Melanie had always been close to him, but when her attentions and affections were diverted to her peers, her father's heart went cold. He was the kind of guy who went out of his way, well beyond most parents, in order to make something work for his daughter, but it turned out to be more the work of attachment than his own autonomous character. His language reflected his change of heart. It was full of "I've had enough, I can't take this anymore," "Nobody should have to put up with this kind of shit." The ultimatums also started flying. Melanie's father felt used, abused, taken for granted, and taken advantage of.

Actually, all parents are used, abused, taken for granted, and taken advantage of. The reason it usually doesn't get to us is again the work of attachment. Take for example a mother cat with nursing kittens. The mother is walked on, bitten, scratched, pushed, and prodded, but for the most part remains remarkably tolerant. But should a kitten that is not hers be introduced to the litter, that tolerance will be sorely lacking unless an attachment forms. The mother cat will physically chastise the kitten for the slightest infraction, no matter how unavoidable it was. Our maturity as human parents and our sense of responsibility can help us transcend such instinctive reactions, but we still have much in common with other creatures of attachment. We, too, are triggered more easily when the attachment has become weakened. The lack of spontaneous mutual attachment is probably what has given stepparents such a bad reputation in the fairy tales of children.

Most of us need the help of attachment to put up with the wear and tear experienced while executing our parental responsibilities. Children generally have no idea of their impact on us, the hurts they may have inflicted or the sacrifices we have made on their behalf. Nor should they—at least not until they learn through their own mature reflection what we have done for them. It is part of the task of parenting to be taken for granted. What makes it all worthwhile is the gesture of affection, the sign of connection, the desire for closeness—not necessarily out of appreciation for our dedication and effort, but from attachment pure and simple. On the other hand, when that attachment is diverted, it can make the burden unbearable. Faced with peer-oriented children, many of us find our parenting instincts blunted. The natural warmth we like to feel toward our children becomes chilled, and we may even feel guilty for not "loving" our children enough.

In the unnatural arena of peer-oriented relationships, this same power of attachment to make one put up with mistreatment backfires. Meant to ease the burden of parenting and to keep parents in the game, among peers it fosters abuse. Children may come to tolerate the violation they experience at the hands of their peers. Parents are often dismayed that their children, recalcitrant at home to even the slightest correction or control, put up with the unreasonable demands of peers and even accept being mistreated by them. Unable to recognize that a friend or classmate doesn't care about her enough to take her feelings into consideration, the peer-oriented child will turn a blind eye or find an excuse that preserves the attachment.

## ATTACHMENT COMMANDS THE CHILD'S ATTENTION

It is immensely frustrating to manage a child who does not pay attention to us. Getting a child to look at us and to listen to us is foundational to all parenting. The parents in our cast of nine were all having difficulty gaining the attention of their children. Melanie's mother complained that sometimes it felt as if she didn't even exist. Sean's parents were tired of being ignored. Kirsten's parents were having difficulty getting their seven-year-old to listen and to take them seriously.

The problems experienced by this group in commanding the attention of their children are not unusual. In actual fact, no person can truly *command* the attention of another. The child's brain assigns priorities for what to attend to by dynamics that are, for the most part, unconscious. If hunger is preeminent, food will grab the child's attention. If the need to get oriented is the most urgent, the child will seek the familiar. If the child is alarmed, her attention will be diverted to scanning for what could be wrong. Attachment, however, is what matters most in the child's world and so it will be central to orchestrating her attention.

Basically, attention follows attachment. The stronger the attachment, the easier it is to secure the child's attention. When attachment is weak, the attention of the child will be correspondingly difficult to engage. One of the telltale signs of a child who isn't paying attention is a parent having continually to raise his voice or repeat things. Some of our most persistent demands as parents have to do with their attention: "Listen to me," "Look at me when I'm talking," "Now look here," "What did I just say?" or most simply, "Pay attention."

When children become peer-oriented, their attention instinctively turns toward peers. It goes against the natural instincts of a peer-oriented child to attend to parents or teachers. The sounds emanating from adults are regarded by the child's attention mechanisms as so much noise and interference, lacking in meaning and relevance to the attachment needs that dominate his emotional life.

Peer orientation creates deficits in the child's attention to adults because adults are not top priority in the attention hierarchy of peer-oriented children. It is no accident that attention deficit disorder was initially considered a school problem, a child's failing to pay attention to the teacher. It is also no accident that the explosion in the number of diagnosed cases of attention deficit disorder has paralleled the evolution of peer orientation in our society and is worse where peer orientation is most predominant — urban centers and inner-city schools. This is not to suggest that all problems in paying attention stem from this source and that there are no other factors involved in ADD. On the other hand, not to recognize the fundamental role of attachment in governing attention is to ignore the reality of many children diagnosed with ADD. Deficits in attachments to adults contribute significantly to deficits in attention to adults. If attachment is disordered, attention will also be disordered.

## ATTACHMENT KEEPS THE CHILD CLOSE TO THE PARENT

Perhaps the most obvious task of attachment is to keep the child close. When the child experiences his need for proximity in physical terms — as very young children do — attachment serves as an invisible leash. Our offspring have this in common with many other creatures of attachment who must keep a parent in sight, hearing, or smell.

Sometimes we find the need for closeness a bit suffocating, especially when the toddler or preschooler panics when we so much as close the bathroom door. For the most part, however, this attachment programming gives us great freedom. Instead of having to keep our eye on the child continuously, we can afford to take the lead and trust in his instincts to make him follow. Like a mother bear with a cub or a feline mother with kittens or mother goose with goslings, we can let attachment do the work of keeping our young close instead of having to herd them or put them in pens.

The child's instincts to keep close to us can get in our way and frustrate us. We do not welcome the work of attachment when it is separation we crave, whether for purposes of work, school, sex, sanity, or sleep. Our society is so topsy-turvy that we may actually come to value the child's willingness to separate more than her instincts for closeness. Unfortunately, we cannot have it both ways. Parents whose young children are not properly attached face a nightmare scenario just keeping the child in sight. We should be thankful for the assistance attachment provides in holding our children close. If we had to do all the work, we would never be able to get on with the sundry other duties that parenting involves. We need to learn to parent in harmony with this design rather than fight against it.

If all goes well, the drive for physical proximity with the parent gradually evolves into a need for emotional connection and contact. The urge to keep the parent in sight changes into the need to know where the parent is. Even adolescents, if well attached, will be asking "Where's dad?" and "When's mom getting home?" and will often exhibit some anxiety when not able to get in touch.

Peer orientation messes with these instincts. There is just as much need for connection and contact in peer-oriented children, but it is now redirected toward each other. Now it's the whereabouts of our replacements that the child becomes anxious about. As a society we have developed a powerful technology for keeping in touch, from cell phones to e-mail to Internet chat lines. Thirteen-year-old Melanie, obsessed with peer contact, was fully engaged in this pursuit. This urgent need to stay in touch interferes not only with family time but with the child's studies, the development of talent, and most certainly with the creative solitude that is so essential for maturation. (For more on maturation and creative solitude, see Chapter 9.)

## ATTACHMENT CREATES A MODEL OUT OF THE PARENT

Adults are often surprised and even hurt when the children under their care do not follow their lead in how they conduct themselves and live their lives. Such disappointment springs from the misbelief that parents and teachers are automatic models for their children and students. In reality, the child accepts as his models only those to whom he is strongly attached.

It is not our lives that make us models, no matter how exemplary, nor is it our sense of responsibility toward the child or our nurturing role in the child's life. It is attachment that makes a child want to be like another person, to take on another's characteristics. Modeling, in short, is an attachment dynamic. By emulating the person to whom he is attached, the child is maintaining psychological closeness with that individual.

The desire for sameness with important attachment figures leads to some of a child's most significant and spontaneous learning experiences, even though closeness, not learning, is the underlying motivation. Such learning occurs without either the parent having much conscious intent of teaching or the child of studying. In the absence of attachment, the learning is labored and the teaching forced. Think of the work that would be involved if each word the child acquired had to be deliberately taught by the parent, each behavior consciously shaped, each attitude intentionally inculcated. The burden of parenting would be overwhelming. Attachment accomplishes these tasks automatically, with relatively little effort required from either parent or child. Attachment provides power-assisted learning— how delightful it is, many people have found, to study a new language when in love with the charming instructor! Whether we know it or not, as parents and teachers we rely heavily on attachment to make models out of us.

When peers replace parents as the dominant attachment figures, they become our child's models without, of course, assuming any responsibility for the end result. Our children copy each other's language, gestures, actions, attitudes, and preferences. The learning is just as impressive, but the content is no longer in our control. The schoolyard is often where this power-assisted learning occurs most. What is learned in this manner may be acceptable when the models are children we like, but quite distressing when children become the models whose behavior or values we find troubling. Worse, any teaching we want to offer our children now becomes labored, deliberate, and painfully slow. The job of parenting becomes immeasurably more complicated when we are not the model our child is emulating.

## ATTACHMENT DESIGNATES THE PARENT AS THE PRIMARY CUE-GIVER

One of the fundamental tasks of parenting is to provide direction and guidance to our children. Every day we point out what works and what doesn't, what is good and what's not, what is expected and what is inappropriate, what to aim for and what to avoid. Until the child becomes capable of self-direction and of following cues from within, he or she needs someone to show the way. Children constantly search for cues to how to be and what to do.

The critical issue is not how astute our teaching is, but who the child's attachment programming appoints to be the guide to follow. It is important to be good at giving direction, but it does not matter how wise or clear-spoken if we are not the ones the child is looking to for cues. That is where the parenting literature has gone wrong. The unstated premise, no longer warranted, is that children are adult-oriented, taking their cues from parents or teachers. The focus of the literature is therefore on how to provide guidance and direction—for example, being clear about expectations, setting well-defined and reasonable limits, articulating the rules, being consistent about consequences, avoiding mixed messages. When children do not follow our cues, it is easy to assume that the problem lies either in the way we are conveying our expectations or in children's ability to receive our messages. That may be so in some situations, but far more likely the problem lies much deeper: as a result of the lost attachment, the child no longer follows our lead.

Providing direction and guidance shouldn't be an arduous task, fraught with frustration. It can, and ought to, happen spontaneously. Whomever serves as the child's compass point comes to serve as the cue-giver as well. It is all part of the orienting reflex. The child's brain will automatically scan for cues from whomever the child is primarily attached to. If a child's attachment brain is oriented to the parent, these cues will come from the parent's face, the parent's reactions, the parent's values, communications, and gestures. The parent is being read and studied carefully for signs that point to what might be wanted or expected. Attachment makes it easy to give direction—sometimes a bit too easy.

When we are not at our best and behave or speak in ways we are not proud of, we may wish that our children were not following our lead quite so automatically and accurately. The power may feel burdensome at times, but somebody will be the designated cue-giver. If not us, then who? At least, as adults and responsible parents, we have the capacity and sense of responsibility to reflect on our actions and, when necessary, repair any damage we may have caused. When peers get the power, they assume no responsibility, nor do they ever feel bad about any negative impact they have. Unlike parents, they do not struggle to grow into the role attachment has assigned them. Even if we are immature and inadequate, being granted the awesome responsibility of being a model and cue-giver is a powerful inducement to extend ourselves and grow up.

If peers replace a parent as the cue-giver, the child will follow the expectations of his peers, as he perceives them. Such a child will follow the demands of his peers just as readily as he would obey the orders of the parent if he, the child, were adult-oriented.

Some parents may avoid giving direction in the naive belief that they have to leave room for the child to develop his own internal guides. It doesn't work like that. Only psychological maturity can grant genuine self-determination. While it is important for their development that children be given choices appropriate to their age and maturity, parents who avoid giving direction on principle end up abdicating their parenting role. In the absence of parental direction most children will seek guidance from a substitute source, likely their peers.

Managing a child who is not following our direction is difficult enough, but trying to control a child under someone else's command is next to impossible. What was meant to replace us is not someone else giving orders but maturity—that is, a grown-up person's own capacity to make decisions and to choose the best course of action for herself.

## ATTACHMENT MAKES THE CHILD WANT TO BE GOOD FOR THE PARENT

The final important way we are assisted by our child's attachment to us is the most significant of all: the child's desire to be good for the parent. It deserves a close look.

The child's eagerness to comply gives the parent formidable power. The difficulties created by its absence are equally formidable. We can see the impetus to be good in the eagerness of pet dogs to behave for their masters, indifferent though they are to the commands of strangers. Trying to manage a dog uninterested in being good for us gives a small inkling of what we are up against when this motivation is lacking in an emotionally much more complex and vulnerable being like the human child.

This desire to be good is one of the first things I look for in a child whose parents are encountering trouble in their parenting. There are a number of reasons for a child to not be good, but by far the most crucial is the absence of the desire itself. Sad to say, some children can never measure up to their parents' expectations because the standards demanded by the parents are hopelessly unrealistic. But if the child's desire itself is lacking, it does not much matter if the expectations are realistic or not. When I queried the parents of Sean, Melanie, and Kirsten, they all reported that their child was short on this motivation. Yet the parents of each could recall a time in the not-too-distant past when the drive to be good had been much more in evidence.

For purposes of child-rearing, the crowning achievement of a working attachment is to instill in a child the desire to be good. When we say of a particular child that he is "good," we think we are describing an innate characteristic of the child. What we don't see is that it's the child's attachment to the adult that fosters that goodness. In this way, we are blind to the power of attachment. The danger in believing that the child's innate personality causes his desire to be good is that we will blame and shame him—we will see him as "bad"—if we find that desire lacking. The impulse to be good arises less from a child's character than from the nature of a child's relationships. If a child is "bad," it's the relationship we need to correct, not the child.

Attachment evokes the desire to be good in a number of ways, each of them influential in its own right. Together they make possible the transmission of standards of acceptable behavior and values from one generation to the next. One source of the child's desire to be good is what I call the "attachment conscience"—a sort of alarm that is innate in the child. It warns her against conduct that would trigger the parent's disfavor. The word *conscience* originates in the Latin verb "to know." I use it here in this more basic meaning, not as a code of morality but as an inner knowledge that protects against a rift with the parent.

The essence of the attachment conscience is separation anxiety. Because attachment matters so much, important nerve centers in the attachment brain operate like alarms, creating a sense of uncomfortable agitation when we face separation from those we are attached to. At first it is the anticipation of physical separation that evokes this response in the child. As attachment becomes more psychological, the experience of emotional separation becomes more anxiety-producing. The child will feel bad when anticipating or experiencing the disapproval or the disappointment of the parent. Anything the child does that could possibly upset the parent, push the parent away, or alienate the parent will evoke anxiety in the child. The attachment conscience will keep the child's behavior within the boundaries set by parental expectations.

The attachment conscience may ultimately evolve into the moral conscience of the child, but its original function is to preserve the connection with whomever serves as the primary attachment. When a child's working attachment changes, the attachment conscience will likely be recalibrated to avoid whatever would cause upset or distancing in the new relationship. Not until a child has developed a selfhood strong enough to form independent values and judgments does a more mature and autonomous conscience evolve, consistent across all situations and relationships.

While it is beneficial for a child to feel bad when anticipating a loss of connection with those who are devoted to him and his well-being and development, it is crucially important for parents to understand that it is unwise to ever exploit this conscience. We must never intentionally make a child feel bad, guilty, or ashamed in order to get him to be good. Abusing the attachment conscience evokes deep insecurities in the child and may induce him to shut it right down for fear of being hurt. The consequences are not worth any short-term gains in behavioral goals.

The attachment conscience may become dysfunctional for reasons other than peer orientation, but the most common cause of it serving the wrong purpose is for it to become skewed toward peers and away from parents. In this circumstance the conscience is still operational, but its natural purpose is subverted. Two undesirable consequences follow. Parents lose the help of this conscience in influencing their children's behavior and, at the same time, the attachment conscience is reset to serve peer relationships. If we find ourselves shocked by the behavioral changes that come in the wake of peer orientation, it is because what is acceptable to peers is vastly different from what is acceptable to parents. Likewise, what alienates peers is a far cry from what alienates parents. The attachment conscience is serving a new master.

When a child tries to find favor with peers instead of parents, the motivation to be good for the parents drops significantly. If the values of the peers differ from those of the parents, the child's behavior will also change accordingly. This change in behavior reveals that the values of the parents had never been truly internalized, genuinely made the child's own. They functioned mostly as instruments of finding favor.

Children do not internalize values—make them their own—until adolescence. Thus the changes in a peer-oriented child's behavior do not mean that his values have changed, only that the direction of his attachment instinct has altered course. Parental values such as studying, working toward a goal, the pursuit of excellence, respect for society, the realization of potential, the development of talent, the pursuit of a passion, the appreciation of culture are often replaced with peer values that are much more immediate and short term. Appearance, entertainment, peer loyalty, spending time together, fitting into the subculture, and getting along with each other will be prized above education and the realization of personal potential. Parents often find themselves arguing about values, not realizing that for their peer-oriented children values are nothing more than the standards that they, the children, must meet in order to gain the acceptance of the peer group.

So it happens that we lose our influence just at the time in our children's lives when it is most appropriate and necessary for us to articulate our values to them and to encourage the internalization of what we believe in. The nurturing of values takes time and discourse. Peer orientation robs parents of that opportunity. In this way peer orientation arrests moral development.

The impulse to be bad is the obverse of the desire to be good. To indicate that such and such would please us or that something our child did made us proud or happy can actually backfire. The bipolar nature of attachment, discussed in Chapter 2, is such that when the negative aspect is active, it can provoke behavior opposite to what is desired. This was certainly true with Melanie and her mother. When a child is resisting contact with us instead of wanting to please, the instincts are to repel and to irritate. Melanie went to great lengths to annoy her mother. It may seem like the peer-oriented child is trying to push our buttons, and in one sense this is very true, except that is instinctive and unintentional. Creatures of attachment are creatures of instinct and impulse. It doesn't feel good or right or proper to seek favor in the eyes of those one is seeking distance from. When looking for the approval of your peers, it is almost unbearable to find favor with adults.

A final warning. A child's desire to be good for the parent is a powerful motivation that makes parenting much easier. It requires careful nurturance and trust. It is a violation of the relationship not to believe in the child's desire when it actually exists, for example to accuse the child of harboring ill intentions when we disapprove of her behavior. Such accusations can easily trigger defenses in the child, harm the relationship, and make her feel like being bad. It is also too risky for the child to continue to want to be good for a parent or teacher who lacks faith in her intention to be good and thinks, therefore, that she, the child, must be tempted with bribes or threatened with sanctions. It's a vicious circle. External motivators for behavior such as rewards and punishments may destroy the precious internal motivation to be good, making leverage by such artificial means necessary by default. As an investment in easy parenting, trusting in a child's desire to be good for us is one of the best.

Many current methods of behavior management, by relying on externally imposed motivations, run roughshod over this delicate drive. The doctrine of so-called natural consequences is one example. This disciplining method is meant to impress upon the child that specific misbehaviors will incur specific sanctions selected by the parent, according to logic that makes sense in the mind of the parent but rarely in the child's. What the parent sees as natural is experienced by the child as arbitrary. If consequences are truly natural, why do they have to be imposed on the child?

Some parents perceive trust as having to do with the end result, not with the basic motivation. In their eyes trust is something to be earned rather than an investment to be made. "How can I trust you," they may say, "if you don't do what you said you would do or if you lied to me?" Even if a child was never able to measure up to our expectations or realize his own intentions, it would still be important to trust in his desire to be good for us. To withdraw that trust is to take the wind out of his sails and to hurt him deeply. If the desire to be good for us is not treasured and nurtured, the child will lose his motivation to keep trying to measure up. It is children's desire to be good for us that warrants our trust, not their ability to perform to our expectations.

# 6

# COUNTERWILL: WHY CHILDREN
# BECOME DISOBEDIENT

"**Y**OU AREN'T MY boss," seven-year-old Kirsten was suddenly telling her bewildered parents whenever they demanded her cooperation. Sean, nine years old and also increasingly recalcitrant, tacked a large and forbidding Keep Out sign on his door. The adolescent Melanie's communication with her parents was reduced to little more than gestures of defiance: a sullen expression, a shrug, or a smirk that became all the more contemptuous as her father issued enraged but ineffectual orders to "wipe that smile off your face."

As I showed in the previous chapter, once our children become peeroriented, attachment turns against us and we lose the power to parent. With these two strikes against them, the parents of Kirsten, Melanie, and Sean were having a rough time already, but the story doesn't end there. There is another instinct that, when skewed by peer orientation, creates havoc in the parent-child relationship and makes life miserable for any adult in charge. It was aptly dubbed "counterwill" by an insightful Austrian psychologist named Otto Rank.

Counterwill is an instinctive, automatic resistance to any sense of being forced. It is triggered whenever a person feels controlled or pressured to do someone else's bidding. It makes its most dramatic appearance in the second year of life—yes, the so-called terrible two's. (If two-year-olds could make up such labels, they would perhaps describe their parents as going through the "terrible thirties.") Counterwill reappears with a vengeance during adolescence but it can be activated at any age—many adults experience it.

In the first part of the twentieth century, Rank had already noted that dealing with counterwill was the parent's most daunting challenge. He was writing at a time when, by and large, children's attachments were still aligned toward adults. So there is nothing abnormal about counterwill in a child, but, as I will shortly explain, it has become abnormally magnified under the influence of peer orientation.

No one likes to be pushed around, including children—or more correctly, *especially* children. Though we are all quite aware of this instinctive response in ourselves, we somehow overlook it when dealing with our young. Understanding counterwill can save a parent much unnecessary confusion and conflict, particularly when it comes to making sense of a peer-oriented child's attitudes and behavior.

Counterwill manifests in thousands of ways. It can show up as the reactive no of the toddler, the "You aren't my boss" of the young child, as balkiness when hurried, as disobedience or defiance. It is visible in the body language of the adolescent. Counterwill is also expressed through passivity, in procrastination, or in doing the opposite of what is expected. It can appear as laziness or lack of motivation. It may be communicated through negativity, belligerence, or argumentativeness, often interpreted by adults as insolence. In many children driven by counterwill we may observe a fascination with transgressing taboos and adopting antisocial attitudes. No matter what it looks like, the underlying dynamic is straightforward—instinctive resistance to being forced.

The simplicity of the dynamic is in sharp contrast to the multitude and complexity of the problems it creates—for parents, for teachers, and for anyone dealing with children. The very fact that something is important to us can make our children feel less like doing it. The more we pressure our children into eating their veggies, cleaning their rooms, brushing their teeth, doing their homework, minding their manners, or getting along with their siblings, the less inclined they are to comply. The more insistently we command them not to eat junk food, the more inclined they are to do it. "Each time you tell me to eat my greens, I feel less like doing it," a self-perceptive fourteen-year-old told his father. The clearer we are about our expectations, the more focused they become in their defiance. All this can be true even in the most normal and natural of circumstances—that is, when children are well attached to the adults charged with their care. When children are not actively attaching to the ones responsible for them, they will experience grown-ups' efforts at maintaining authority as "bossing around." By displacing the child's natural attachments, peer orientation magnifies the resistance out of all measure. The counterwill instinct can get quite out of hand.

## COUNTERWILL GROWS AS ATTACHMENT WANES

The basic human resistance to coercion is usually tempered, if not preempted, by attachment. This, too, we know from our own experience: when we're in love, hardly any expectation by our loved one seems unreasonable. We are far more likely to balk at the demands of someone we don't feel connected with. A child who wants to be close to us will likely receive our expectations as an opportunity to measure up. Cues about how to be and what to do help such a child find favor in the parent's eyes.

Divorced from the attachment dynamic, it is a different story indeed, especially for those not mature enough to know their own minds. Expectations are now a source of pressure. To be told what to do is to feel pushed around. To obey is to feel as if one has capitulated. Even relatively mature adults may react that way, let alone the developing child. To give a command to a preschooler with whom one does not have a relationship is to invite being defied or, at best, being ignored. The little one has no inclination to obey someone with whom he does not feel connected. It simply does not feel right to do the bidding of strangers, those outside the child's circle of attachments.

For immature adolescents the dynamic is exactly the same, even if their ways of expressing it may not be nearly as cutely innocent. In situations when they are habitually told what to do by persons to whom they are not attached, counterwill can easily become entrenched as their fundamental response to the adult world. An intensely peer-oriented fourteen-year-old who had been sent to a boarding school because counterwill had made her unmanageable ended up being kicked out of the school for the same reason. I asked why she had committed some of the atrocious acts attributed to her. Her answer was a shrug and a matter-of-fact "because we weren't supposed to." This imperative seemed so self-evident to her that, in her perception, my question hardly deserved to be answered.

Asked what matters the most to them, peer-oriented and counterwill-driven children often reply, "To not let anyone push us around." So pervasive and severe is their counterwill that to adults they seem incorrigible and impossible to manage. Clinicians diagnose such children with oppositional defiant disorder. Yet it is not the oppositionality—the counterwill—that is out of order but the child's attachments. These children are only being true to their instinct in defying people to whom they do not feel connected. The more peer-oriented a child, the more resistant to the adults in charge. What we label as behavioral disorders in individual children are really signs of a societal dysfunction.

The counterwill instinct flies in the face of our notions about how children should be. We operate under the impression that children should be universally receptive to direction by the responsible adults. Children are naturally compliant all right, but only in the context of connection and only when attachment power is sufficient.

By undermining a child's attachment with parents, peer orientation turns the counterwill instinct against the very people the child should be looking to for guidance and direction. Peer-oriented children instinctively resist even the parents' most reasonable expectations. They balk, "work to rule," counter, disagree, or do the opposite of what is wanted.

Parents don't even have to say anything to provoke counterwill in a peer-oriented child. If anyone can read our minds concerning what we would like them to do, it is our children. When we the parents are replaced by peers, this knowledge of our will does not go away. What disappears is the attachment to us that would make our will palatable. The desire to comply is replaced by its opposite. Without a single word from the parent the peer-oriented child will feel imposed on, pressured, or manipulated.

Underlying the difficulties facing the parents of Kirsten, Sean, and Melanie was this counterwill dynamic, distorted and magnified by peer orientation. Simple requests resulted in these children getting their backs up. Push came to shove. Expectations backfired. The more important something was to the parents, the less inclined the children were to deliver. The more commanding Melanie's father tried to be, the more rebellious his daughter became. It wasn't so much that the parents were doing anything wrong as that their children's counterwill instinct had been made pervasive—and even perverse—by peer orientation.

## THE NATURAL PURPOSE OF COUNTERWILL

As vexing as dealing with an oppositional child can be for adults, in its appropriate context counterwill, like all natural instincts in their natural setting, exists for a positive and even necessary purpose. It serves a twofold developmental function. Its primary role is as a defense that repels the commands and influence of those outside the child's attachment circle. It protects the child from being misled and coerced by strangers.

Counterwill also fosters the growth of the young person's internal will and autonomy. We all begin life utterly helpless and dependent, but the outcome of natural development is the maturation of a self-motivated and self-regulated individual with a genuine will of her own. The long transition from infancy to adulthood begins with the very young child's tentative moves toward separation from the parents. Counterwill first appears in the toddler to help in that task of individuation. In essence, the child erects a wall of no's. Behind this wall, the child can gradually learn her likes and dislikes, aversions and preferences, without being overwhelmed by the far more powerful will of the parent. Counterwill may be likened to the small fence one places around a newly planted lawn to protect it from being stepped on. Because of the tenderness and tentativeness of the new emergent growth, a protective barrier has to be in place until the child's own ideas, meanings, initiatives, and perspectives are rooted enough and strong enough to take being trampled on without being destroyed. Without that protective fence, the child's incipient will cannot survive. In adolescence, counterwill serves the same goal, helping the young person loosen his psychological dependence on the family. It comes at a time when the sense of self is having to emerge out of the cocoon of the family. Figuring out what we want has to begin with having the freedom to not want. By keeping out the parent's expectations and demands, counterwill helps make room for the growth of the child's own self-generated motivations and inclinations. Thus, counterwill is a normal human dynamic that exists in all children, even those appropriately attached.

For most well-attached children, counterwill remains a repeated but fleeting experience. It will be limited to situations when the force that the adult is applying to bring the child into line is greater than the attachment power the adult possesses in that given situation. Some such moments are unavoidable in parenting. The wise and intuitive parent will keep them to the necessary minimum, to times when circumstances or the child's well-being demand that the parent impose his will openly. If we are unconscious of both the dynamic of attachment and that of counterwill, we may not be sensitive to where the threshold between the two lies. We cross it inadvertently even when there is no call to do so.

We may believe, for example, that our child is stubborn or willful and that we have to break him of his defiant ways. Yet young children can hardly be said to have a will at all, if by that is meant a person's capacity to know what he wants and to stick to that goal despite setbacks or distractions. "But my child is strong-willed," many parents insist. "When he decides that he wants something he just keeps at it until I cannot say no, or until I get very angry." What is really being described here is not will but a rigid, obsessive clinging to this or that desire. An obsession may resemble will in its persistence but has nothing in common with it. Its power comes from the unconscious and it rules the individual, whereas a person with true will is in command of his intentions. The child's oppositionality is not an expression of will. What it denotes is the absence of will, which allows a person only to react, but not to act from a free and conscious process of choosing.

It is common to mistake counterwill for strength on the part of the child, as the child's purposeful attempt to get his own way. What is strong is the defensive reaction, not the child. The weaker the will, the more powerful the counterwill. If the child was indeed strong in her own self, she would not be so threatened by the parent. Instead of being the one doing the pushing, it is the child who feels pushed around. Her brazenness does not come from genuine independence but from the lack of it.

Counterwill happens *to* the child rather than being instigated *by* her. It may take the child as much by surprise as the parent and is really the manifestation of a universal principle, that for every force there is a counterforce. We see the same law in physics where, for example, for every centripetal force there has to be a centrifugal one. Since counterwill is a counterforce, we invite it into being every time our wish to impose something on our child exceeds his desire to connect with us.

The best reason for children to experience counterwill is when it arises not as automatic oppositionality, but as a healthy drive for independence. The child will resist being helped in order to do it herself; will resist being told what to do in order to find her own reasons for doing things. She will resist direction in order to find her own way; to discover her own mind, to find her own momentum and initiative. The child will resist the "shoulds" of the parent in order to discover her own preferences. But, as I will explain, that shift toward genuine independence can happen only when a child is absolutely secure in his attachment to the adults in his life (see Chapter 9).

A five-year-old safely grounded in his relationship with his parents might react to a the sky-is-blue kind of statement by retorting adamantly that it is not. It may seem to the parent that the child is blatantly contrary or trying to be difficult. In reality, the child's brain is simply blocking out any ideas or thoughts that have not originated within him. Anything that is alien to him is resisted in order to make room for him to come up with his own ideas. The final content will most likely be the same—the sky is blue—but when it comes to being one's own person, originality is what counts.

When counterwill is serving the quest for autonomy, it operates much like a psychological immune system, reacting defensively to anything that does not originate within the child. As long as the parent makes some room for the child to become his own person and nurtures his need for autonomy as well as for attachment, developmental progress will be made. Even this counterwill may not be easy to handle, as Otto Rank pointed out, but it isn't pervasive—does not distort most of our child's interactions with us—and it is certainly there for a good purpose. It serves the ultimate developmental agenda of mature independence.

If development unfolds optimally and the child makes headway in becoming her own person, the need for attachment wanes. As it does, the maturing child will be even more sensitive to coercion and even less amenable to being bossed around. Such a child will feel demeaned when treated as if he or she does not have his own thoughts and opinions, boundaries, values and goals, decisions and aspirations. She will resist adamantly when not acknowledged as a separate person. Again, this is a good thing. Counterwill is serving the purpose of protecting the child against becoming an extension of anyone else, even the parent. It helps to deliver an autonomous, emergent, independent being, full of vitality and able to function outside of attachments.

As genuine independence develops and maturation occurs, counterwill fades. With maturation human beings gain the capacity to endure mixed emotions. They can be in conflicting states of mind at the same time: wanting to be independent but committed also to preserving the attachment relationship. Ultimately, the truly mature person with a genuine will of his own need not mount an automatic opposition to the will of another: he can afford to heed the other when it makes sense to do so, or to go his own way when it does not.

## THE FALSE INDEPENDENCE OF
## THE PEER-ORIENTED CHILD

As ever, peer orientation throws a monkey wrench into the natural developmental pattern. Rather than serving autonomy, counterwill supports only the more primitive purpose of keeping the child from being bossed around by those with whom she has no wish to be close. For peer-oriented children, those people are us—their parents and teachers. Rather than preparing the way to genuine independence, counterwill protects the dependence on peers. And here is the ultimate irony: a dynamic that originally served to forge room for independent functioning comes, under the influence of peer orientation, to destroy the very basis of independence—the child's healthy relationship with the parent.

In our society, such peer-distorted counterwill is often mistaken for the real thing, for the healthy human striving for autonomy. We assume that the peer-oriented adolescent's oppositional reactions represent natural teenage rebellion. It is easy to confuse the two. There are the usual signs of resistance: the talking back, the refusal to cooperate, the incessant arguing, the noncompliance, the territorial battles, the barricades erected to keep the parents out, the antisocial attitudes, the you-can't-control-me messages. Counterwill in the service of peer attachment, however, is vastly different from the natural counterwill that supports true independence. In a maturing child the desire for attachment and the quest for autonomy mingle, creating a host of mixed feelings. Times of more reactive counterwill are balanced by times of seeking closeness. When the counterwill is a result of peer-orientation, the resistance is more blatant and unmitigated by any moves toward proximity with the parents. The child is rarely aware of conflicting impulses—the pull is all one way, toward the peers.

There is a foolproof way to distinguish peer-distorted counterwill from the genuine drive for autonomy: the maturing, individuating child resists coercion whatever the source may be, including pressure from peers. In healthy rebellion, true independence is the goal. One does not seek freedom from one person only to succumb to the influence and will of another. When counterwill is the result of skewed attachments, the liberty that the child strives for is not the liberty to be his true self but the opportunity to conform to his peers. To do so, he will suppress his own feelings and camouflage his own opinions, should they differ from those of his peers.

Are we saying that it may not be natural, for example, that a teenager may want to stay out late with his friends? No, the teen may want to hang out with his pals not because he is driven by peer orientation, but simply because on occasion that's just what he feels like doing. The question is, is he willing to discuss the matter with his parents? Is he respectful of their perspective? Is he able to say no to his friends when he has other responsibilities or family events or when he simply may prefer being on his own?

The peer-oriented teenager will brook no obstacle and experiences intense frustration when his need for peer contact is thwarted. He is unable to assert himself in the face of peer expectations and will, proportionately, resent and oppose his parents' desires.

Adults who misread this primitive and perverted form of counterwill as healthy teenage self-assertion may prematurely back away from the parenting role. While it's wise to give adolescents space to be themselves, to allow them to learn from their own mistakes, many parents just throw in the towel. Out of sheer exasperation or frustration, usually unannounced and without ceremony, they retire nonetheless. To back off prematurely, however, is unwittingly to abandon a child who still needs us dearly but doesn't know that she does. If we saw these peer-oriented adolescents as the dependents they truly are and realized how much they needed our parenting, we would be determined to regain our parenting power. We should be wooing such children back from their peers.

## THE MYTH OF THE OMNIPOTENT CHILD

Another mistake is to interpret the child's opposition as a power play or as striving for omnipotence.* It is understandable, when feeling a lack of power ourselves, to project a will to power onto the child. If I am not in control, the child must be; if I do not have the power, the child must have it; if I am not in the driver's seat, the child has to be. Instead of assuming responsibility for my own sense of weakness, I see the child as striving for control. In the extreme, even babies can be seen to have all the power: to control one's schedules, to sabotage one's plans, to rob one's sleep, to rule the roost.

The problem with seeing our children as having power is that we miss how much they truly need us. Even if a child *is* trying to control us, he is doing so out of a need and a dependence on us to make things work. If he was truly powerful, he would have no need to get us to do his bidding.

Faced with a child they perceive as demanding, some parents become defensive and move to protect themselves. As adults, we react to feelings of being coerced much as children do—balking, resisting, opposing, and countering. Our own counterwill is provoked, leading to a power struggle with our children that becomes really more a battle of counterwills than a

---

*One child psychiatrist went so far as to write a book entitled *The Omnipotent Child*. He was referring to toddlers!

battle of wills. The sad part about this is that the child loses the parent she desperately needs. Our resistance only multiplies the child's demands and erodes the attachment relationship that is our best and only hope.

Taking counterwill for a show of strength both triggers and justifies the use of psychological force. We strive to meet perceived strength with strength. Our demeanor inflates, our voices rise, and we up the ante with whatever leverage we can command. The greater the force we impose, the more counterwill our reaction will provoke. Should our reaction trigger anxiety, which serves as the child's psychological alarm that an important attachment is being threatened, preservation of closeness will become her foremost goal. The frightened child will scurry to make it up to us and to get back into our good graces. We may believe we have attained our goal of "good behavior," but such capitulation is not without cost. The relationship will be weakened by the insecurity caused by our anger and our threats. The more force we use, the more wear and tear on the relationship. The weaker the relationship becomes, the more prone we are to being replaced—nowadays, most often by peers. Not only is peer orientation a major cause of counterwill, but our reactions to counterwill can foster peer orientation.

## WHY FORCE AND MANIPULATION BACKFIRE

It is instinctive, when experiencing insufficient power for the task at hand, whether it is moving a rock or moving a child, to look for some leverage. Parental efforts to gain leverage generally take two forms: bribery or coercion. If a simple direction such as "I'd like you to set the table" doesn't do, we may add an incentive, for example, "If you set the table for me, I'll let you have your favorite dessert." Or if it isn't enough to remind the child that it is time to do homework, we may threaten to withdraw some privilege. Or we may add a coercive tone to our voice or assume a more authoritarian demeanor. The search for leverage is never-ending: sanctions, rewards, abrogation of privileges; the forbidding of computer time, toys, or allowance; separation from the parent or separation from friends; the limitation or abolition of television time, car privileges, and so on and so on. It is not uncommon to hear someone complain about having run out of ideas for what still might remain to be taken away from the child.

As our power to parent decreases, our preoccupation with leverage increases. Euphemisms abound: bribes are called variously rewards, incentives, and positive reinforcement; threats and punishments are rechristened warnings, natural consequences, and negative reinforcements; applying psychological force is often referred to as modifying behavior or teaching a lesson. These euphemisms camouflage attempts to motivate the child by external pressure because his intrinsic motivation is deemed inadequate. Attachment is natural and arises from within; leverage is contrived and imposed from without. In any other realm, we would see the use of leverage as manipulation. In parenting, such means of getting a child to follow our will have become embraced by many as normal and appropriate.

All attempts to use leverage to motivate a child involve the use of psychological force, whether we employ "positive" force as in rewards or "negative" force as in punishments. We apply force whenever we trade on a child's likes or when we exploit a child's dislikes and insecurities in order to get her to do our will. We resort to leverage when we have nothing else to work with—no intrinsic motivation to tap, no attachment for us to lean on. Such tactics, if they are ever to be employed, should be a last resort, not our first response and certainly not our modus operandi. Unfortunately, when children become peer-oriented, we as parents are driven to leverage-seeking in desperation.

Manipulation, whether in the form of rewards or punishments, may succeed in getting the child to comply temporarily, but we cannot by this method make the desired behavior become part of anyone's intrinsic personality. Whether it is to say thank-you or sorry, to share with another, to create a gift or card, to clean up a room, to be appreciative, to do homework, or to practice piano, the more the behavior has been coerced, the less likely it is to occur voluntarily. And the less the behavior occurs spontaneously, the more inclined parents and teachers are to contrive some leverage. Thus begins a spiraling cycle of force and counterwill that necessitates the use of more and more leverage. The true power base for parenting is eroded.

Plenty of evidence both in the laboratory and in real life attests to the power of counterwill to sabotage shallow behavioral goals pursued by means of psychological force or manipulation. One particular experiment involved preschool children who loved playing with Magic Markers. These children were divided into various groups: one group was promised an attractive certificate if they used the markers; one group was not promised anything but was rewarded for using the markers with the same certificate; one group was neither promised nor given a reward. When tested several weeks later but without any rewards being mentioned, the two groups in which positive coercion was used were far less inclined to play with the

Magic Markers.[1] The counterwill instinct ensured that the use of force would backfire. In a similar experiment, the psychologist Edward Deci observed the behavior of two groups of college students vis-à-vis a puzzle game they had originally all been equally intrigued by. One group was to receive a monetary reward each time a puzzle was solved; the other was given no external incentive. Once the payments stopped, the paid group proved far more likely to abandon the game than their unpaid counterparts. "Rewards may increase the likelihood of behaviors," Dr. Deci writes, "but only so long as the rewards keep coming. Stop the pay, stop the play."[2]

It is easy to misinterpret the child's counterwill as a drive for power. We may never be fully in control of our circumstances, but to raise children and to face their counterwill on a daily basis is to have our powerlessness driven home to us consistently. In present-day society it is neither surprising nor unusual for parents to feel tyrannized and powerless. With the sense of impotence we experience when child-adult attachments are not strong enough, we begin to see our children as manipulative, controlling, and even powerful.

We need to get past the symptoms. If all we perceive is the resistance or the insolence, we will respond with anger, frustration, and force. We must see that the child is only reacting instinctively whenever he feels he is being pushed and pulled. Beyond the counterwill we need to recognize the weakened attachment. The defiance is not the essence of the problem; the root cause is the peer orientation that makes counterwill backfire on adults and robs it of its natural purpose.

As we will discuss in Part 4, the best response to a child's counterwill is a stronger parental relationship and less reliance on force.

# THE FLATLINING OF CULTURE

THE FOLLOWING IS the verbatim copy of an exchange, on MSN Messenger, between two young teenagers (their MSN identities are in italics):

> *then she said RECTUM!! that's my sons name* says: "hey."
> *Crontasaurus and Rippitar Join The Barnyard Tai Chi Club* says: "sup?"
> *then she said RECTUM!! that's my sons name* says: "??"
> *Crontasaurus and Rippitar Join The Barnyard Tai Chi Club* says: "hey."
> *then she said RECTUM!! that's my sons name* says: "sup?"

Three features of this electronic dialogue, quite typical for what passes as correspondence among today's adolescents, are striking. First, the careful construction of the long and nonsensical identifying pseudonyms, tinged with mockery and irreverence. Image, not content, is what matters. Second, by vivid contrast, the contraction of language to virtually inarticulate monosyllables. And finally, the utter emptiness of what is being said: contact without genuine communication. "Hey" is the universal greeting. "Sup" substitutes for "what's up" as the replacement for "how are you" or "how is it going"—with no invitation to share information of genuine significance to either participant. Such "conversations" can and do go on at great length without anything more meaningful being said. It's tribal language, foreign to adults, and it has the implicit purpose of making a connection while revealing nothing of value about the self.

"Today's teens are a tribe apart," wrote the journalist Patricia Hersch in her 1999 book on adolescence in America. As befits a tribe, teens have their own language, values, meanings, music, dress codes, and identifying marks, such as body piercing and tattoos. Parents may have felt in previous times as if their teenagers were out of control, but the tribal behavior of adolescents today is unprecedented. We may, for example, see the street-dueling and brawling of the young Capulets and Montagues in *Romeo and Juliet* as tribal warfare. And it was, with one crucial difference between Shakespeare's young heroes and today's teens: the Shakespearean characters identified with the tribes—family groupings—of their parents and conducted their hostilities along family lines. Nor was the central conflict of the play intergenerational: the young lovers disobeyed their parents but did not reject them, wanting only to bring them together for the sake of their own love for each other. They were aided by supportive adults, such as the friar who performed their secret marriage ceremony. Today's teen tribes have no connection with adult society. In Leonard Bernstein's *West Side Story*, the modern American take on the Romeo and Juliet tale, the feuding teen gangs are completely isolated from the adult world and are bitterly hostile to it.

Although we have lulled ourselves into believing that this tribalization of youth is an innocuous process, it is a historically new phenomenon with a disruptive influence on social life. It underlies the frustration many parents feel at their inability to pass on their traditions to their children.

In the separate tribe many of our children have joined, the transmission of values and culture flows horizontally, from one unlearned and immature person to another. This process, which can be thought of as the flatlining of culture, is, under our very eyes, eroding one of the underpinnings of civilized social activity. A certain degree of tension between generations is a natural part of development but is usually resolved in ways that allow for children to mature in harmony with the culture of their elders. Young people can have free self-expression without forgetting or disrespecting universal values handed down vertically, from one generation to the next. That is not what we are seeing today.

"Children throughout Western civilization," declared an MTV announcer not long ago, "are coming to look and act more like each other than their own parents or grandparents." While this statement was in the nature of a network boast during an anniversary broadcast, it contains an element of truth alarming in its implications.

The transmission of culture assures the survival of the particular forms given to our existence and expression as human beings. It goes much beyond our customs and traditions and symbols to include how we express ourselves in gestures and language, the way we adorn ourselves in dress and decoration, what and how and when we celebrate. Culture also defines our rituals around contact and connection, greetings and good-byes, belonging and loyalty, love and intimacy. Central to any culture is its food—how food is prepared and eaten, the attitudes toward food, and the functions food serves. The music people make and the music they listen to is an integral part of any culture.

The transmission of culture is, normally, an automatic part of child-rearing. In addition to facilitating dependence, shielding against external stress, and giving birth to independence, attachment also is the conduit of culture. As long as the child is properly attaching to the adults responsible, the culture flows into the child. To put it another way, the attaching child becomes spontaneously informed, in the sense of absorbing the cultural forms of the adult. According to Howard Gardner, a leading American developmentalist, more is spontaneously absorbed from the parents in the first four years of life than during all the rest of a person's formal education put together.[1]

When attachment is working, the transmission of culture does not require deliberate instruction or teaching on the part of the adult or even conscious learning on the part of the child. The child's hunger for connection and inclination to seek cues from adults take care of it. If the child is helped to attain genuine individuality and a mature independence of mind, the passing down of culture from one generation to another is not a process of mindless imitation or blind obedience. Culture is a vehicle for true self-expression. The flowering of individual creativity takes place in the context of culture.

When a child becomes peer-oriented, the transmission lines of civilization are downed. The new models to emulate are other children or peer groups or the latest pop icons. Appearance, attitudes, dress, and demeanor all adapt accordingly. Even children's language changes—more impoverished, less articulate about their observations and experience, less expressive of meaning and nuance.

Peer-oriented children are not devoid of culture, but the culture they are enrolled in is generated by their peer orientation. Although this culture is broadcast through media controlled by adults, it is the children and youth whose tastes and preferences it must satisfy. They, the young, wield the spending power that determines the profits of the culture industry—

even if it is the parents' incomes that are being disposed of in the process. Advertisers know subtly well how to exploit the power of peer imitation as they make their pitch to ever-younger groups of customers via the mass electronic media. In this way, it is our youth who dictate hairstyles and fashion, youth to whom music must appeal, youth who primarily drive the box office. Youth determine the cultural icons of our age. The adults who cater to the expectations of peer-oriented youth may control the market and profit from it, but as agents of cultural transmission they are simply pandering to the debased cultural tastes of children disconnected from healthy adult contact. Peer culture arises from children and evolves with them as they age. For reasons I will explain in Part 3, peer orientation breeds aggression and an unhealthy, precocious sexuality. The result is the aggressively hostile and hypersexualized youth culture, propagated by the mass media, to which children are already exposed by early adolescence. Today's rock videos shock even adults who themselves grew up under the influence of the "sexual revolution." As the onset of peer-orientation emerges earlier and earlier, so does the culture it creates. The butt-shaking and belly-button-baring Spice Girls pop phenomenon of the late 1990s, as of this writing a rapidly fading memory, seems in retrospect a nostalgically innocent cultural expression compared with the pornographically eroti-cized pop idols served up to today's preadolescents.

Although a youth culture was in evidence by the 1950s, the first obvious and dramatic manifestation of a culture generated by peer-orientation was the hippie counterculture of the 1960s and 1970s. The Canadian media theorist Marshall McLuhan called it "the new tribalism of the Electric Age." Hair and dress and music played a significant part in shaping this culture, but what defined it more than anything was its glorification of the peer attachment that gave rise to it. Friends took precedence over family. Physical contact and connection with peers were pursued; the brother-hood of the pop tribe was declared, as in the generation-based "Woodstock nation." The peer group was the true home. "Don't trust anyone over thirty" became the byword of youth who went far beyond a healthy cri-tique of their elders to a militant rejection of tradition. The degeneration of that culture into alienation and drug use, on the one hand, and its co-optation for commercial purposes by the very mainstream institutions it was rebelling against were almost predictable.

The wisdom of well-seasoned cultures has accumulated over hundreds and sometimes thousands of years. Healthy cultures also contain rituals and customs and ways of doing things that protect us from ourselves and safeguard values important to human life, even when we are not conscious of what such values are. An evolved culture needs to have some art and music that one can grow into, symbols that convey deeper meanings to existence and models that inspire greatness. Most important of all, a culture must protect its essence and its ability to reproduce itself—the attachment of children to their parents. The culture generated by peer orientation contains no wisdom, does not protect its members from themselves, creates only fleeting fads, and worships idols hollow of value or meaning. It symbolizes only the undeveloped ego of callow youth and destroys child-parent attachments. We may observe the cheapening of cultural values with each new peer-oriented generation. For all its self-delusion and smug isolation from the adult world, the Woodstock "tribe" still embraced universal values of peace, freedom, and brotherhood. Today's mass musical gatherings are about little more than style, ego, tribal exuberance, and dollars.

The culture generated by peer-orientation is sterile in the strict sense of that word: it is unable to reproduce itself or to transmit values that can serve future generations. There are very few third generation hippies. Whatever its nostalgic appeal, that culture did not have much staying power. Peer culture is momentary, transient, and created daily, a "culture du jour," as it were. The content of peer culture resonates with the psychology of our peer-oriented children and adults who are arrested in their own development. In one sense it is fortunate that peer culture cannot be passed on to future generations, since its only redeeming aspect is that it is fresh every decade. It does not edify or nurture or even remotely evoke the best in us or in our children.

The peer culture, concerned only with what is fashionable at the moment, lacks any sense of tradition or history. As peer orientation rises, young people's appreciation of history wanes, even of recent history. For them, present and future exist in a vacuum with no connection to the past. The implications are alarming for the prospects of any informed political and social decision-making flowing from such ignorance. A current example is South Africa today, where the end of apartheid has brought not only political freedom but, on the negative side, rapid and rampant Westernization and the advent of globalized peer culture. The tension between the generations is already intensifying. "Our parents are trying to educate us about the past," one South African teenager told a Canadian newspaper reporter. "We're forced to hear about racists and politics. . . ." For his part, Steve Mokwena, a thirty-six-year-old historian and a veteran of the anti-apartheid struggle, is described by the journalist as being "from a different world than the young people he now works with." "They're being force-fed on a diet of American pop trash. It's very worrying," said Mokwena—in his mid-thirties hardly a hoary patriarch.[2]

You might argue that peer orientation, perhaps, can bring us to the genuine globalization of culture, of a universal civilization that no longer divides the world into "us and them." Didn't the MTV broadcaster brag that children all over television's world resembled one another more than their parents and grandparents? Could this not be the way to the future, a way to transcend the cultures that divide us and to establish a worldwide culture of connection and peace? We think not.

Despite the superficial similarities created by global technology, the dynamics of peer-orientation are more likely to promote division rather than a healthy universality. One need only to look at the extreme tribalization of the youth gangs, the social forms entered into by the most peer-oriented among our children. Seeking to be the same as someone else immediately triggers the need to be different from others. As the similarities within the chosen group strengthen, the differences from those outside the groups are accentuated to the point of hostility. Each group is solidified and reinforced by mutual emulation and cue-taking. In this way, tribes have formed spontaneously since the beginning of time. The crucial difference is that traditional tribal culture could be passed down, whereas these tribes of today are defined and limited by barriers among the generations.

The school milieu is rife with such dynamics. When immature children cut off from their adult moorings mingle with one another, groups soon form spontaneously, often along the more obvious dividing lines of grade and gender and race. Within these larger groupings certain subcultures emerge: sometimes along the lines of dress and appearance, and sometimes along those of shared interests, attitudes, or abilities, as in groups of jocks, brains, and computer nerds. Sometimes they form among peer-oriented subcultures like skateboarders, bikers, and skinheads. Many of these subcultures are reinforced and shaped by the media and supported by cult costumes, symbols, movies, music, and language. If the tip of the peer-orientation iceberg are the gangs and the gang wannabes, at the base are the cliques. Like the two MSN correspondents at the beginning of this chapter, immature beings revolving around one another invent their own language and modes of expression that impoverish their self-expression and cut them off from others. Such phenomena may have appeared before, of course, but not nearly to the same extent we are witnessing today.

The result is the tribalization noted by Patricia Hersch. Children displaced from their families, unconnected to their teachers, and not yet mature enough to relate to one another as separate beings, automatically regroup to satisfy their instinctive drive for attachment. The culture of the group is either invented or borrowed from the peer culture at large. It does not take children very long to know what tribe they belong to, what the rules are, whom they can talk to, and whom they must keep at a distance. Despite our attempts to teach our children respect for individual differences and to instill in them a sense of belonging to a cohesive civilization, we are fragmenting at an alarming rate into tribal chaos. Our very own children are leading the way. The time we as parents and educators spend trying to teach our children social tolerance, acceptance, and etiquette would be much better invested in cultivating a connection with them. Children nurtured in traditional hierarchies of attachment are not nearly as susceptible to the spontaneous forces of tribalization. The social values we wish to inculcate can be transmitted only across existing lines of attachment.

The culture created by peer orientation does not mix well with other cultures. Because peer orientation exists unto itself, so does the culture it creates. It operates much more like a cult than a culture. Immature beings who embrace the culture generated by peer orientation become cut off from people of other cultures. Peer-oriented youth actually glory in excluding traditional values and historical connections. People from differing cultures that have been transmitted vertically retain the capacity to relate to one another respectfully, even if in practice that capacity is often overwhelmed by the historical or political conflicts in which human beings become caught up. Beneath the particular cultural expressions they can mutually recognize the universality of human values and cherish the richness of diversity. Peer-oriented kids are, however, inclined to hang out with one another exclusively. They set themselves apart from those not like them. As our peer-oriented children reach adolescence, many parents find themselves feeling as if their very own children are barely recognizable with their tribal music, clothing, language, rituals, and body decorations. "Tattooing and piercing, once shocking, are now merely generational signposts in a culture that constantly redraws the line between acceptable and disallowed behavior," a Canadian journalist pointed out in 2003.[3]

Many of our children are growing up bereft of the universal culture that produced the timeless creations of humankind: *The Bhagavad Gita*; the writings of Rumi and Dante, Shakespeare and Cervantes and Faulkner, or of the best and most innovative of living authors; the music of Beethoven and Mahler; or even the great translations of the Bible. They know only what is current and popular, appreciate only what they can share with their peers.

True universality in the positive sense of mutual respect, curiosity, and shared human values does not require a globalized culture created by peer-orientation. It requires psychological maturity—a maturity that cannot result from didactic education, only from healthy development. As we will next discuss, only adults can help children grow up in this way. And only in healthy relationships with adult mentors—parents, teachers, elders, artistic, musical and intellectual creators—can children receive their birthright, the universal and age-honored cultural legacy of humankind. Only in such relationships can they fully develop their own capacities for free and individual and fresh cultural expression.

# PART THREE

# STUCK IN IMMATURITY: HOW PEER ORIENTATION STUNTS HEALTHY DEVELOPMENT

# THE DANGEROUS FLIGHT
# FROM FEELING

Walking through the halls of my son's high school during lunch hour recently, I was struck by how similar it felt to being in the halls and lunchrooms of the juvenile prisons in which I used to work. The posturing, the gestures, the tone, the words, and the interaction among peers I witnessed in this teenage throng all bespoke an eerie invulnerability. These kids seemed incapable of being hurt. Their demeanor bespoke a confidence, even bravado that seemed unassailable but shallow at the same time.

The ultimate ethic in the peer culture is "cool"—the complete absence of emotional openness. The most esteemed among the peer group affect a disconcertingly unruffled appearance, exhibit little or no fear, seem to be immune to shame, and are given to muttering things like "doesn't matter," "don't care," and "whatever."

The reality is quite different. Humans are the most vulnerable—from the Latin *vulnerare*, to wound—of all creatures. We are not only vulnerable physically, but psychologically as well. What, then, accounts for the discrepancy? How can young humans who are in fact so vulnerable appear so opposite? Is their toughness, their "cool" demeanor, an act or is it for real? Is it a mask that can be doffed when they get to safety or is it the true face of peer orientation?

When I first encountered this subculture of adolescent invulnerability, I assumed it was an act. The human psyche can develop powerful defenses against a conscious sense of vulnerability, defenses that become ingrained in the emotional circuitry of the brain. I preferred to think that these children, if given the chance, would remove their armor and reveal their softer, more genuinely human side. Occasionally this expectation proved correct, but more often than not I discovered the invulnerability of adolescents was no act, no pretense. Many of these children did not have hurt feelings, they felt no pain. That is not to say that they were incapable of being wounded, but as far as their consciously experienced feelings were concerned, there was no mask to take off.

Children able to experience emotions of sadness, fear, loss, and rejection will often hide such feelings from their peers to avoid exposing themselves to ridicule and attack. Invulnerability is a camouflage they adopt to blend in with the crowd but will quickly remove in the company of those with whom they have the safety to be their true selves. These are not the kids I am most concerned about, although I certainly do have a concern about the impact an atmosphere of invulnerability will have on their learning and development. In such an environment genuine curiosity cannot thrive, questions cannot be freely asked, naive enthusiasm for learning cannot be expressed. Risks are not taken in such an environment, nor can passion for life and creativity find their outlets.

The kids most deeply affected and at greatest risk for psychological harm are the ones who aspire to be tough and invulnerable, not just in school but in general. These children cannot don and doff the armor as needed. Defense is not something they do, it is who they are. This emotional hardening is most obvious in delinquents and gang members and street kids, but is also a significant dynamic in the common everyday variety of peer orientation that exists in the typical American home.

## PEER-ORIENTED KIDS ARE MORE VULNERABLE

The only reason for a child not to be aware of his own vulnerability is that it has become too much to bear, his wounds too hurtful to feel. In other words, children overwhelmed by emotional hurt in the past are likely to become inured to this same experience in the future.

The relationship between psychological wounds and the *flight from vulnerability* is quite obvious in children whose experience of emotional pain has been profound. Most likely to develop this extreme type of defensive emotional hardening are children from orphanages or multiple foster homes, children who have experienced significant losses or have suffered abuse and neglect. Given the trauma they have endured, it is easy to appreciate why such children would have developed powerful unconscious defenses.

What is surprising is that, without any comparable trauma, many children who have been peer-oriented for some time can manifest the same level of defensiveness. It seems that peer-oriented kids have a need to protect themselves against vulnerability to as great a degree as traumatized children. Why should that be, in the absence of any overtly similar experiences?

Before discussing the reasons for the increased fragility and emotional stiffening of peer-oriented children, we need to clarify the meaning of the phrase *defended against vulnerability* and its near synonym, *flight from vulnerability*. We mean by them the brain's instinctive defensive reactions to being overwhelmed by a sense of vulnerability. These unconscious defensive reactions are evoked against a consciousness of vulnerability, not against actual vulnerability. The human brain is not capable of preventing a child from being wounded, only from feeling wounded. The terms *defended against vulnerability* and *flight from vulnerability* encapsulate these meanings. They convey a sense of a child's losing touch with thoughts and emotions that make her feel vulnerable, a diminished awareness of the human susceptibility to be emotionally wounded. Everyone can experience such emotional closing down at times. A child becomes defended against vulnerability when being shut down is no longer just a temporary reaction but becomes a persistent state.

There are four reasons peer-oriented kids are more susceptible to emotional wounds than adult-oriented ones. The net effect is a flight from vulnerability disturbingly similar to the emotional hardening of traumatized children.

## PEER-ORIENTED CHILDREN LOSE THEIR NATURAL SHIELD AGAINST STRESS

The first reason why peer-oriented children have to harden emotionally is that they have lost their natural source of power and self-confidence and, at the same time, their natural shield against intolerable hurt and pain.

Apart from the steady onslaught of tragedies and traumas occurring everywhere, the child's personal world is one of intense interactions and events that can wound: being ignored, not being important, being excluded, not measuring up, experiencing disapproval, not being liked, not being preferred, being shamed and ridiculed. What protects the child from experiencing the brunt of all this stress is an attachment with a parent. It is attachment that matters: as long as the child is not attached to those who belittle him, there is relatively little damage done. The taunts can hurt and cause tears at the time, but the effect will not be long lasting. When the parent is the compass point, it is the messages he or she gives that are relevant. When tragedy and trauma happen, the child looks to the parent for clues whether or not to be concerned. As long as their attachments are safe, the sky could collapse and the world fall apart, but children would be relatively protected from feeling dangerously vulnerable. Roberto Benigni's movie, *Life Is Beautiful*, about a Jewish father's efforts to shield his son from the horrors of racism and genocide, illustrates that point most poignantly. Attachment protects the child from the outside world.

One father told me how he had witnessed the power of attachment to keep a child safe when his son, whom we'll call Braden, was about five years old. "Braden wanted to play soccer in the local community league. On the very first day of practice, some older kids gave him a rough time. When I heard their voices taunting and ridiculing him, I quickly turned into a protective father bear. I had every intention of giving these young bullies an external attitude adjustment when I observed Braden face off with them, stretching himself to his full height, putting his hands on his hips and sticking his chest out as far as it would go. I heard him say something like, 'I am not a stupid little jerk! My daddy says I'm a soccer player.' And that seemed to be that." Braden's idea of what his father thought of him protected him more effectively than the father ever could have by direct intervention. His father's perceptions of him took precedence. He could deflect the insults of peers. By contrast, a peer-oriented child who no longer looks to adults for his sense of self-valuation has no such protection.

There is a flip side to this dynamic, of course. To the degree that this boy's attachment to his father protects him against hurtful interaction with others, it also sensitizes him to the father's own words and gestures. If he, the parent, belittled him, shamed him, poured contempt on him, Braden would be devastated. His attachment to his parents renders him highly vulnerable in relationship to them but less vulnerable in relationship to others. There is an inside and an outside to attachment: the vulnerability is on the inside, the invulnerability on the outside. Attachment is both a shield and a sword. Attachment divides the world into those who can hurt you and those who can't. Attachment and vulnerability—these two great themes of human existence—go hand in hand.

An obvious part of our job as parents is to defend our children against being physically wounded. Although the bruising is not always so visible, the capacity to be hurt is even greater in the psychological arena. Even we adults, as relatively mature creatures, can be violently thrown off our course or become immobilized by the emotional pain of disrupted attachments. If we as adults can get hurt in this way, how much more can children, who are far more dependent, far more in need of their attachments.

Attachment is a child's most pressing need and most powerful drive, and yet it is attachment that sets the child up for getting hurt. Like two sides of a coin, we cannot have one without the other. The more attached the child, the more capable of being wounded. Attachment is vulnerable territory. And that leads us to the second reason for the heightened emotional defensiveness of peer-oriented kids.

## PEER-ORIENTED KIDS BECOME SENSITIZED TO INSENSITIVE INTERACTIONS OF CHILDREN

Just as an adult-oriented child is more vulnerable in relationship to his parents and teachers, peer-oriented kids are more so in relationship to one another. Having lost their parental attachment shields, they become highly sensitized to the actions and communication of other children. The problem is that children's natural interaction is anything but careful and considerate and civilized. When peers replace parents, this careless and irresponsible interaction takes on a potency it was never meant to have. Sensitivities and sensibilities are easily overwhelmed. We have only to imagine how we as adults would fare if subjected by our friends to the kind of social interaction children have to endure each and every day—the petty betrayals, the shunning, the contempt, the sheer lack of dependability. It is no wonder that peer-oriented kids shut down in the face of vulnerability.

The literature on the impact of peer rejection on children, based on extensive research, is very clear about the negative consequences, employing words like shattering, crippling, devastating, mortifying.[1] Suicides among children are escalating, and the literature indicates that the rejection of peers is a growing cause. I have observed firsthand the lives of numerous adults and children crippled by treatment suffered at the hands of their peers. The very first client in my psychology practice was an adult victim of peer abuse back when he was in elementary school. For some reason unknown to him, he became the chosen scapegoat of a number of frustrated children who picked on him incessantly. He developed such serious compulsions and obsessions that he was unable to cope with normal life.

For example, he could not abide any reference to the number 57 because 1957 was the worst year of his abuse by peers. If contaminated by that number, he would need to perform complex cleansing rituals that made normal living impossible. Peer ostracization and abuse have crippled the lives of many such childhood scapegoats. (Recent studies attest that such phenomena are rapidly escalating under the influence of peer orientation, and we will look at them more closely in Chapters 10 and 11, on aggression and bullying.)

The primary culprit is assumed to be peer rejection: shunning, exclusion, shaming, taunting, mocking, bullying. The conclusion reached by some experts is that peer acceptance is absolutely necessary for a child's emotional health and well-being, and that there is nothing worse than not being liked by peers. It is assumed that peer rejection is an automatic sentence to lifelong self-doubt. Many parents today live in fear of their children's not having friends, not being esteemed by their peers. This way of thinking fails to consider two fundamental questions: What renders a child so vulnerable in the first place? And why is this vulnerability increasing?

It is absolutely true that children snub, ignore, shun, shame, taunt, and mock. Children have always done these things when not sufficiently supervised by the adults in charge. But it is attachment, not the insensitive behavior or language of peers, that creates vulnerability. The current focus on the impact of peer rejection and peer acceptance has completely overlooked the role of attachment. If the child is attached primarily to the parents, it is parental acceptance that is vital to emotional health and well-being, and not being liked by parents is the devastating blow to self-esteem. The capacity of children to be inhumane has probably not changed, but, as research shows, the wounding of our children by one another is increasing. If many kids are damaged these days by the insensitivity of their peers, it is not necessarily because children today are more cruel than in the past, but because peer orientation has made them more susceptible to one anothers taunts and emotional assaults. Our failure to keep our children attached to us and to the other adults responsible for them has not only taken away their shields but put a sword in the hands of their peers. When peers replace parents, children lose their vital protection against the thoughtlessness of others. The vulnerability of a child in such circumstances can easily be overwhelmed. The resulting pain is more than many children can bear.

Studies have been unequivocal in their findings that the best protection for a child, even through adolescence, is a strong attachment with an adult. The most impressive of these studies involved ninety thousand adolescents from eighty different communities chosen to make the sample as representative of the United States as possible. The primary finding was that teenagers with strong emotional ties to their parents were much less likely to exhibit drug and alcohol problems, attempt suicide, or engage in violent behavior and early sexual activity.[2] Such adolescents, in other words, were at greatly reduced risk for the problems that stem from being defended against vulnerability. Shielding them from stress and protecting their emotional health and functioning were strong attachments with their parents. This was also the conclusion of the noted American psychologist Julius Segal, a brilliant pioneer of research into what makes young people resilient. Summarizing studies from around the world, he concluded that the most important factor keeping children from being overwhelmed by stress was "the presence in their lives of a charismatic adult—a person with whom they identify and from whom they gather strength."[3] As Dr. Segal has also said, "Nothing will work in the absence of an indestructible link of caring between parent and child."

Peers should never have come to matter that much—certainly not more than parents or teachers or other adult attachment figures. Taunts and rejection by peers sting, of course, but they shouldn't cut to the quick, should not be so devastating. The profound dejection of an excluded child reveals a much more serious attachment problem than it does a peer-rejection problem.

In response to the intensifying cruelty of children to one another, schools all over this continent are rushing to design programs to inculcate social responsibility in youngsters. We are barking up the wrong tree when we try to make children responsible for other children. In my view it is completely unrealistic to believe we can in this way eradicate peer exclusion and rejection and insulting communication. We should, instead, be working to take the sting out of such natural manifestations of immaturity by reestablishing the power of adults to protect children from themselves and from one another.

## MANIFESTATIONS OF VULNERABILITY ARE SHAMED AND EXPLOITED BY PEERS

Peer-oriented young people thus face two grave psychological risks that more than suffice to make vulnerability unbearable and provoke their brains into defensive action: having lost the parental attachment shield, and having the powerful attachment sword wielded by careless and irresponsible children. A third blow against feeling deeply and openly—and the third reason for the emotional shutdown of the peer-oriented child—is that any sign of vulnerability in a child tends to be attacked by those who are already shut down against vulnerability.

To give an example from the extreme end of the spectrum, in my work with violent young offenders, one of my primary objectives was to melt their defenses against vulnerability so they could begin to feel their wounds. If a session was successful and I was able to help them get past the defenses to some of the underlying pain, their faces and voices would soften and their eyes would water. For most of these kids, these tears were the first in many years. Especially when someone isn't used to crying, it can markedly affect the face and eyes. When I first began, I was naive enough to send kids back into the prison population after their sessions. It is not difficult to guess what happened. Because the vulnerability was still written on their faces, it attracted the attention of the other inmates. Those who were defended against their own vulnerability felt compelled to attack. They assaulted vulnerability as if it was the enemy. I soon learned to take defensive measures and help my clients make sure their vulnerability wasn't showing. Fortunately, I had a washroom next to my office in the prison. Sometimes kids spent up to an hour pouring cold water over their faces, attempting to wipe out any vestiges of emotion that would give them away. Even if their defenses had softened a bit, they still had to wear a mask of invulnerability to keep from being wounded even further. Part of my job was to help them differentiate between the mask of invulnerability that they had to wear in such a place to keep from being victimized and, on the other hand, the internalized defenses against vulnerability that would keep them from feeling deeply and profoundly.

The same dynamic, obviously not to this extreme, operates in the world dominated by peer-oriented children. Vulnerability is usually attacked, not with fists but with shaming. Many children learn quickly to cover up any signs of weakness, sensitivity, and fragility, as well as alarm, fear, eagerness, neediness, or even curiosity. Above all, they must never disclose that the teasing has hit its mark.

Carl Jung explained that we tend to attack in others what we are most uncomfortable with in ourselves. When vulnerability is the enemy, it is attacked wherever it is perceived, even in a best friend. Signs of alarm may provoke verbal taunts such as "fraidy cat" or "chicken." Tears evoke ridicule. Expressions of curiosity can precipitate the rolling of eyes and accusations of being weird or nerdy. Manifestations of tenderness can result in incessant teasing. Revealing that something caused hurt or really caring about something is risky around someone uncomfortable with his vulnerability. In the company of the desensitized, any show of emotional openness is likely to be targeted.

## PEER RELATIONSHIPS ARE INHERENTLY INSECURE

There is yet a fourth and even more fundamental cause forcing peer-oriented kids to escape their heightened susceptibility to emotional wounding.

The vulnerability engendered by peer orientation can be overwhelming even when children are not hurting one another. This vulnerability is built into the highly insecure nature of peer-oriented relationships. Vulnerability does not have to do only with what is happening but with what could happen—with the inherent insecurity of attachment. What we have, we can lose, and the greater the value of what we have, the greater the potential loss. We may be able to achieve closeness in a relationship, but we cannot secure it in the sense of holding on to it—not like securing a rope or a boat or a fixed interest–bearing government bond. One has very little control over what happens in a relationship, whether we will still be wanted and loved tomorrow.

Although the possibility of loss is present in any relationship, we parents strive to give our children what they are constitutionally unable to give to one another: a connection that is not based on their pleasing us, making us feel good, or reciprocating in any way. In other words, we offer our children precisely what is missing in peer attachments: unconditional acceptance.

Human beings have an intuitive understanding of the point at which vulnerability is too much to bear. Vulnerability due to fear of loss is inherent in peer relationships. In peer relationships there is no maturity to lean on, no commitment to depend on, no sense of responsibility for another human being. The child is left with the stark reality of insecure attachment: What if I don't connect with my peers? What if I cannot make the relationship work? What if I don't want to go along with things my buddies do, if my mom doesn't let me go, or if my friend likes so and so more than she likes me? Such are the ever-present anxieties of peer-oriented children, never far below the surface. Peer-oriented children are obsessed with who likes whom, who prefers whom, who wants to be with whom. There is no room for missteps, for perceived disloyalty, disagreement, differences, or noncompliance. True individuality is crushed by the need to maintain the relationship at all costs. Yet no matter how hard the child works, when peers replace parents the sense of insecurity can escalate until it is too much to endure. That is often when the numbness sets in, the defensive shut down occurs and the children no longer appear vulnerable. They become emotionally frozen by the need to defend themselves against the pain of loss, even before it actually occurs. Similar dynamics come powerfully into play in the sexual "love" relationships of older teenagers (see Chapter 12).

In *Separation*, the second volume of his great trilogy on attachment, John Bowlby described what had been observed when ten small children in residential nurseries were reunited with their mothers after separations lasting from twelve days to twenty-one weeks. The separations were in every case due to family emergencies and the absence of other caregivers, and in no case due to any intent on the parents' part to abandon the child.

In the first few days following the mother's departure the children were anxious, looking everywhere for the missing parent. That phase was followed by apparent resignation, even depression on the part of the child, to be replaced by what seemed like the return of normalcy. The children would begin to play, react to caregivers, accept food and other nurturing. The true emotional cost of the trauma of loss became evident only when the mothers returned. On meeting the mother for the first time after the days or weeks away, every one of the ten children showed significant alienation. Two seemed not to recognize their mothers. The other eight turned away or even walked away from her. Most of them either cried or came close to tears; a number alternated between a tearful and an expressionless face. The withdrawal dynamic has been called "detachment" by John Bowlby.[4] Such detachment has a defensive purpose. It has one meaning: so hurtful was it for me to experience your absence that to avoid such pain again, I will encase myself in a shell of hardened emotion, impervious to love—and therefore to pain. I never want to feel that hurt again.

Bowlby also pointed out that the parent may be physically present but emotionally absent owing to stress, anxiety, depression, or preoccupation with other matters. From the point of view of the child, it hardly matters. His encoded reactions will be the same, because for him the real issue is not merely the parent's physical presence but her or his emotional accessibility. A child who suffers much insecurity in his relationship with his parents will adopt the invulnerability of defensive detachment as his primary way of being. When parents are the child's working attachment, their love and sense of responsibility will usually ensure that they do not force the child into adopting such desperate measures. Peers have no such awareness, no such compunctions, and no such responsibility. The threat of abandonment is ever present in peer-oriented interactions, and it is with emotional detachment that children automatically respond.

No wonder, then, that *cool* is the governing ethic in peer culture, the ultimate virtue. Although the word *cool* has many meanings, it predominately connotes an air of invulnerability. Where peer orientation is intense, there is no sign of vulnerability in the talk, in the walk, in the dress, or in the attitudes.

My cowriter was, before becoming a physician, a high school teacher. Gabor recalls that when he read John Steinbeck's *Of Mice and Men* with his tenth-grade class, the students utterly lacked empathy with the two poverty-stricken and simple working-men who are the book's protagonists. "But they are so stupid," many of the students said. "They just got what they deserved." These teenagers exhibited little appreciation of tragedy and no respect for people's dignity in bearing pain.

It is easy to blame television or the movies or rap music for desensitizing our children to human suffering, to violence, and even to death. Yet the fundamental invulnerability does not come from commercialized culture, reprehensible as it is for pandering to and exploiting children's emotional hardening and immaturity. The invulnerability of peer-oriented kids is fueled from the inside. Even if there were no movies or television programs to shape its expression, it still would spring forth spontaneously as the modus operandi of peer-oriented youth. Though peer-oriented children can come from all over the world and belong to an infinite number of subcultures, the theme of invulnerability is universal in youth culture. Fashions may come and go, music can change form, the language may vary, but cool detachment and emotional shutdown seem to permeate it all. The pervasiveness of this culture is a powerful testimony to the desperate flight from vulnerability of its members.

Also bearing witness to the unbearable nature of the vulnerability experienced by peer-oriented kids is the preponderance of vulnerability-quelling drugs. Peer-oriented kids will do anything to avoid the human feelings of aloneness, suffering, and pain, and to escape feeling hurt, exposed, alarmed, insecure, inadequate, or self-conscious. The older and more peer-oriented the kids, the more drugs seem to be an inherent part of their lifestyle. Peer orientation creates an appetite for anything that would reduce vulnerability. Drugs are emotional painkillers. And, in another way, they help young people escape from the benumbed state imposed by their defensive emotional detachment. With the shutdown of emotions come boredom and alienation. Drugs provide an artificial stimulation to the emotionally jaded. They heighten sensation and provide a false sense of engagement without incurring the risks of genuine openness. In fact, the same drug can play seemingly opposite functions in an individual. Alcohol and marijuana, for example, can numb or, on the other hand, free the brain and mind from social inhibitions. Other drugs are stimulants—cocaine, amphetamines, and ecstasy; the very name of the latter speaks volumes about exactly what is missing in the psychic life of our emotionally incapacitated young people.

The psychological function served by these drugs is often overlooked by well-meaning adults who perceive the problem to be coming from outside the individual, through peer pressure and youth culture mores. It is not just a matter of getting our children to say no. The problem lies much deeper. As long as we do not confront and reverse peer orientation among our children, we are creating an insatiable appetite for these drugs. The affinity for vulnerability-reducing drugs originates from deep within the defended soul. Our children's emotional safety can come only from us: then they will not be driven to escape their feelings and to rely on the anesthetic effects of drugs. Their need to feel alive and excited can and should arise from within themselves, from their own innately limitless capacity to be engaged with the universe.

This brings us back to the essential hierarchical nature of attachment. The more the child needs attachment to function, the more important it is that she attaches to those responsible for her. Only then can the vulnerability that is inherent in emotional attachment be endured. Children don't need friends, they need parents, grandparents, adults who will assume the responsibility to hold on to them. The more children are attached to caring adults, the more they are able to interact with peers without being overwhelmed by the vulnerability involved. The less peers matter, the more the vulnerability of peer relationships can be endured. It is exactly those children who don't need friends who are more capable of having friends without losing their ability to feel deeply and vulnerably.

But why should we want our children to remain open to their own vulnerability? What is amiss when detachment freezes the emotions in order to protect the child? Intuitively we all know that it is better to feel than to not feel. Our emotions are not a luxury but an essential aspect of our makeup. We have them not just for the pleasure of feeling but because they have crucial survival value. They orient us, interpret the world for us, give us vital information without which we cannot thrive. They tell us what is dangerous and what is benign, what threatens our existence and what will nurture our growth. Imagine how disabled we would be if we could not see or hear or taste or sense heat or cold or physical pain. To shut down emotions is to lose an indispensable part of our sensory apparatus and, beyond that, an indispensable part of who we are. Emotions are what make life worthwhile, exciting, challenging, and meaningful. They drive our explorations of the world, motivate our discoveries, and fuel our growth. Down to the very cellular level, human beings are either in defensive mode or in growth mode, but they cannot be in both at the same time. When children become invulnerable, they cease to relate to life as infinite possibility, to themselves as boundless potential, and to the world as a welcoming and nurturing arena for their self-expression. The invulnerability imposed by peer orientation imprisons children in their limitations and fears. No wonder so many of them these days are being treated for depression, anxiety, and other disorders.

The love, attention, and security only adults can offer liberates children from the need to make themselves invulnerable and restores to them that potential for life and adventure that can never come from risky activities, extreme sports, or drugs. Without that safety our children are forced to sacrifice their capacity to grow and mature psychologically, to enter into meaningful relationships, and to pursue their deepest and most powerful urges for self-expression. In the final analysis, the flight from vulnerability is a flight from the self. If we do not hold our children close to us, the ultimate cost is the loss of their ability to hold on to their own truest selves.

# STUCK IN IMMATURITY

"I'M TOTALLY FED up," Sarah's mother said, upset about her daughter's inconsistency and unpredictability. "She doesn't follow through with anything, no matter how hard we try to make things work for her." One repeated situation particularly disturbed Sarah's parents. They would extend themselves to make possible some fervently expressed desire of hers, only to find that she bolted at the first moment of frustration or failure. She quit her figure skating class at the end of her second lesson after they had carefully saved the money for the fees and arranged their schedules to accommodate her timetable. Sarah was also very impulsive, impatient, and would lose her temper easily. She kept on promising to be good but often failed to follow through.

Peter's mother and father were also concerned. Their son was chronically impatient and irritable, at times getting quite nasty with his sister as well as his parents. "He doesn't even seem to be aware," Peter's father told me, "that what he says or does has any impact on the rest of the family." Peter was also argumentative and oppositional. He lacked any long-term aspirations. He had no passion for anything except Nintendo and computer games. The concept of work seemed to mean nothing to him, whether it was schoolwork, home study, or chores around the house. "What worries me most," said the father, "is that Peter doesn't seem worried at all." The boy showed no concern about his lack of direction and meaningful goals.

In somewhat different ways, Peter and Sarah exhibited a similar constellation of traits. Both children were impulsive. Both appeared to know how they should conduct themselves, but neither actually behaved in accordance with what they knew. Both were unreflective, failed to think before acting, and were given to swing-of-the-pendulum reactions. Each set of parents wanted to know if they should be concerned. To Sarah's parents, my answer was probably not. Sarah was only four years old: these traits went with the territory. If everything unfolded as it should, the next few years of development would bring significant differences in Sarah's attitude and behavior. Peter's parents did have reason to be uneasy, however. He was fourteen and, in this way at least, his personality had not changed since he was a preschooler.

Both Sarah and Peter manifested what I have come to dub the *preschooler syndrome*, behaviors appropriate for any preschool child. At this stage of development a number of psychological functions are not yet integrated in the child—a lack of integrative functioning that is a red flag for psychological immaturity. The only ones, of course, who have the developmental "right" to act like preschoolers are preschoolers. In an older child or adult such lack of integration indicates an immaturity that is out of phase with age.

Physical growth and adult physiological functioning are not automatically accompanied by psychological and emotional maturation. Robert Bly, in his book *The Sibling Society*, exposes immaturity as being endemic in our society. "People don't bother to grow up, and we are all fish swimming in a tank of half-adults," he writes.[1] In today's world the preschooler syndrome affects many children well past the preschool years, and may even be seen in teenagers and adults. Many adults have not attained maturity—have not mastered being independent, self-motivated individuals capable of tending their own emotional needs and of respecting the needs of others.

Among the several reasons why maturity is less and less prevalent today, peer orientation is probably the main culprit. Immaturity and peer orientation go hand in hand. The earlier the onset of peer orientation in a child's life and the more intense the preoccupation with peers, the greater the likelihood of being destined to perpetual childishness.

Peter was highly peer-oriented. It wasn't clear what came first: Had his immaturity made him so susceptible to becoming peer-oriented or was it his early peer orientation that was the cause of his arrested development? The causality can go in both directions, but once formed, peer orientation locks the problem in. Either way, peer-oriented kids fail to grow up.

## WHAT IT MEANS TO BE IMMATURE

As we mature, our brain develops the ability to mix things together, to hold different perceptions, senses, thoughts, feelings, and impulses all at the same time without becoming confused in thinking or paralyzed in action. This is the capacity I called "integrative functioning" when, just above, I mentioned the preschooler syndrome. Reaching this point in development has a tremendous transforming and civilizing effect on personality and behavior. The attributes of childishness, like impulsiveness and egocentrism, fade away and a much more balanced personality begins to emerge. One cannot teach the brain to do this; the integrative capacity must be developed, grown into. The ancient Romans had a word for this kind of mix: *temper*. That verb now means "to regulate" or "to moderate," but originally referred to the mingling of different ingredients to make clay. Both Sarah and Peter were "untempered" in experience and expression. Being untempered—unable to tolerate mixed feelings at the same time—is the hallmark of the immature.

For instance, Sarah was quite affectionate toward her parents, but like most children would get frustrated from time to time. When frustrated, she would be given to tantrums even to the point of saying "I hate you" to her mother. Sarah's frustrations with her mother, at her developmental level, were never tempered by affection, just as her frustrations at falling on the ice were not tempered by her desire to figure skate. Hence her impulsiveness. Similarly, when Peter erupted, it would be with insults and name-calling. Although predictably and repeatedly he would get into trouble, his apprehension at the negative consequences was eclipsed by whatever intense frustration he was experiencing at that moment. Again, the feelings failed to mix. Both these children lost their tempers in the true meaning of that word and, as a result, their reactions were strident, insolent, and unmitigated.

Along the same lines, Peter could not assimilate the idea of work because the concept requires mixed feelings. Work is often not very attractive, but we generally do it because we can mix our resistance to it in the moment with a commitment or purpose we may have in mind for the long term. Too immature to hold on to a goal beyond immediate satisfaction, Peter worked only when he felt like it and that wasn't very often. He was conscious of no more than one feeling at a time. In this sense, he was no different from any preschooler. His failure to endure conflicting thoughts, feelings, and purposes in his consciousness was a legacy of his peer orientation.

## NATURE'S BLUEPRINT FOR GROWTH

In our customary headlong rush to figure out what to do about this or that problem, we often ignore the first essential step of looking, reflecting, and understanding. We can ill afford to omit that step when it comes to rearing children in today's chaotic world. We must know how things work so we can understand what can go wrong—that's a necessity for prevention or, if needed, a remedy. What follows is a thumbnail sketch of maturation, a process every parent and teacher should have a working knowledge of. For many it will simply affirm what they have already grasped intuitively.

How do young human beings mature? One of the most significant breakthroughs of developmental theory came in the 1950s when scientists found that there is a consistent and predictable order to the process of maturation, whenever and wherever it occurs. The first phase involves a kind of splitting, or differentiation, followed by a second phase which brings ever increasing integration of the separated elements. This sequence holds true whether the organism is plant or animal and whether the domain is biological or psychological and whether the entity is a single cell or the complex entity we call the self.

Maturation proceeds first through the process of division, teasing things apart until they are distinct and independent. Only then will development mix these same distinct and separate elements together. It is simple and, at the same time, profound—a process we see even at the most basic level. The embryo first grows by dividing into separate cells, each one with its own nucleus and distinct boundaries. Then, once the individual cells have separated sufficiently so that they are not in danger of fusing, the focus of development becomes the interaction between them. Groups of cells become integrated into functioning organs. In turn, the distinct organs develop separately and then become organized and integrated into body systems—for example, the heart and blood vessels form the cardiovascular system. The same pattern is followed with the two hemispheres of the brain. The developing brain regions at first function quite independently of each other physiologically and electrically, but then become gradually integrated. As they do, the child exhibits new skills and behavior.[2] This process continues well into the teenage years and even beyond.

Maturation in the psychological realm involves the differentiation of the elements of consciousness—thoughts, feelings, impulses, values, opinions, preferences, interests, intentions, aspirations. Differentiation needs to happen before these elements of consciousness can be mixed to produce tempered experience and expression. It is the same in the realm of relationships: maturation requires that the child first becomes unique and separate from other individuals. The better differentiated she becomes, the more she is able to mix with others without losing her sense of self.

More fundamentally, a sense of self first needs to separate from inner experience, a capacity entirely absent in the young child. The child has to be able to know that she is not identical with whatever feeling happens to be active in her at any particular moment. She can feel something without her actions being necessarily dominated by that feeling. She can be aware of other, conflicting feelings, or of thoughts, values, commitments that might run counter to the feeling of the moment. She can choose.

Both Peter and Sarah lacked a relationship with themselves because this prerequisite division had not yet occurred. They were not given to re-flecting on their inner experience, agreeing or disagreeing with them-selves, approving or disapproving of what they saw within. Because their feelings and thoughts were not differentiated enough to withstand mixing, they were capable of only one feeling or impulse at a time. Neither of them was given to statements like "Part of me feels this way and part of me feels that way." Neither of them had "on the other hand" kind of experi-ences, nor felt ambivalent about erupting in frustration or about avoiding things. Without the capacity for reflection, they were defined by the inner experience of the moment. They immediately acted out whatever emo-tions arose in them. They could be their inner experience but they could not see it. This inability made them impulsive, egocentric, reactive, and impatient. Because frustration did not mix with caring, they had no pa-tience. Because anger did not mix with love, they showed no forgiveness. Because frustration did not mix with either fear or affection, they lost their tempers. In short, they lacked maturity.

It would have been unreasonable to expect Sarah to be capable of mixed feelings or for her to be anything other than untempered in her ex-pression. She was too young. It was certainly reasonable to expect self-reflection and the capacity to tolerate mixed impulses and emotions of Peter, but completely unrealistic as well. He was no more mature than Sarah.

I felt confident in reassuring Sarah's parents that there was plenty of evi-dence of a very active maturing process going on within her. She exhibited encouraging signs of the differentiation process at work: she was eager to do things by herself and loved to figure things out on her own. She defi-nitely wanted to be her own person and have her own thoughts, ideas, and reasons for doing things. She also had a wonderful venturing-forth kind of energy—a curiosity about things she was not familiar with or attached to, an eagerness to explore the unknown, and a fascination with anything new or novel. Furthermore, she engaged in solitary play that was imaginative, creative, and completely self-satisfying. These telltale signs of the maturing process put to rest any concern about Sarah's failing to develop. Her personality was maturing and, in its own time, the fruit would come. Patience was what was called for.

I could not find any similar vital signs of emergent life in Peter. There was no creative solitude, no desire to figure things out for himself, no pride in being self-sufficient, no attempt to be his own person. He was preoccupied by boundaries with his parents, but this was not about truly individuating, only about keeping his parents out of his life. His resistance to leaning on his parents was not motivated by a desire to do things himself. He was oppositional and contrary but, as we discussed in Chapter 6, only from the intensity of his peer attachments and not from a genuine drive toward independence.

Maturation is spontaneous but not inevitable. It is like a computer program preinstalled in the hard drive but not necessarily activated. Unless Peter got unstuck, he was well on his way to becoming one of those adults still caught in the preschooler syndrome. But how to get children like Peter unstuck? What activates the process of maturation?

## HOW MATURATION CAN BE FOSTERED

Although parents and teachers are forever telling children to "grow up," maturation cannot be commanded. One cannot teach a child to be an individual or train a child to be his own person. This is the work of maturation and maturation alone. We can nurture the process, provide the right conditions, remove the impediments, but we can no more make a child grow up than we can order the plants in our garden to grow.

Dealing with immature children, we may need to show them how to act, draw the boundaries of what is acceptable, and articulate what our expectations are. Children who do not understand fairness have to be taught to take turns. Children not yet mature enough to appreciate the impact of their actions must be provided with rules and prescriptions for acceptable conduct. But such scripted behavior mustn't be confused with the real thing. One cannot be any more mature than one truly is, only act that way when appropriately cued. To take turns because it is right to do so is certainly civil, but to take turns out of a genuine sense of fairness can only come from maturity. To say sorry may be appropriate to the situation, but to assume responsibility for one's actions can come only from the process of individuation. There is no substitute for genuine maturation, no short-cut to getting there. Behavior can be prescribed or imposed, but maturity comes from the heart and mind. The real challenge for parents is to help kids grow up, not simply to look like grown-ups.

If discipline is no cure for immaturity and if scripting is helpful but insufficient, how can we help our children mature? For years, develop-mentalists puzzled over the conditions that activated maturation. The breakthrough came only when researchers discovered the fundamental importance of attachment.

Surprising as it may be to say, the story of maturation is quite straight-forward and self-evident. Like so much else in child development, it be-gins with attachment. As I explained in Chapter 2, attachment is the first priority of living things. It is only when there is some release from this preoccupation that maturation can occur. In plants, the roots must first take hold for growth to commence and bearing fruit to become a possibil-ity. For children, the ultimate agenda of becoming viable as a separate being can take over only when their needs are met for attachment, for nur-turing contact, and for being able to depend on the relationship uncondi-tionally. Few parents, and even fewer experts, understand this intuitively. "When I became a parent," one thoughtful father who did understand said to me, "I saw that the world seemed absolutely convinced that you must form your children—actively form their characters rather than simply cre-ate an environment in which they can develop and thrive. Nobody seemed to get that if you give them the loving connection they need, they will flourish."

The key to activating maturation is to take care of the attachment needs of the child. To foster independence we must first invite dependence; to promote individuation we must provide a sense of belonging and unity; to help the child separate we must assume the responsibility for keeping the child close. We help a child let go by providing more contact and connec-tion than he himself is seeking. When he asks for a hug, we give him a warmer one than he is giving us. We liberate children not by making them work for our love but by letting them rest in it. We help a child face the separation involved in going to sleep or going to school by satisfying his need for closeness. Thus the story of maturation is one of paradox: *depen-dence and attachment foster independence and genuine separation.*

Attachment is the womb of maturation. Just as the biological womb gives birth to a separate being in the physical sense, attachment gives birth to a separate being in the psychological sense. Following physical birth, the developmental agenda is to form an emotional attachment womb for the child from which he can be born once again as an autonomous individual, capable of functioning without being dominated by attachment drives. Humans never outgrow their need to connect with others, nor should they, but mature, truly individual people are not controlled by these needs. Becoming such a separate being takes the whole of a childhood, which in our times stretches to at least the end of the teenage years and perhaps beyond.

We need to release a child from preoccupation with attachment so he can pursue the natural agenda of independent maturation. The secret to doing so is to make sure that the child does not need to work to get his needs met for contact and closeness, to find his bearings, to orient. Children need to have their attachment needs satiated; only then can a shift of energy occur toward individuation, the process of becoming a truly individual person. Only then is the child freed to venture forward, to grow emotionally.

Attachment hunger is very much like physical hunger. The need for food never goes away, just as the child's need for attachment never ends. As parents we free the child from the pursuit of physical nurturance. We assume responsibility for feeding the child as well as providing a sense of security about the provision. No matter how much food a child has at the moment, if there is no sense of confidence in the supply, getting food will continue to be the top priority. A child is not free to proceed with his learning and his life until the food issues are taken care of, and we parents do that as a matter of course. Our duty ought to be equally transparent to us in satisfying the child's attachment hunger.

In his book *On Becoming a Person*, the psychotherapist Carl Rogers describes a warm, caring attitude for which he adopted the phrase *unconditional positive regard* because, he said, "It has no conditions of worth attached to it." This is a caring, wrote Rogers, "which is not possessive, which demands no personal gratification. It is an atmosphere which simply demonstrates *I care; not I care for you if you behave thus and so.*"[3] Rogers was summing up the qualities of a good therapist in relation to her/his clients. Substitute parent for therapist and child for client, and we have an eloquent description of what is needed in a parent-child relationship. Unconditional parental love is the indispensable nutrient for the child's healthy emotional growth. The first task is to create space in the child's heart for the certainty that she is precisely the person the parents want and love. She does not have to do anything or be any different to earn that love — in fact, she cannot do anything, since that love cannot be won or lost. It is not conditional. It is just there, regardless of which side the child is acting from—"good" or "bad." The child can be ornery, unpleasant, whiny, uncooperative, and plain rude, and the parent still lets her feel loved. Ways have to be found to convey the unacceptability of certain behaviors without making the child herself feel unaccepted. She has to be able to bring her unrest, her least likable characteristics to the parent and still receive the parent's absolutely satisfying, security-inducing unconditional love.

A child needs to experience enough security, enough unconditional love, for the required shift of energy to occur. It's as if the brain says, "Thank you very much, that is what we needed, and now we can get on with the real task of development, with becoming a separate being. I don't have to keep hunting for fuel; my tank has been refilled, so now I can get on the road again." Nothing could be more important in the developmental scheme of things.

The father of eleven-year-old Evan, a friend of my cowriter, had just completed a weekend seminar on family relationships and was now, on a Monday morning, walking with his son on the way to school. He had been pressuring Evan to continue with his karate class, an activity the boy was resisting. "You know, Evan," the father said to him, "if you stay in karate I'm going to love you. And you know what else? If you don't stay in karate I'm going to love you just as much." The child didn't say anything for a few minutes. Then, suddenly, he looked up at the overcast sky and smiled at his father. "Isn't it a beautiful day, Dad?" he said. "Aren't those beautiful clouds up there?" After a few more moments of silence, he added, "I think I'll get my black belt." And he has continued with his martial arts studies.

Even adults can experience the effects of this developmental shifting of gears, given the right conditions. One situation that can produce a surge of emergent energy is the experience of being deeply in love and also feeling very secure in that love. People freshly in love experience a renewal of interests and curiosity, an acute sense of uniqueness and individuality, and an awakening of a spirit of discovery. It doesn't come from someone pushing us to be mature and independent but from being deeply fulfilled and satiated in our attachment needs.

Impeding the development of so many of our children is their inability to make that shift from seeking satisfaction of their attachment hunger to the emergence of independent, exuberant engagement with their world. There are five reasons, important for parents and educators to understand, for why peer orientation robs children of the capacity to become satiated.

## PEER ORIENTATION STUNTS GROWTH IN FIVE SIGNIFICANT WAYS

### Parental Nurturance Cannot Get Through

One effect of peer orientation is that the love and nurturance we have for our children cannot get through. This was certainly the case in Peter's situation and for many of the parents I have conferred with. There was no doubt that Peter's parents loved him, wanted the best for him, and were willing to sacrifice for him. However, they, like many parents in their situation, found it difficult to maintain love in the absence of any kind of reciprocity from their son, and even more daunting when he actively rejected their overtures, rebuffed their affection, and resented any communication of interest on their part. Peter was simply not allowing his parents' warmth and caring to sink in.

I see so many situations where a child is in the midst of plenty, a virtual banquet spread out before him, but is suffering from psychological malnourishment because of attachment problems. You cannot feed someone who is not sitting at your table. All the love in the world would not be enough to take the child to the turning point—the umbilical cord needs to be hooked up for the nourishment to get through. It is impossible to satiate the attachment needs of a child who is not actively attaching to the person willing and able to provide for those needs. When a child replaces parents with peers as the primary attachment figures, it is to peers she will look for emotional nurturing. Plainly put, it is exceptional for peer attachments to ever satisfy that attachment hunger. The developmental shift of energy never occurs. Because there is no move from attachment to individuation, peer orientation and immaturity go hand and hand.

### Peer Attachments, Being Insecure, Cannot Bring a Child to Rest

Peer relationships connect immature beings. As I pointed out in the previous chapter, they are inherently insecure. They cannot allow a child to rest from the relentless foraging for approval, love, and significance. The child is never free from the pursuit of closeness. Instead of rest, peer orientation brings agitation. The more peer-oriented the child, the more pervasive and chronic the underlying restlessness becomes. No matter how much contact and connection exist with peers, proximity can never be taken for granted or held fast. A child feeding off his popularity with others—or suffering the lack of it—is conscious of every nuance, threatened by every unfavorable word, look, gesture. With peers, the turning point is never reached: the pursuit of closeness never shifts into venturing forth as a sepa-

rate being. Owing to their highly conditional nature, peer relationships—
with few exceptions—cannot promote the growth of the child's emerging
self. One exception would be the friendship of children who are secure in
their adult attachments; in such cases the acceptance and companion-
ship of a peer can add to a child's sense of security. Feeling fundamentally
safe in his adult relationships, such a child gets an extra glow from peer
friendships—not having to depend on them, he need not feel threatened
by their inherent instability.

### Peer-Oriented Children Are Unable to Feel Fulfilled

There is yet another reason why peer-oriented kids are insatiable. In order
to reach the turning point, a child must not only be fulfilled, but this fulfillment must sink in. It has to register somehow in the child's brain that
the longing for closeness and connectedness is being met. This registration
is not cognitive or even conscious, but deeply emotional. It is emotion that
moves the child and shifts the energy from one developmental agenda to
another, from attachment to individuation. The problem is that, for fulfillment to sink in, the child must be able to feel deeply and vulnerably—an
experience most peer-oriented kids will be defended against. For the reasons discussed in the last chapter, peer-oriented children cannot permit
themselves to feel their vulnerability.

It may seem strange that feelings of fulfillment would require openness
to feelings of vulnerability. There is no hurt or pain in fulfillment—quite
the opposite. Yet there is an underlying emotional logic to this phenomenon. For the child to feel full he must first feel empty, to feel helped the
child must first feel in need of help, to feel complete he must have felt in-
complete. To experience the joy of reunion one must first experience the
ache of loss, to be comforted one must first have felt hurt. Satiation may
be a very pleasant experience, but the prerequisite is to be able to feel vulnerability. When a child loses the ability to feel her attachment voids, the
child also loses the ability to feel nurtured and fulfilled. One of the first
things I check for in my assessment of children is the existence of feelings
of missing and loss. It is indicative of emotional health for children to be
able to sense what is missing and to know what the emptiness is about. As
soon as they are able to articulate, they should be able to say things like "I
miss daddy," "It hurt me that grandma didn't notice me," "It didn't seem
like you were interested in my story," "I don't think so and so likes me."

Many children today are too defended, too emotionally closed, to experience such vulnerable emotions. Children are affected by what is missing
whether they feel it or not, but only when they can feel and know what is

missing can they be released from their pursuit of attachment. Parents of such children are not able to take them to the turning point or bring them to a place of rest. If a child becomes defended against vulnerability as a result of peer orientation, he is made insatiable in relation to the parents as well. That is the tragedy of peer orientation—it renders our love and affection so useless and unfulfilling.

For children who are insatiable, nothing is ever enough. No matter what one does, how much one tries to make things work, how much attention and approval is given, the turning point is never reached. For parents this is extremely discouraging and exhausting. Nothing is as satisfying to a parent as the sense of being the source of fulfillment for a child. Millions of parents are cheated of such an experience because their children are either looking elsewhere for nurturance or are too defended against vulnerability to be capable of satiation. Insatiability keeps our children stuck in first gear developmentally, stuck in immaturity, unable to transcend basic instincts. They are thwarted from ever finding rest and remain ever dependent on someone or something outside themselves for satisfaction. Neither the discipline imposed by parents nor the love felt by them can cure this condition. The only hope is to bring children back into the attachment fold where they belong and then soften them up to where our love can actually penetrate and nurture.

What happens when insatiability dominates a person's emotional functioning? The process of maturation is preempted by an obsession or an addiction, in this case for peer connection. Peer contact whets the appetite without nourishing. It titillates without satisfying. The end result of peer contact is usually an urgent desire for more. The more the child gets, the more he craves. The mother of an eight-year-old girl mused, "I don't get it—the more time my daughter spends with her friends, the more demanding she becomes to get together with them. How much time does she really need for social interaction, anyway?" Likewise, the parents of a young adolescent complained that "as soon as our son comes home from camp, he gets on the phone right away to call the kids he's just been with. Yet it's the family he hasn't seen for two weeks." The obsession with peer contact is always worse after exposure to peers, whether it is at school or in playtimes, sleepovers, class retreats, outings, or camps. If peer contact satiated, times of peer interaction would lead automatically to increased self-generated play, creative solitude, or individual reflection.

Many parents confuse this insatiable behavior with a valid need for peer interaction. Over and over I hear some variation of "but my child is absolutely obsessed with getting together with friends. It would be cruel to deprive him." Actually, it would be more cruel and irresponsible to indulge what so clearly fuels the obsession. The only attachment that children truly need is the kind that nurtures and satisfies them and can bring them to rest. The more demanding the child is, the more he is indicating a runaway obsession. It is not strength that the child manifests but the desperation of a hunger that only increases with more peer contact.

### Peer-Oriented Children Cannot Let Go

My focus so far in this chapter has been on the satiation of attachment hunger as the key to releasing a child from preoccupation with attachment. Yet there are people who have matured well without ever having enjoyed, as children, a nurturing attachment with an adult. How can this be? The explanation is that there is a second key to unlocking the maturation process. One could call it "the back door to maturation," as it is far less obvious and in many ways the opposite of satiation. This emotional turning point comes when, instead of being fulfilled by what works, the child's brain registers that the attachment hunger is not going to be satisfied in this situation or at this time. The futility that sinks in arises from failed aspirations—not getting daddy's attention or being special to grandma, a failure to make a friend or to have someone to play with. It may be caused by a child's inability to escape feeling alone, or to be the biggest and best, matter the most to someone, to find a lost pet, keep mommy home, or to prevent the family from moving. The list of potentially futile desires could extend from the most mundane example of a thwarted drive for closeness with someone to the most profound loss of attachment.

Our emotional circuitry is programmed to release us from the pursuit of contact and closeness not only when attachment hunger is fulfilled but also when we truly get that the desire for its fulfillment is futile. Letting go of a desire we are attached to is most difficult even for adults, whether it be the wish that everyone like us or that a particular person love us, or that we become politically powerful. Not until we accept that what we have been trying to do cannot be done and fully experience the disappointment and sadness that follow can we move on with our lives. As immature creatures of attachment, children naturally experience the urges to hold on, to make contact, to demand attention, to possess the person attached to. A child may even become consumed by this desire to the point that it dominates her functioning. Only when the futility registers deep within the emotional brain will the urgency relax and the clinging end. On the other hand, if the futility fails to sink in, the child will remain gripped by obsessive attachment needs and will persist in pursuing the unattainable.

As with fulfillment, futility must sink in for the shift in energy to occur, the shift that leads to acceptance, from frustration to a sense of peace with how things are. It is not enough to register it intellectually, it must be felt deeply and vulnerably, in the very heart of the limbic system, at the core of the brain's emotional circuitry. Futility is a vulnerable feeling, bringing us face-to-face with the limits of our control and with what we cannot change. Feelings of futility are some of the first to go when a child becomes defended against vulnerability. As a result, peer-oriented kids are extremely short on such emotions. Despite the fact that their peer relationships are so fraught with frustration and loss, they seldom talk about feelings of disappointment, sadness, and grief. As we will see in a later chapter, the inability to go from frustration to futility, from "mad to sad," is a major source of aggression and violence.

In children, one of the most obvious signs of futility sinking in is the eyes watering. There is a little organ in the brain that orchestrates this telltale sign. We often learn to hide our tears as adults, but the impulse to cry is hardwired to feelings of futility. Of course, there are other experiences that can move us to tears as well, like something in our eye, onions, physical pain, and frustration. The tears of futility are set off by different neurological circuitry and are psychologically unique. They feel different on our cheeks. They are accompanied by a shift in energy: a healthy sadness, a backing-off from trying to change things. Tears of futility actually bring a release, a sense that something has come to an end. They signal that the brain truly apprehends that something is not working and must be let go of. A toddler who, for example, drops his ice cream cone but is able to find his tears and sadness in the arms of a loving adult will accept his loss, brighten up quickly, and move on to his next adventure in the world.

It is only natural that a child would be moved to tears by the experience of something unsuccessful in her attachments. In this, too, peer-oriented kids are far from natural. They are more likely to be dry-eyed when it comes to futility, and the worse things are in their peer relationships, the more entrenched becomes their unconscious resistance to accepting the futility of things. When we stop crying, it's as if the brain's capacity to process emotions—normally quite flexible and responsive—becomes rigid. It loses its plasticity, its ability to develop. Without futility, as without satiation, maturation is impossible.

### Peer Orientation Crushes Individuality

Peer orientation threatens maturation in another crucial way: it crushes individuality. Before we explore why, we must briefly point out the important distinction between individuality and individualism. *Individuality* is the fruit of the process of becoming a psychologically separate being that culminates in the full flowering of one's uniqueness. Psychologists call this process differentiation or individuation. To be an individual is to have one's own meanings, one's own ideas and boundaries. It is to value one's own preferences, principles, intentions, perspectives, and goals. It is to stand in a place occupied by no other. *Individualism* is the philosophy that puts the rights and interests of a person ahead of the rights and interests of the community. Individuality, on the other hand, is the foundation of true community because only authentically mature individuals can fully cooperate in a way that respects and celebrates the uniqueness of others. Ironically, peer orientation may fuel individualism even as it undermines true individuality.

Budding individuality and emerging independence require protection, both from the reactions of others and from the power of one's own drive to attach to others at all costs. There is something very vulnerable about newly emergent psychological growth in all its manifestations: interest, curiosity, uniqueness, creativity, originality, wide-eyed wonder, new ideas, doing it oneself, experimenting, exploring, and so on. Such emergence has a tentative and timid character, like a turtle sticking its head out of a shell. To venture forth in all our naked originality is to be totally exposed to the reactions of others. If the reaction is too critical or negative, this show of emergence quickly dissipates. Only a highly mature person can brave the reactions of those who do not recognize or value independence of thought, being, and action.

Children cannot be expected to welcome signs of maturation in another child. It is not their responsibility and, in any case, they are too driven by attachment to honor individuality. How could they know that developing one's own intentions is the seed of future values? That dividing the world into "mine" and "not mine" is not antisocial but the necessary beginning of individuation? That wanting to be the author of one's work and the originator of one's ideas is the way to becoming one's own person? Children do not care much about such things in one another. It takes an adult to recognize the seeds of maturity, to make room for individuality, and to value the early signs of independence. It takes an adult to see individuality as a sacred trust and to give it whatever protection it needs.

Still, if the only problem was children's inability to encourage and celebrate one another's individuality, peer interaction would not be so hard on emerging personhood. Unfortunately, the problem is much worse than that. Immature people tend to trample on any individuality that dares show itself. In a child's world it is not immaturity but rather the maturing processes that are suspect and a source of shame. The *emergent* child—the child who is self-motivated and not driven by needs for peer contact—seems like an anomaly, irregular, a little off the beaten track. The words that peer-oriented kids use for such a child are highly critical, words like weird, stupid, retarded, freak, and geek. Immature children do not understand why these emergent, maturing others are trying so hard to get along, why they seek solitude sometimes instead of company, why they can be curious and interested about things that don't involve others, why they ask questions in class. There must be something wrong with these kids and for that they deserve to be shamed. The stronger a child's peer orientation, the more intensely she will resent and assault another kid's individuality.

Just as individuation is threatened from the outside by the reactions of peers, it's also undermined by the internal dynamics of the peer-oriented child. Individuality is hard on peer attachments. Few peer-oriented relationships can bear the weight of the child becoming his own person, having his own preferences, speaking his own mind, expressing his own judgments, making his own decisions. When attachment to peers is the primary concern, individuality must be sacrificed. To the immature child this sacrifice seems only right. Editing her personality, diminishing her true self-expression, and suppressing any conflicting opinions or values seem like the natural course of action. She must not allow her individuality to come between herself and her peers. To immature beings, friendship—by which they mean peer attachment—must always come before the self. Creatures of attachment would willingly sell their birthright of individuality for some token acceptance from peers, without any idea of the developmental sacrilege they had just committed. Not until there is viability as a separate being does a self-preserving instinct even form.

Kate is the mother of seven-year-old Claire, whom she home-schools. "Quite a neat and unique little person at seven," says Kate of her daughter, "with independence of spirit. Yet after more than a few hours with her peers, she comes back not exactly herself. Her language is not her own and she takes on the mannerisms of her friends. Then it takes a couple of hours for her Claire-self to reemerge. But as she gets older, the more and more she is able to maintain herself."

During my daughter Tamara's peer-oriented years she could not express her opinions or even entertain thoughts that would lead to conflict with her friends. I could almost see her shrink to fit within the parameters of whatever relationship she was preserving. When I encouraged her to be herself with Shannon—the girl who had become her primary orientation—she had great difficulty even comprehending what I meant. Although Tamara excelled academically, she was embarrassed by her accomplishments and took great pains to hide her marks from her peers. Any peer-oriented child knows the deal: don't say or do anything that could reflect badly on others and risk pushing them away. She knew intuitively that these relationships could not take her weight, yet instead of allowing development to take its course, she attempted to make herself small enough to fit.

The world our children live in is becoming increasingly unfriendly to the natural processes of maturing. In the peer-oriented universe, maturation and individuation are seen as the enemies of attachment. Uniqueness and individuality become impediments to success in the peer culture.

It is our job, as parents, to cultivate attachments with our children that make room for individuation. A child's individuality should never be the price exacted for warmth and closeness. We have to give our children what they cannot give to one another: the freedom to be themselves in the context of loving acceptance—an acceptance that immature peers are unable to offer but one that we adults can and must provide.

# A LEGACY OF AGGRESSION

NINE-YEAR-OLD Helen stood in front of a mirror one day and took vicious cuts from her dark locks, leaving herself nearly hairless in the front. When Helen's mother, bewildered and alarmed, demanded to know what that behavior had been about, the child aimed the sharp end of the scissors at her and screamed insults.

Fifteen-year-old Emily was sent by her mother to see me because she was cutting and slashing herself. Her attacking impulses were directed not just against herself. Nothing and no one escaped her seething sarcasm and hostility, except her friends. She even mocked the titles on my bookshelf. Although I found her witticisms refreshing and her intelligence impressive, it was hard to stomach the way she trashed her parents and her younger brother. Mercilessly critical, she badmouthed them incessantly. Her hostility was unrelenting.

Helen's parents are friends of mine. In the year prior to this unexpected outburst of aggression from their daughter they had gone through a very difficult period in their marriage. Their time and energy had been absorbed by their relationship troubles, leaving Helen to scrounge for emotional contact from her peers, where she was unsuccessful.

As Emily's experience illustrates, even had Helen achieved her goal of peer acceptance, her emotional needs would still have remained unsatisfied. Emily had, at the age of ten, become very peer-oriented in the wake of her mother's battle with cancer. Unable to handle the vulnerability evoked by the possibility of losing her, Emily had reacted by pushing her mother away. The void created by backing out of her maternal attachment had become filled with peers. These peers now meant everything to her. The aggression expressed in her actions, words, and attitudes followed. Attacking family members is all too typical of peer-oriented children, leaving parents and siblings wounded. In most cases, the attacks will not be physical, but the verbal assaults and emotional hostility can be extremely wearing, alienating, and hurtful.

Aggression is one of the most common complaints raised by parents and teachers these days. It was the main concern of the parents of Kirsten, Melanie, and Sean. While aggression is not always related to peer orientation, the more peer-oriented the child, the more likely aggression will be part of the picture.

As peer orientation increases in a society, so will childhood aggression. There were six thousand violent incidents reported by the New York City school board in 1993 compared with one single violent incident in 1961.[1] The number of serious assaults among Canadian youth have climbed fivefold in the last fifty years, while in the United States, it's up sevenfold.[2] The increasing abuse of parents by their children was the subject of the recent Cottrell report to Health Canada.[3] In one survey, four out of five teachers reported having been attacked by students, if not physically then by intimidating threats and verbal assaults.[4] When the definition of aggression is expanded to include self-attack, the suicide statistics become very disturbing. Attempts with fatal outcomes have tripled among children in the past fifty years. Suicides among ten- to fourteen-year-olds have been increasing at the fastest rate.[5]

Many adults today are hesitant to confront groups of youths they do not know, for fear of being attacked. Such apprehension was virtually unknown a generation or two ago. Those of us who have been around for a while can sense the difference a few decades have made.

Media reports of aggression in children abound: "Spurned teen returns to party with gun, killing three," "Youth swarmed by teens, in critical condition," "Gang of children, ages 10 to 13, engaged in violent crimes," "Flunked student returns to school, killing teacher." In an October 2002 account of the fatal assault by a group of youths ranging in age from ten to eighteen on a thirty-six-year-old man in Chicago, the Associated Press quotes a witness as saying, "They were pounding on him [with rakes, milk cartons and bats] and hollering, saying, 'Hey, let me use that . . .' It was like a game to them." Within a few weeks of that bloody event, two murders by teenagers in the adjacent western provinces shocked the Canadian public. The body of a thirty-nine-year-old wife and mother of three was found amid the remains of a deliberately set fire at the family's home in Maple Ridge, British Columbia. A few hours later police pulled over a fifteen-year-old in the dead woman's automobile. "He was at the wheel, smoking a cigar. Five others youths were in the car." The teenager was charged with first-degree murder. Notable in this account is the apparent nonchalance of this child-murderer, in the company of his peers.*

Violent atrocities by teenagers against one another have become the stuff of headlines: at Columbine High School in Colorado; in Tabor, Alberta; in Liverpool, England. But to focus on the grim statistics and media stories of bloody violence is to miss the full impact of children's aggression in our society. The most telling signs of the groundswell of aggression and violence are not in the headlines but in the peer culture—the language, the music, the games, the art, and the entertainment of choice. A culture reflects the dynamics of its participants, and the culture of peer-oriented children is increasingly a culture of aggression and violence. The appetite for violence is reflected in the vicarious enjoyment of it not only in music and movies but in the schoolyards and school halls. Children fuel hostilities among their peers rather than defuse them, encourage others to fight rather than dissuade them from violence. The perpetrators are only the tip of the iceberg. In one schoolyard study, researchers found that most schoolchildren were likely to passively support or actively encourage acts of bullying and aggression; fewer than one in eight attempted to intervene. So ingrained have the culture and psychology of violence become that peers in general expressed more respect and liking for the bullies than for the victims.[6]

The most prevalent forms of childhood and teenage aggression are not the fights and assaults that are the focus of studies or statistics but the attacking gestures, words, and actions that are the daily modes of interaction among peer-oriented kids. The attacks may be emotional, vented in hostility, antagonism, and contempt. They may be expressed in rude gestures or the rolling of the eyes, or in words through insults and put-downs. The attack can be in the tone of voice, in a mocking gesture, in the glare of the eyes, in the posture of the body, in the sarcasm of a comment, or in the coldness of a response. Aggression can be directed toward others or expressed through tantrums and fits. It can also be directed toward oneself in self-deprecation like "I'm so stupid," self-hostility like "I hate myself," head

---

*The teenager has since been convicted of the crime. His life story is one of early abandonment, a serial loss of adult attachments, and consequent entrenchment in the peer group.

banging, self-harm, and suicidal thoughts and impulses. Attacks can be directed toward existence itself, such as "I'm going to kill you" or "I'm going to kill myself." Attacks on existence can also be psychological, as in ostracism, in pretending that another does not exist or refusing to acknowledge someone's presence. The list is endless. In other words, the essence of aggression transcends the blatantly violent forms that have become the subject of the widespread but futile "zero tolerance" policies currently being adopted in schools and other institutions that deal with large numbers of children. Given the pervasive nature of aggression, zero tolerance is shallow in concept and impossible to realize in practice.

Aggression, like love, is in the nature of the underlying motivation — what moves you. In the case of aggression, it is the impulse to attack. Where does all this aggression come from? What is driving children's aggression to new heights? Why are peer-oriented children so prone to violence? The answers lie not in the statistics but in understanding what the roots of aggression are and how peer orientation nurtures these roots. Only by making sense of aggression can we truly make sense of its escalation in the world in which our children live.

Peer orientation is not the root cause of aggression. Toddlers and preschoolers and other children who are not the least bit peer-oriented can be aggressive. Aggression and violence have been part of human history since the beginning of time. Aggression is one of the oldest and most challenging of human problems; peer orientation is relatively new. But peer orientation powerfully stokes the fires of aggression and foments it into violence.

## THE DRIVING FORCE OF AGGRESSION

What moves a person to attack? Frustration. Frustration is the fuel of aggression. Of course, frustration will no more automatically lead to aggression than a supply of oxygen will automatically cause a fire. As we will see, frustration can lead to other outcomes as well, quite incompatible with aggression. Only in the absence of a more civilized resolution to frustration does its increase lead to aggression. Peer orientation not only increases frustration in a child but also decreases the likelihood of finding peaceful alternatives to aggression.

Frustration is the emotion we feel when something doesn't work. What doesn't work may be a toy, a job, one's body, a conversation, a demand, a relationship, the coffeemaker, or the scissors. Whatever it is, the more it matters to us that "it" should work, the more stirred up we become when it doesn't. Frustration is a deep and primitive emotion, so primitive, in fact, that it exists in other animals as well. Frustration is not something that is necessarily conscious, but like any emotion it will move us nonetheless.

There are many triggers for frustration, but because what matters most to children—as to many adults—is attachment, the greatest source of frustration is attachments that do not work: loss of contact, thwarted connection, too much separation, feeling spurned, losing a loved one, a lack of belonging or of being understood. Because we are generally unconscious of attachment, we are also often unconscious of the link between our frustration and our attachments not working.

The close link between attachment frustration and aggression was driven home to me when my son Shay was three years old. Shay was very attached to me and had experienced relatively little prolonged separation from me until I accepted an invitation from across the continent to do a five-day course for educators. On my return, Shay's aggression had increased from his age-appropriate base level of two or three incidents a day to more like twenty to thirty a day. I didn't need to ask him why he was having tantrums or biting and hitting and throwing things—it so happened that the topic of the seminar I had just given was the roots of aggression and violence. Nor could he have told me. It was attachment frustration pure and simple, welling up from deep within. The mother of Helen, the girl mentioned at the beginning of this chapter, suffered a serious depression when Helen was three years old. Both she and her husband became less available to their daughter during the long dark months of her mood disorder. Then suddenly, for no ostensible reason, Helen began to strike out at other children at the playground, children she didn't even know. It was her attachment frustration erupting into aggressive behavior.

When peers replace parents, the source of their frustration changes as well and, in most cases, will increase rather than decrease. Peers whose primary attachments are to one another are frustrated because they have a hard time keeping close. They do not live with one another and so suffer separation continually. There is never any certainty about finding favor with peers; being chosen today is no guarantee of being chosen tomorrow. If mattering to peers is what matters most, there will be frustration around every corner: calls not returned, being overlooked or ignored, being replaced by another, being slighted or put down. A child can never rest securely in the sense that he is accepted or thought special by his peers. Furthermore, peer relationships rarely can withstand a child's true psychological weight. The child must edit herself constantly, being careful not to reveal differences or disagree too vehemently. Anger and resentment must be swallowed if closeness is to be preserved. There is no secure home base, no shield from stress, no forgiving love, no commitment to rely on, no sense of being intimately known in the peer relationship. The frustration in such a milieu is intense, even when things are working relatively well. Add some rejection and some ostracism, and the frustration goes over the top. No wonder that the language of our peer-oriented children turns foul and the themes of their music and entertainment take aggressive turns. It is also little wonder that so many of these children attack themselves, mutilate their bodies, and contemplate suicide. Less obviously but more pervasively, many more kids are uncomfortable with themselves. Consciously or unconsciously, they are highly critical of their own attributes. That, too, is a form of aggression against the self.

Children who are stuck with frustration seek opportunities to attack and are highly engaged by attacking themes in music, literature, art, and entertainment. My cowriter recalls being shocked when one of his sons, then on the verge of adolescence, began to watch violent wrestling programs on television and took to wearing costumes that evoked a horror movie protagonist, the lethally sharp-nailed Freddie Kruger. This boy, at that time in his life, lacked a secure enough attachment with his parents and was caught up in some extremely frustrating relationships with peers.

As many parents have ruefully experienced, once a child's attachment brain has seized on peers, attempts to thwart this agenda can evoke intense frustration indeed. Limitations and restrictions imposed by parents can unleash a torrent of attacking language and behavior that can be highly distressing. Eleven-year-old Matthew was a case in point. He had replaced his parents with a solitary peer, Jason. The two were inseparable. Matthew requested that he be allowed to go to a Halloween overnight party at Jason's house. When his parents refused, Matthew erupted in such emotional hostility and verbal aggression that his parents become frightened of what he might do. That is when they consulted me and discovered his underlying peer orientation. An anguished note Matthew wrote to his parents captured some of his frustration and resulting aggression.

> Now, please just think for a minute about the situation here. Say Jason wants to do something with someone, he would normally call me. But he won't even bother now because you won't let me. So instead he becomes more acquainted with other people, which normally would be okay but now he won't be friends with me. That makes me pretty fucking mad!!!!!!!! It makes me so mad I want to hurt someone and I mean really

fuck them up. . . . I'll swear to god your little boy you love so much will be no more. I'll fucking kill myself if I have to! Perhaps I'll slit my rists. . . . ONCE I HAVE NO FRIENDS, I HAVE NO LIFE.

There is no end of fuel for the fires of aggression in a peer-oriented child.

It is not a given that frustration must lead to aggression. The healthy response to frustration is to attempt to change things. If that proves impossible, we can accept how things are and adapt creatively to a situation that cannot be changed. If such adaptation doesn't occur, the impulses to attack can still be kept in check by tempering thoughts and feelings—in other words, by mature self-regulation. It is quite possible to become intensely frustrated and yet not be driven to attack. In peer-oriented children, acceptable outcomes to frustration are likely to be blocked in ways I will now explain. These children become aggressive by default.

There are three major deficiencies in peer relationships that lead to frustration being bottled up until it erupts in aggression.

## HOW PEER ORIENTATION FOMENTS AGGRESSION

### Peer-Oriented Children Are Less Able to Effect Change

When we feel frustrated, our first inclination is to change whatever isn't working for us. We can try to accomplish this by making demands on others, attempting to alter our own behavior, or by a variety of other means. Having moved us to action, frustration will have done its duty.

The problem is that life brings many frustrations that are beyond us: we cannot alter time or change the past or undo what we have done. We cannot avoid death, make good experiences last, cheat on reality, make something work that won't, or induce someone to cooperate with us when they may not feel like it. We are unable to always make things fair or to guarantee our own or another's safety. Of all these unavoidable frustrations the most threatening for children is that they cannot make themselves psychologically and emotionally secure. These extremely important needs—to be wanted, invited, liked, loved, and special—are out of their control.

As long as we parents are successful in holding on to our children, they need not be confronted with this deep futility, fundamental to human existence. It is not that we can forever protect them from reality, but children should not have to face challenges they are not ready for. Peer-oriented children are not so lucky. Given the degree of frustration they experience, they become desperate to change things, to somehow secure their attachments. Some become compulsively demanding in their relationships with one another. Some become preoccupied with making themselves more attractive in the eyes of their peers—hence the large increase in the demand for cosmetic surgery among young people and hence, too, their obsession with being fashionably chic at earlier and earlier ages. Some become bossy, others charmers or entertainers. Some bend over backward, turning into psychological pretzels to preserve a sense of closeness with their peers. Perpetually dissatisfied, these children are out of touch with the source of their discontent and rail against a reality they have no control over. Of course, the same dynamics may also occur in children's relationships with adults—and all too often do—but they are absolutely guaranteed to be present in peer-oriented relationships.

No matter how much the peer-oriented child attempts to change things by making demands, altering her appearance, making things work for others; no matter how she tones down her true personality or compromises herself, she will find only fleeting relief. She'll find no lasting relief from the unrelenting attachment frustration, and there will be the added frustration of continually hitting against this wall of impossibility. Her frustration, rather than coming to an end, moves one step closer to being transformed into aggression, as in the cases of Helen and Emily, mentioned at the beginning of this chapter.

### Peer-Oriented Children Are Less Able to Adapt

Frustration that comes up against impassable obstacles is meant to dissolve into feelings of futility. In this way frustration engenders adaptation, causing us to change ourselves when we are unable to change the circumstances that thwart us. A child moved to adapt does not attack: adaptation and aggression, both potential outcomes of frustration, are incompatible.

This frustration-to-futility dynamic is most transparent in toddlers. A toddler makes demands that the parent, usually for valid reasons, is unwilling or unable to meet. After some unsuccessful attempts at changing things, the toddler should be moved to tears of futility. That response is a very good thing. The energy is being transformed from trying to change things to letting go. If some of the frustration had already erupted into attack, those feelings, too, change from mad to sad. Once the transformation to feelings of futility occurs, the child comes to rest. When frustration is not converted by this process, the child will not quit trying to get his way. Unless distracted or indulged, the toddler is likely to keep struggling against the futility and erupt in attack until exhaustion sets in. Only feelings of futility can enable someone to quit a course of action that does not work and dissolve the frustration involved.

The brain must register that something doesn't work. It's not enough to *think* something does not work—it must be *felt*. We have all had the experience of knowing something isn't working but continuing to repeat the same action over and over. For example, many of us as parents have said to a child: "If I've told you once, I've told you a thousand times . . ." If, instead, we allowed our own sense of futility to sink in, we would not persist in parenting behaviors that we know don't work and will not work, no matter how many times we repeat them.

Adaptation is a deeply unconscious and emotional process orchestrated not by the thinking parts of the cerebral cortex but by the limbic system, the brain's emotional apparatus. For example, when we have lost a loved one, whether due to death or simply to the ending of a relationship, it is not enough that we know they are absent for adaptation to occur. We must come to terms with this emotionally, through waves and waves of felt futility. Only when the futility sinks in and we apprehend on the deepest emotional level the impossibility of preserving physical and emotional contact with someone forever gone from our lives do the tears come and adaptation begins. This process may take years. When, for a young child, the wall of futility is erected to a snack before supper, adaptation should take only a few moments—that is, mad should move to sad very quickly. In the case of having to share mommy with a sibling, such adaptation may take a bit longer. But if tears of futility never come, adaptation will not occur. Whether our eyes water or not, the most common feelings of futility are sadness, disappointment, and grief. Fortunately, even when we have learned to suppress our tears, sadness and disappointment can still do their work in facilitating adaptation if we are able to experience futility inwardly. The dilemma of peer-oriented children is that feelings of futility involve vulnerability: to feel futility is to come to terms with the limits of our power and control. In the peer-oriented child's flight from vulnerability feelings of futility are the first to be suppressed. In a culture of cool, tears of futility are a source of shame. Deficient in feelings of futility, peer-oriented kids are much more prone to aggression.

Peer orientation both gives rise to frustration and takes away the tears that would be the antidote. Helen, for instance, had lost her tears and now was full of emotional hostility toward her mother. Emily never shed a tear over her mother's cancer. Instead of tears of futility, she shed drops of blood from cutting herself. Instead of sadness and disappointment, she was full of sarcasm and contempt. She chose the violence of heavy metal rather than the melancholy kind of music that would have reflected and soothed her anguish. Children in increasing numbers face the futility of making things work with their peers but, too hardened to let futility sink in, end up attacking themselves and others.

When futility doesn't sink in there is also a failure to let go and a failure to accept existing limits. Without adaptation there is no resilience in the face of adversity, no resourcefulness in the absence of direction, and no ability to recover from past trauma.

Peer-oriented kids are stuck between a rock and a hard place: the rock is the things they can't change and the hard place is in their own hearts.

### Peer-Oriented Kids Have Fewer Mixed Feelings About Attacking

Frustration may also be kept from turning into aggression if the impulses to attack are checked by opposing impulses, thoughts, intentions, and feelings. When it comes to aggression, ambivalence is a very good thing. Peer-oriented children are much less likely to feel ambivalent about attacking.

Normally, keeping attack impulses in check are intentions not to hurt, a desire to be good, a fear of retaliation, or a concern about the consequences. Also mitigating aggression is a sense of alarm about alienating those we're attached to, feelings of affection, and even a desire for self-control. Once the impulses to attack arise, what keeps the child civilized is being simultaneously moved in an opposing direction. The conflicting motivations spark a civilizing consciousness that enables self-control. With ambivalence lacking and the urge to attack at the fore, nothing stops inappropriate impulses from being acted out.

Why are peer-oriented children much less likely to feel ambivalent about attacking? First, owing to their arrested development, they are more likely to have a nature untamed by mixed feelings and conflicting impulses. This is the preschool syndrome discussed in Chapter 9—impulsiveness stemming from psychological immaturity. It doesn't matter what an impulsive child knows, how good his intentions may be, how often he has been lectured, how punishing the consequences may be; once his frustration has accumulated sufficiently, all these will be eclipsed by his urge to attack.

The second reason why peer-oriented children are less likely to feel ambivalent is the absence of the mitigating force of attachment. As I explained in Chapter 2, the bipolar nature of primitive attachment drives us to repel those to whom we are not attracted. When, to satisfy the child's attachment hunger, connection and closeness are sought from peers, virtually everyone else is left open to attack—siblings, parents, and teachers.

Also subject to attack are those peers to whom the child is not interested in attaching. Once more, such aggression can take many forms other than physical attack: badmouthing, mocking, ignoring, backbiting, emotional hostility, name-calling, put-downs, antagonism, contempt.

Thus peer orientation triggers impulses to attack and, at the same time, it removes the natural immunity for family members and other adults responsible for the child. Hence the increasing abuse of parents by their children and of teachers by their students.

Another powerful tempering influence is psychological alarm. A significant portion of the brain is devoted to an elaborate alarm system. Anxiety is an emotional alarm that warns us of danger, whether from attack or the threat of being separated from those who matter to us. Apprehension about getting into trouble, fear of getting hurt, concern about consequences, anxiety about alienating loved ones are mechanisms meant to move a child to caution. Attacking is risky business. The very thought of it, in a child capable of mixed emotions, should evoke feelings of alarm that help keep her aggression in check.

The difficulty with feeling alarmed is that it makes us also feel vulnerable. In fact, the realization that something bad could happen to us is the very essence of vulnerability. Because of their flight from vulnerability, many peer-oriented children lose their feelings of fear. They may still become alarmed on a physiological level, but consciously they no longer experience the sense of alarm or the vulnerability that goes along with it. They no longer talk about being frightened or nervous or scared.

Once feelings of alarm are numbed, the chemistry of alarm—the rush of adrenaline—can become appealing and even addictive. Children whose emotions are shut down as their defense against vulnerability can actually court danger for the adrenaline rush it creates—hence, no doubt, the surging popularity of "extreme sports."

The more intensely peer-oriented a child, the less likely he is to feel apprehensive and cautious. Brain research reveals that up to one third of our adolescent delinquents no longer have normal brain activity in the area where alarm is supposed to register. Without a functioning trigger in the brain for alarm a person's impulses to attack are likely to erupt in violent forms.

The impact of alcohol illustrates this relationship. The sense of alarm that holds aggressive impulses in check is numbed by alcohol, whether the alarm is about getting hurt or getting into trouble or about alienating someone important to us. When a person ingests alcohol, the parts of his brain that normally inhibit aggression are suppressed. It should be no surprise that alcohol is involved in a high percentage of violent crimes.[7] Kids think alcohol gives them "balls"; in reality, it only takes away their fear. The brain, however, is fully capable of numbing our feelings of alarm without any assistance from alcohol or other drugs, and will do so if the circumstances are too overwhelming. Emotional self-numbing is the goal of too many of our peer-oriented children. Of course, once peer-oriented children reach adolescence, they are also more likely to drink, increasing the probability of aggression.

Trying to douse the fires of aggression in our peer-oriented children is itself an exercise in futility. Until this futility sinks in, however, and we find our own sadness about this state of affairs, we are unlikely to change our ways. We are in a dreadful predicament with our peer-oriented children. The more they become so, the more inclined they are to aggression but also the less responsive to our discipline. The more aggressive they are, the more alienated and absent we become, leaving a still greater void to be filled with their peers. Our automatic tendency, under such circumstances, is to focus our attention and efforts on the aggression rather than on the underlying issue of our children's misdirected attachments. No matter how upsetting and alienating the problem, we cannot afford to make aggression the central focus. Our only hope of turning things around is to reclaim our children and to restore their attachment to us.

# THE MAKING OF
# BULLIES AND VICTIMS

Bullies have always been with us, as anyone familiar with the swaggering but cowardly character Flashman from the Victorian boys' classic *Tom Brown's School Days* will know. We can all recall episodes of bullying from our childhood, whether we were participants, witnesses, or victims. For all that, the phenomenon of bullying has only very recently reached such proportions as to become a subject for widespread social alarm. According to the *New York Times*, "in one of the largest studies ever of child development, researchers at the [U.S.] National Institutes of Health reported that about a quarter of all middle-school children were either perpetrators or victims (or in some cases, both) of serious and chronic bullying, behavior that included threats, ridicule, name calling, punching, slapping, jeering and sneering."[1]

It is rare now to find a school district in North America that has not found it necessary to institute antibullying programs or issue edicts of "zero tolerance" against bullying behavior. Yet the sources of bullying are little understood. The measures proposed to deal with it are predictably ineffective because, as usual, they seek to address behaviors rather than causes. In 2001, for example, the *New York Times* reported that, in the aftermath of a deadly high school shooting provoked by episodes of bullying in Santee, California, the Washington State Senate passed legislation aimed at cracking down on the problem. According to the report, "the bill's supporters say it may just help to avert more violence, but skeptics noted that the California high school where the shooting occurred already had antibullying programs, including provisions for anonymous tips about students making threats, and programs to help teenagers get along, like one called 'Names can really hurt us.' "[2]

In a study mentioned in the previous chapter, researchers from York University studied videotapes of fifty-three episodes of playground bullying among elementary school students and found that more than half the time the bystanders observed the taunting and the violence passively while nearly a quarter of the time some of them joined in picking on the victim.[3]

A murder that drew international attention in 1997, that of the Victoria, British Columbia, teenager Reena Virk by her peers, was nightmarishly reminiscent of the *Lord of the Flies*. Reena was fourteen years old at the time of her death, and her accused killers were within a year or two of being her contemporaries. As in the William Golding novel, a group of adolescents turned on the most vulnerable of their group, their frustrations and rage not fully vented until her body lay battered and drowned. One of the murderers reportedly smoked a cigarette while nonchalantly holding the victim's head under the water. Many who didn't directly participate witnessed the beating, no one making any strong effort to intervene, no one afterward being moved to report the incident to the authorities. No adult found out about the killing for several days.

In *Lord of the Flies*, a group of British choirboys are marooned on a tropical island. Left to their own devices, they spontaneously divide into bullies and bullied, to the point of murder. The interpretation many have put on the Golding novel is that children harbor an untamed savagery underneath a thin veneer of civilization and that only the force of authority can keep their innate brutalizing impulse in check. This impression is reinforced by the proliferation of media reports of kids victimizing other kids. Although it is true that the non-presence of adults in children's lives is a major cause of bullying, the real dynamic involves not missing adult authority but the dearth of adult attachments. More accurately, the waning of adult authority is directly related to the weakening of attachments with adults and their displacement by peer attachments. With bullying, as with the legacy of violence in general, we see the effects of peer orientation. We can actually observe the same phenomenon in the animal world.

In a laboratory of monkeys at the U.S. National Institutes of Health a group of infants was separated from adults and, by default, reared only by one another. Unlike with adult-raised monkeys, a large number of these peer-oriented animals displayed bullying behavior and became impulsive, aggressive, and self-destructive.[4]

In a South African wildlife reserve, park rangers become concerned about the slaughter of rare white rhinos. Poachers were originally blamed, but it later transpired that a group of rogue young elephants was responsible. The episode drew so much attention that it was reported on the TV program "60 Minutes." An Internet account provides details:

> The story began a decade ago when the park could no longer sustain the population of elephants. [Rangers] decided to kill many of the adult elephants whose young were old enough to survive without them. And so, the young elephants grew up fatherless.
>
> As time went on, many of these young elephants roamed together in gangs and began to do things elephants normally don't do. They threw sticks and water at rhinos and acted like the neighborhood bullies. . . . A few young males grew especially violent, knocking down rhinos and stepping or kneeling on them, crushing the life out of them. . . .
>
> The solution was to bring in a large male to lead them and to counteract their bully behaviors. Soon the new male established dominance and put the young bulls in their place. The killing stopped.

In both of these cases we see that bullying among animals followed the destruction of the natural generational hierarchy. Among human children as well, the bullying phenomenon is a direct product of the subversion of the natural hierarchy, following on the loss of adult relationships. In *Lord of the Flies* the children are left to their own devices in the wake of a plane crash that none of their caregiving adults survive. In the killing of Reena Virk in Victoria, both the victim and her attackers were young people from troubled family backgrounds who were intensely peer-oriented, having lost emotional attachments with adults. Even the Victorian-era bully Flashman was the product of a system that took very young boys out of their homes and placed them in institutions where peer values dominated their social life and relationships. Bullying has always been an endemic feature of British boys' schools.

The underlying problem is not the behavior itself but the loss of the natural attachment hierarchy with adults in charge. When youngsters can no longer look to parents to orient by, they are reduced to instinct and impulse. As I'll discuss, an instinct to dominate arises when there is a loss of appropriate attachments. Unfortunately, the dynamics of bullying behavior, so deeply rooted in instinct and emotion, are often overlooked. Only what's immediately visible to us, the bullying behavior and its deplorable impact on the victims, draw everyone's concern.

What's especially grabbing our attention is the epidemic of bullying in our schools. The traditional North American stereotype of the bully as a social misfit, socially disadvantaged, preying on the weak and the vulnerable but ostracized by the mainstream no longer holds. In our children's world, bullies are not outcasts. They often enjoy a large supporting cast, at least in school. A study published in 2000 by the American Psychological Association found that "many highly aggressive and anti-social boys in elementary school are rewarded with popularity." The main author of this research was Philip Rodkin, a professor at Duke University in North Carolina. "When we think of aggressive kids, we tend to think of kids who are losers, stigmatized and out of control," Dr. Rodkin said. "But about one third of these aggressive kids are ringleaders of groups in the classroom. These kids can have a lot of influence on their peers and on the classroom as a whole, even if they're a minority, because of their high status."[5]

It is popular but misguided to believe that bullying originates in a moral failure or stems from abuse in the home or a lack of discipline or from exposure to violence in the entertainment media. Some aspects of bullying may arise from such sources, but bullying itself, I am convinced, is fundamentally an outcome of a failure of attachment. In each of the earlier examples, the children and animals had been orphaned, physically or emotionally and psychologically. To study the effect of peer-rearing, the monkeys had been separated from their parents; the elephants' parents had been killed in a cull. The adults in *Lord of the Flies* had died, and the Victoria teens were cut off from their parents. They all—animals and children alike—suffered from an intolerable attachment void. Their bullying behavior was an expression of immature beings not properly ensconced in a natural hierarchy of attachments. What research exists supports just such a conclusion. One study reported in the *New York Times* suggested that the more time young children spent in peer company and away from parents, the more prone they were to develop bullying behavior. According to the *Times* article, "Youngsters who spent more than 30 hours a week away from mommy had a 17 percent chance of ending up as garden-variety bullies and troublemakers, compared to only 6 percent of children who spent less than 10 hours a week in day care."[6]

## DOMINATION WITHOUT CARING

Why do a child's subverted attachments predispose him to becoming a bully or, for that matter, to becoming a victim? I have explained that the primary role of attachment in human life is to make it possible for a mature, nurturing adult to take care of an immature and needy young child.

To this end, the first item of business in any attachment relationship is to establish a working hierarchy. As discussed in Chapter 5, under normal circumstances the attachment brain assigns the child to a dependent mode while the adult takes a dominant role. However, the instinct to assume either a dominant or a dependent position can be activated in any attachment relationship, even if both parties are immature and neither is in a position to look after the other's needs. The dependent looks up to the other to be cared for, while the dominant one assumes the responsibility for the well-being of the other. Between children and adults, the appropriate division of roles is obvious, or ought to be. When the subjects are children and children, the outcome can be disastrous. Some children seek dominance without assuming any responsibility for those who submit to them, while other children become submissive to those who cannot nurture them. The result of peer orientation is that powerful attachment urges force immature kids who should be on equal terms with one another into an unnatural hierarchy of dominance and submission.

Some dominating children do in fact become the mother hens, looking out for the younger ones, taking care of the needy ones, defending the vulnerable, and protecting the weak. There are heartwarming stories of children taking care of children in the absence of adults. Alpha children may be bossy and prescriptive and inclined to order their brood around, but it is for the purpose of taking care of their dependents and executing their responsibilities. Somebody must do it, and these children rise to the occasion. Despite their bossy ways, they are not bullies. They do not pick on the weak, only on those who mess with the children they are taking care of. They don't attack vulnerability when they see it, but only those who would take advantage of it. They have no mean streak, only a fiercely protective instinct. They may indeed fight or argue but not to elevate their position, only to defend their dependents. The American classic, *The Boxcar Children* by Gertrude Chandler Warner, is a beloved fictional account of children assuming responsibility for one another. Four orphaned brothers and sisters decide to care for one another rather than to seek shelter with a grandfather none of them know. Henry, the oldest, even finds work to help support his siblings.

Children (or adults) become bullies when the striving for dominance is *not* coupled with the instinctual sense of responsibility for those lower in the pecking order. The needs of others are demeaned rather than served, vulnerability is not safeguarded but exploited, weakness evokes mocking instead of helping and, in place of concern, handicaps trigger ridicule.

Dominance does not elicit caretaking because the bully's flight from vulnerability is usually so desperate that he (or she) has become hardened against feelings of caring and responsibility. Bullies are, above all, psychologically shut down against an awareness of anything that would increase their sense of vulnerability—anything that would open them to experiencing consciously their capacity to be emotionally wounded. Bullies are blind to their shortcomings and mistakes. For bullies, invulnerability is a virtue—being tearless and fearless. To care is to be emotionally invested in something or someone. To feel responsible is to be open to feelings of inadequacy and guilt. "I don't care" and "It's not my fault" are the mantras of the bully.

Bullying arises when the attachment-driven need to dominate one's peers is combined with a hardening against the feelings of caring and responsibility that should accompany a dominant role. The bully's defense against vulnerability bends domination in a destructive direction.

It is no wonder that bullying has burgeoned in the world of our children.

## WHAT DRIVES BULLIES TO DOMINATE

A person who dominates is far less vulnerable than one in a dependent position, and so the children who are the most emotionally shut down are also the ones most predisposed to seek dominance over others.

To be sure, some kids are psychologically set to become bullies before ever being peer-oriented. In such cases, peer orientation, even if not the cause, provides ample opportunity for the child to act out his impulses to bully.

Sometimes the drive for dominance can be traced to a painful experience while the child was in a dependent role. When a parent or caregiver has abused her position of responsibility by lording over the child, by trampling on his dignity, by hurting him, it is not surprising that he would develop a wish to avoid a dependent position at all cost. In any new attachment situation, he will instinctively seek the top spot. As a young boy, Frank had lived with a stepfather who beat him regularly. When peers replaced parents as the attachments that mattered to him, this twelve-year-old was desperate to come out on top. He emulated exactly what was done to him. In this way, and not through genes, can bullies beget bullies.

A child may also be predisposed to become a bully if the parent has failed to give her the secure sense that there is a competent, benign, and powerful adult in charge. The child, as much as she may resist parental direction and strive for more autonomy than she can handle, yearns to feel that she is in the hands of someone strong enough and wise enough to take care of her. The failure of parents to establish attachment dominance seems to be escalating, due in part to contemporary parenting practices and the devaluation of parenting intuition. It seems that many parents put their children in the lead, looking to them for cues on how to parent. Some parents hope to avoid upset and frustration by doing everything in their power to make things work for their children. Children parented in such a manner never come up against the necessary frustration that accompanies facing the impossible. They are deprived of the experience of transforming frustration into feelings of futility, of letting go and adapting. Other parents confuse respect for their children with indulging their wants instead of meeting their needs. Still others seek to empower their children by giving them choices and explanations when what the child really needs is to be allowed to express his frustration at having some of his desires disappointed by reality, to be given the latitude to rail against something that won't give. Still other parents look to their children to fulfill their own attachment needs. Many parents in today's highly unstable socioeconomic climate are present for their children physically but are too preoccupied with the stresses of their lives to be fully present emotionally.

If parents are too needy or too passive or too uncertain to assert their dominance, the attachment instincts are going to move the child into that dominance position by default. Such children can become bossy and controlling. As one five-year-old put it to his mother, "How can you say you love me when you don't do what I tell you to?" Another preschooler whispered in her mother's ear, "If you don't listen to me, I'm going to kill you when I grow up." When parents fail to take their rightful positions in the relationship with their children, the attachment becomes inverted. If my own practice is any indication, children are coming increasingly to bully their parents. When these children become peer-oriented, their brain naturally selects the dominant mode. They will go on to bully their peers.

## HOW BULLIES SEEK DOMINANCE OVER OTHERS

The establishment of dominance can take many forms. The most direct way of elevating oneself is to boast or brag, presenting oneself as the biggest, the best, the most important. The most common way of elevating oneself, however, is to put others down, and the bully is usually preoccupied with showing others who's boss and keeping them in line. The tools of the trade are plentiful: condescension, contempt, insults, belittling and demeaning, humiliating, taunting and teasing, shaming. The bully instinctively scans for the insecurity in others and seeks to exploit it for her gain. Bullies take great pleasure in making others look silly or stupid or in making them feel ashamed. To inflate themselves, they instinctively deflate others. They don't have to learn how to achieve such ends: the necessary techniques arise spontaneously from the psychology of the bully.

What a bully wants, of course, is what every child wants: something to satisfy the hunger for attachment. For the bully, such satisfaction must be accomplished in the least vulnerable way possible. Of the six ways of attaching I listed in Chapter 2, being the same as someone is the least vulnerable.* On the other side of this coin, differences become the primary targets of insult. Anything that stands out, anything that renders a child unique, anything that is not valued in the peer culture makes that child a target for the bully. Bullies are repulsed by differences and they dominate by attacking the differentness of others. Another of the less vulnerable ways of attaching is to be significant, to be important in the eyes of someone. In their grasp for superiority, bullies exploit any apparent inferiority in others, just as they mock and devalue any perceived superiority in others. Bullies cannot stand anyone to be more important than they are.

Another way of achieving dominance is to intimidate. By provoking fear, the bully gains the upper hand. He is therefore preoccupied with alarming others through threats, dares, stories, and scare tactics. To consolidate his position, the bully must never be seen as being afraid of anything. Some adolescents go to ridiculous lengths to prove their fearlessness, burning or cutting themselves and showing their scars to prove they are not afraid. The power of these instincts must not be underestimated. Talking sense into such children is impossible, because our sense makes no sense to them.

One of the most primitive ways to establish dominance, of course, is to gain physical superiority. A teenager testifying at a Toronto trial in which he and three of his peers were accused of having beaten a fifteen-year-old boy to death reported that his friends had engaged in bragging after the assault. They were "bigging themselves up," he said.

There used to be significant gender differences in this contest for domination as well as many culturally defined rules for how to do it. Peer orientation has reduced the gender differences, stripped the contest of its

*See "The Six Ways of Attaching," Chapter 2. The vulnerable ways of attaching, such as psychological openness and intimacy, are anathema to the bully.

socially accepted rules, and made the pursuit of dominance more desperate than ever. Girls are now also establishing domination through physically attacking others. Sometimes this girl fighting is interpreted as girls being less prim and proper, less inhibited than in times past—an expression, in other words, of "girl power." That is far from the case; girls bullying each other is a sign of emotional regression, not of liberation.

Yet another way of attaining dominance is to demand deference, the bully's signature behavior. Children perceive the bully as having to get her own way and stopping at nothing to achieve this end. What makes bullies so demanding? Again, we need to look to the dynamics of attachment and vulnerability. Although they are not aware of it, bullies are full of frustration because of the loss of their attachments with adults and their impoverished attachments with peers. Too psychologically defended to know the reason for their discontent, they make demands that are far removed from the sources of their frustration. They are trapped. They can never demand what they truly need—warmth, love, relationship. Deference, or the external trappings of it, is a poor substitute. Thus, whatever bullies receive in response to what they demand—no matter how fully their demands are met—can never satisfy the fundamental hunger for emotional nourishment. Their attempts to fulfill their craving are fruitless, but since they cannot permit themselves to experience the true futility of it all, they cannot let go. The bully's demands are perpetual.

Deference is demanded because it is such a powerful sign of loyalty and submission. It does not seem to matter to the bully that the signs of deference are given not from the heart but only on demand or under threat. Bullies don't hesitate to demand what they cannot command, to take what is not freely given. The futility of such an endeavor never sinks in; the bully is unable to differentiate between the external signs of respect and the real thing, or to grasp that closeness and contact given on demand are not genuine and can never satisfy. Since the deference he extorts forcibly fails to satiate, both the bully's hunger for attachment and his frustration grow ever more intense. What he really wants—emotionally satisfying relationships—he can never get in these ways.

## WHAT TRIGGERS A BULLY'S ATTACK

The bully is provoked to attack whenever his demands, even if unstated, are frustrated. For example, bullies are extremely sensitive to lack of deference. Even looking at him in the wrong way can trigger a reaction. Walking through a hallway containing bullies is like walking through a mine-field, trying ever so carefully to avoid making a wrong move for fear of setting something off. Unfortunately, it is not always clear what that wrong move is until too late. For one child, Justine, it was brushing up against a bully's tray in the cafeteria. For Franca, it was dancing with a boy the class bully had marked as her own. For both of these girls, their mistakes earned them months of threats and harassment, making their lives miserable and affecting their marks despite the fact that both children were pretty savvy, usually able to stay out of harm's way.

Many children are completely incapable of living without getting into trouble in a world where bullies reign. Unfortunately, one of the primary impacts of peer orientation is to provoke defenses against the vulnerability required to read signs of hostility and rejection. When the alarm system is muted, children are less able to read the cues that should move them to caution. In this way, peer orientation not only creates bullies but prepares the victims. These unfortunate children are forever walking into harm's way. This was the story with Reena Virk, the beating and drowning victim in Victoria. She was intensely peer-oriented, but defended against feeling the wounds of her rejection. The more she experienced rejection, the more desperately she tried to belong. Even near the very end, she was reportedly begging her enemies to be nice to her and pleading with them that she loved them. Instead of being alarmed and moved to caution, she blindly walked toward her own demise. This dynamic, in less severe forms, is repeated hundreds of times every day in schoolyards across our continent. Children are walking into danger because they've successfully tuned out the social cues of rejection and the spoken or unspoken messages that should alarm them.

In addition to perceived disrespect or nonsubmission, the other primary trigger for bullying is a show of vulnerability. A child must never show a bully how he can be wounded or he will pay for his mistake. Reveal that something hurts and the bully will turn the knife. Reveal what is important, and the bully will find a way of spoiling it. To appear needy, eager, or enthusiastic is to make oneself a target. Most of our children know this and carefully camouflage their vulnerability around those who might attack it. They can't say they miss us or they would become the laughingstock of their peers. They must not admit to being hurt by a comment or they will be taunted unmercifully. They can't confess to sensitivity or the teasing will never stop. They must learn to hide their fear, never show alarm, deny their hurt. To survive in the world where bullies reign, our children must carefully cover all traces of vulnerability, erase all signs of caring. No doubt, that is why so many children suppress any feelings of empathy for the victims of bullying.

In the skewed hierarchies created by peer orientation, some of the children become submissive. In this, they are governed by instinct as much as those driven to dominate. Faced with a dominating peer, submissive children automatically show deference. Part of demonstrating submission is to show vulnerability, much as a wolf in a pack turns over to expose its throat to the more powerful leader. The wolf is presenting the most vulnerable part of his body, indicating submission. This behavior is deeply rooted in attachment instinct. Under natural circumstances, showing one's vulnerability should beget caretaking. Saying that something hurts should elicit tenderness. In the eyes of the bully, however, such unabashed vulnerability is like a red flag to a bull, inflaming the urge to attack. Both the victims and their bullies are only following their unconscious instincts, but with dreadful consequences to the victims.

## BACKING INTO ATTACHMENTS

Among the dark predispositions of bullies is a peculiar process that I call "backing into attachments." An emotionally healthy person approaches attachments in a straightforward fashion, head on, as it were. He expresses his needs and desires openly, revealing vulnerability. For the bully, it is much too risky to seek closeness openly. It would be far too frightening for a peer-oriented bully to say "I like you," "You are important to me," "I miss you when you're not here," "I want you to be my friend." The bully can never admit to his insatiable hunger for connection, nor can he even feel it consciously much of the time.

So how does the bully attach? Remember that attachment has both negative and positive sides. I described this in Chapter 2 as the bipolar nature of attachment. Here, then, is a second negative way to establish connection. The bully attempts to move nearer to those whose closeness he craves by pushing away from people with whom he doesn't want to have contact. Though indirect and much less effective, this approach also carries far less risk of getting hurt or rejected. It allows the bully to never appear to care about the outcome, never to betray any emotional investment in a desired relationship. Instead of voicing her yearning for contact with the desired individual directly, the bully will resist contact with others, ostentatiously ignoring and shunning them, especially in the presence of the person she is really pursuing. In place of imitating the ones she secretly wishes to pursue, she mocks and mimics others. Emotionally too frozen to open up to those who count, bullies keep secrets from those who don't count to them—or will even create secrets about them.

Thus emerges the personality of the bully: distancing one person to get close to another, pouring contempt here to establish a relationship there, shunning and ostracizing some people to cement a connection with others. There is danger in loving but none in loathing, risk in admiration but not in contempt, vulnerability in wanting to be like someone else but none in mocking those who are different. Bullies instinctively take the least vulnerable route to their destination.

Those on the receiving end of this instinct-driven behavior are often at a loss to make sense of it. "Why me?" "What did I do to deserve this kind of treatment?" "Why does he pick on me when I'm trying to mind my own business?" No wonder they're confused and bewildered. The truth of the matter is that it is rarely about them. The targets are only a means to an end. Someone has to serve that purpose for the bully. It is nothing personal; it rarely ever is. The only prerequisite for being picked on is to not be someone the bully is attaching to. Unfortunately, when the unwitting pawns in this attachment strategy take such treatment to heart, their psychological devastation is all the greater. It is difficult to keep some of the children targeted by bullies from assuming that something must be wrong with them, or that they are somehow responsible for how they are being treated. If the children targeted are not shielded by strong attachments to adults, they are at great risk of being emotionally wounded, for a deeply defensive emotional shutdown, for depression or worse.

As the bully population increases, so will the likelihood of children's finding themselves targeted. Wherever two or more peer-oriented children are gathered, they are likely to back into their attachments with each other by ostracizing others. "Don't you just hate her?" "There goes that loser." "She's such a snob." "The guy's a jerk." The trash talk can be incessant. In the eyes of adults such behavior can be bewildering since, in another setting, these same children can be polite, charming, and engaging. Some children's personalities can turn on a dime, depending on whom they happen to be with and toward which pole, negative or positive, the attachment magnet is being pulled.

## THE UNMAKING OF A BULLY

It is important to remember that bullying is not intentional. Children don't want to be bullies, nor do they even need to learn how, for bullying can arise spontaneously within any culture. It is a mistake to believe that a bully's aggressive behavior reflects her true personality. Bullies are not simply bad eggs but rather eggs with hard shells, eggs that parents and teachers have been unable to hatch into separate beings. Bullying is the outcome of the interaction between the two most significant psychological dynamics in the emotional brain of human beings: attachment and defendedness. These powerful dynamics camouflage the child's innate personality.

If we are to rescue the bully, we must first put the bully in his place—not in the sense of teaching him a lesson, punishing him, or belittling him, but in the sense of reintegrating him into a natural hierarchy of attachment. The bully's only hope is to attach to some adult who in turn is willing to assume the responsibility for nurturing the bully's emotional needs. Underneath the tough exterior is a deeply wounded and profoundly alone young person whose veneer of toughness evaporates in the presence of a truly caring adult. "I once asked a bully how it felt, having everyone afraid of him," a middle school counselor told me. " 'I have many friends,' he replied, 'but really I have no friends at all.' And when he said that, he just began to sob."

When a bully no longer feels bereft, no longer has to fend for himself to satisfy his hunger for attachment, bullying becomes redundant. In the film version of *The Two Towers*, the second part of the *Lord of the Rings* trilogy, we see a poignant example of how aggressive behavior becomes superfluous to a person once his attachment needs are met. Gollum, a slimy, twisted, and emotionally starved creature, full of bitterness and hatred, engages in an internal dialogue with himself when he becomes attached to the hobbit Frodo, whom he calls "Master." "We don't need you anymore," he says to his distrustful, manipulative, and even murderous other self, *"Master is taking care of us now."*

If, in summary, we were to describe the essence of the bully, we would speak of a tough shell of hardened emotion protecting a very sensitive creature of attachment, highly immature and hugely dependent, who seeks the dominant position. Although this behavior can be caused by other circumstances, it is a predictable result of peer orientation that both leads to and exacerbates bullying and, among children today, is the most prevalent source of bullying. All the attributes of bullies stem from the combination of these two powerful dynamics: attachment that is intense, inverted, and displaced and a desperate flight from vulnerability. The offspring of this union is the bully: a tough, mean, highly demanding kid who picks on others, taunts, teases, threatens, and intimidates. In addition, the bully is sensitive to slight, easily provoked, fearless and tearless, preying on weakness and vulnerability.

Peer orientation breeds both bullies and their victims. We have been dangerously naive in thinking that by putting children together we would foster egalitarian values and relating. Instead we have paved the way for the formation of new and damaging attachment hierarchies. We are creating a community that sets the stage for a *Lord of the Flies* situation. Peer orientation is making orphans of our children and turning our schools into day orphanages, so to speak. School is now a place where peer-oriented children are together, relatively free of adult supervision, in the lunchrooms, halls, and schoolyards. Because of the powerful attachment reorganization that takes place in the wake of peer orientation, schools have also become bully factories—unwittingly and inadvertently but still tragically.

Most approaches to bullying fall short because they lack insight into the underlying dynamics. Those who perceive bullying as a behavior problem think they can extinguish the behavior by imposing sanctions and consequences. Not only do the negative consequences fail to sink in, but they fuel the frustration and alienate the bullies even more. It is not the bully who is strong but the dynamics that create the bully. In the peer culture the supply of potential victims is also inexhaustible.

The only way to unmake the bully is to reverse the dynamics that made her in the first place: reintegrate the child into a proper attachment hierarchy and then proceed to soften her defenses and fulfill her attachment hunger. Although this may be a daunting task, it is the only solution that offers the possibility of success. Current methods that focus on discouraging bullying behavior or, alternatively, on exhorting children to behave toward one another in civil ways miss the root of the problem: the lack of vulnerable dependence on caregiving adults. Until we see bullying as the attachment disorder it truly is, our remedies are unlikely to make much difference.

Similarly, the best way to protect the victims is also to reintegrate them into depending on the adults who are responsible for them so they can feel their vulnerability and have their tears about what isn't working for them. It is most often the children who are too peer-oriented to lean on adults who are at greatest risk.

I recently participated in a Canadian national television special on bullying that included a number of parents whose children had committed suicide in response to being bullied. Also on the program was a girl whose life had been made miserable by bullying. The mother of the girl recounted that the daughter would burst into tears almost every day after school and talk about her distressing experiences. After the show, the hostess of the program expressed concern to me that this girl might also be at risk for taking her life. On the contrary, I responded, her dependence on her mother and the words and tears she spilled in the safety of their relationship were her salvation. The kids who had taken their lives were enigmas to their parents. Their suicides had been complete surprises. These sad victims had become too peer-oriented to talk to their parents about what was happening and too defended against their vulnerability to find their tears about the trauma they were experiencing. Their frustration mounted until it could no longer be contained. In these particular cases, the children attacked themselves rather than others. In this way, too, the bullies and the bullied are often cut from the same cloth—both lack adequate attachments with nurturing adults. No matter what unhappiness they may at times feel, children are not at risk for attacking themselves or others as long as they are able to lean on their parents, deal with what distresses them, and respond with the appropriate feelings of futility.

Some people, including those regarded as experts, see the problem of bullying as a failure in the transmission of moral values. The perception is true, as far as it goes, but not at all in the sense usually assumed. The failure is not one of teaching our kids the values of caring and consideration. Such human values emerge naturally in children who feel deeply and vulnerably enough. It is not the breakdown in the moral education of the bully that is the problem but a breakdown in the basic values of attachment and vulnerability in mainstream society. If these core values were taken to heart, peer orientation would not proliferate or beget bullies and victims.

# A SEXUAL TURN

THIRTEEN-YEAR-OLD Jessica confided to her friend Stacey that kids at school were pressuring her to perform oral sex on a male classmate at an upcoming party. "They say it's how I can prove that I belong with their group," she said. Jessica wasn't sure how she felt about the matter. Sexually she had no interest in the boy, but she was tickled at being at the center of all this attention. The question—Would she do it or wouldn't she?—was the subject of much titillated speculation at school. She was overweight and never a member of the in-crowd. Stacey, herself bewildered by the responsibility of advising her friend on such an emotionally charged matter, told her own father about Jessica's dilemma. The father, after some consideration, thought it best to inform Jessica's parents. They were shocked, having had no idea either of their daughter's precarious social situation or of the pressure she was facing to become sexually active. By the time they approached Jessica with their concerns, the act had been done. She had succumbed—in this case, not even to the sexual demands of a boy she was trying to please or hoping to develop a relationship with, but purely to the persuasion of her peer group.

As we all realize, sex is rarely about just sex—in the case of Jessica, it certainly wasn't. Sometimes it is about a hunger to be desired. It may be an escape from boredom or loneliness. It may also be a way of staking territory or claiming a possession, or may serve as an attempt to lock into an exclusive relationship with another. Sex can be a powerful symbol of status and recognition. It can be about scoring or about belonging or fitting in or clinging and holding on. It may be about dominance or submission or may function to please someone. Sex, in some cases, reflects a lack of boundaries and an inability to say no. It can, of course, express love, heartfelt passion, and true intimacy. Nearly always, in one form or another, sex is about attachment. In the lives of our adolescents it is, most often, an expression of unfulfilled attachment needs.

The age of first sexual activity is becoming younger and younger. According to a 1997 study by the Centers for Disease Control, over twice as many ninth-grade girls (6.5 percent) than twelfth graders reported having had sex before the age of thirteen. Among American boys in the ninth grade, nearly 15 percent admitted to sexual activity before age thirteen, well over twice the number among twelfth graders. The story is the same in Canada, where a study published in 2000 found that more than 13 percent of girls in the 1990s had sex before they were fifteen, double the comparable statistic from the early 1980s.[1] There is anecdotal evidence both in the United States and Canada that a large number of teenagers engage in oral sex as a substitute for intercourse without recognizing that they have had sex at all. "There is this disturbing shift in attitude of oral sex, anal intercourse, everything *but . . .*" Eleanor Maticka-Tyndale, a professor of sociology at the University of Windsor, has said.

A nineteen-year-old baseball prospect, a draft pick of the Los Angeles Dodgers for 2003, was found guilty of inviting sexual touching by a minor and sentenced to forty-five days in jail. On one occasion the young athlete had had two girls, ages twelve and thirteen, perform oral sex on him. At his successful appeal he argued that he had not initiated the contact, the girls had. And why? The two alleged victims told the court that it was routine in their community for seventh-grade girls to offer oral sex to boys. One of them said that she participated because "everyone else was doing it and [she] didn't want to be left out."[2]

Coupled with the troubling precocity of sexual activity is the debasement of sexuality. There is a great difference between sexual contact as an expression of genuine intimacy and sexual contact as a primitive attachment dynamic. The result of the latter is, inevitably, dissatisfaction and an addictive promiscuity, as seventeen-year-old Nicholas experienced.

"Something's not right," Nicholas began. "Everything is working for me—I have plenty of sex, but I guess I've never really made love. My friends all look up to me for the kind of girls I can score with. But I'm not very good at what you call the intimacy thing. In the morning I never know what to say to a girl. All I want to do is call up one of my buddies and brag." Nicholas's dilemma may be said to be the age-old Don Juan syndrome many males have suffered from, but it's one faced these days by many young men whose sexual initiation and history occur in the context of the peer culture.

Both Nicholas and Jessica were intensely peer-oriented. In Nicholas's words, "I don't feel connected with my family. In fact, my friends are much more of a family to me than my real family is. I don't even want to be around them anymore." I knew Nicholas and his family quite well. He had three sisters and parents who couldn't have loved him more. But he wasn't feeding at their table; he was looking to his peers to fulfill his attachment hunger. For two years during this boy's adolescence his father, a professional, became completely preoccupied by his career while his mother experienced a stress-induced depression. Such a relatively short period during this crucial time in Nicholas's life was enough to create an attachment void that came to be filled by the peer group. That is how susceptible children are today, in a culture that no longer provides substitute adult attachments when, for whatever reason, the family ties even temporarily weaken.

Jessica was also emotionally detached from her parents. I could hardly get her to talk about them, and when she did, it was only in terms of their interference in her life—a life that revolved around her peers. Her peer orientation was manifest in her insatiable hunger for acceptance, an obsession with instant messaging via the Internet, and her utter disdain for adult values such as schoolwork and learning. According to her, nothing was more important than being liked, wanted, and pursued by her friends.

For Nicholas, sex was about conquest and trophies, about coming out on top, about increasing his status with his buddies. For his apparently willing female partners, sex may have been an affirmation of attractiveness, a stamp of approval on being an object of desire, an experience of intimate proximity, or a sign of belonging and exclusiveness. For Jessica, oral sex was a social initiation rite, a tariff she had to pay for being admitted to a social club she longed to join.

For fourteen-year-old Heather sex was about making guys her own, attracting their attention and affection, beating the competition. Heather was another highly peer-oriented child, quite popular and fiercely proud of her ability to interest boys. She became sexually active at age twelve, something she managed to keep hidden from her parents. By the time she came to see me, sent by her parents because they found her unmanageable, she was unusually experienced for her age. She bragged to me about how, before going to high school, she had "worked" three separate elementary schools at the same time, scouting them out for "the hottest guys" and making them hers through her sexual prowess and precocity. Her voice was full of contempt for the girls who couldn't pull this off, claiming they were stupid and nothing but losers. She called one of her current sexual partners her boyfriend but did not seem the least bit guilty about her disloyalty to him. "We don't talk much," she said, "and what he doesn't know won't hurt him," adding that what really bothered her was that he was half an inch shorter than she was. "Besides, the sex with the other guys is just physical." She identified her boyfriend as the one person in the world she felt the closest to, but this closeness did not seem to include a sense of either emotional or psychological intimacy.

How divorced from intimacy teenage sex can become is illustrated by the following anecdote from Dr. Elaine Wynne, a physician who works at a youth clinic. "A fifteen-year-old girl came in for a routine checkup and a Pap test," Dr. Wynne told me. "As I was doing the pelvic exam she casually mentioned that she couldn't tell if her boyfriend ejaculated during sex. It turned out this was of concern to her. 'Have you thought of asking him?' I said. 'Are you kidding?' she responded. 'That's way too personal a question to ask!' "

It is disturbing to witness what sex does to peer-oriented kids and what peer orientation does to sexuality. Not all peer-oriented adolescents will be sexually active, of course, or act out their sexuality in the same way, but the culture they will be immersed in is steeped in a bizarrely distorted sexuality—pseudo-sophistication without maturity, physical playing out of intimacy without any psychological readiness to cope with the consequences.

Physical factors such as physiological maturation and "raging hormones" do not by themselves explain teenage sexuality. To fully understand the precocious sexual behavior of young people we have to look again at three concepts I introduced in earlier chapters: attachment, vulnerability, and maturation. The key, as always, is attachment. The critical factor is not the sexual awakening of adolescence; it is that the peer-oriented adolescent is a sexual being who is apt to use anything at his disposal to satisfy his need to attach. The less vulnerability and maturity are present, the more likely the drive to attach will find sexual expression.

## SEX AS AN EXPRESSION OF ATTACHMENT HUNGER

In the natural order of things, sex happens between mature beings, not between children and those responsible for them. When children seek emotional closeness with adults, sexual interaction is highly unlikely. But should these same children become peer-oriented, the very same hunger for contact is subject to becoming sexualized. Sex becomes an instrument of peer attachment. Children who have replaced their parents with peers are the most likely to be sexually preoccupied or active. Those lacking a sense of intimacy with their parents are the ones most needing to seek intimacy with their peers, but now through sex rather than through feelings or words. This was certainly true of Nicholas, Heather, and Jessica, cut off from loving parents by their peer orientation. They were using sex with their peers to try to satisfy their hunger for connection and for affection.

Sex is a ready-made instrument for those driven to satisfy primitive attachment needs. In Chapter 2, I listed the six ways of attaching, the first of which was through the physical senses. If a child is looking for closeness primarily by means of physical contact, sex is very effective. If attachment is sought in sameness, the child's behavior will conform to values of the peer group, as in the cases of Jessica and the two young girls who provided oral sex to the baseball player. For a person seeking the third way of attaching—exclusive belonging and loyalty—sexual interaction will be very enticing. If a child is drawn to the fourth way—being significant to someone—then affirmation of status or attractiveness will become the prime objective and sex a useful tool for keeping score. Of course, sexual contact can also represent warm feelings and genuine intimacy, but for immature, peer-oriented teenagers it rarely does—as much as they would like to think so. They lack the vulnerability and the maturity for their sexuality to reach these two highest forms of attaching, as I will shortly explain.

Current fashion styles in dress, makeup, and demeanor promote the sexualization of young girls who are in no way ready for mature sexual activity. Looks, with their charged sexual component, have become a primary measure of self-worth, according to Joan Jacobs Brumberg, a historian at Cornell University and author of *The Body Project*, a history of American girlhood. Brumberg told *Newsweek* magazine that fifty years ago, when girls talked about self-improvement, they had in mind academic achievement or some contribution to society. Now, she says, appearance is foremost. "In adolescent girls' private diaries and journals, the body is the consistent preoccupation, second only to peer-relationships."[3] Of course, even the phrase "second only to" misses the mark, since the obsession with body image is a direct result of peer orientation and its by-product, the sexualization of adolescence.

Without knowing it, teenagers are playing with fire when they sexualize their attachments. Sex is not a simple instrument to be used for one's own purposes. It is not possible for adolescents to walk away from sex unscathed and casually, without something essentially human being disturbed. Sex is a potent bonding agent, human contact cement, evoking a sense of union and fusion, creating one flesh. Regardless of how brief or innocent the sexual interaction, sex operates to make couples out of the participants. Ready or not, willing or not, aware or not, it attaches each of those who engage in it. Studies have confirmed what most of us will have found out on our own, that making love has a natural bonding effect, evoking powerful emotions of attachment in the human brain.[4]

The results are all too predictable when the sexualized attachment hunger of peer-oriented kids combines with the serious bonding effect of even "casual" sex. Unwanted teenage pregnancies are escalating in countries where peer orientation abounds, despite our attempts at sex education and birth control. According to the statistics, the teenage pregnancy rates are highest in the United States, followed by Britain and Canada.[5] The sexual activity of peer-oriented children is not about making love or making babies, but about seeking in each other's arms what they should be looking for in the relationship with their parents—contact and connection. When this happens with peers, babies can be the unwelcome result—and in many cases, the unfortunate victims, being born to immature parents in no way prepared to nurture them emotionally or even physically.

## SEXUALITY AND THE FLIGHT FROM VULNERABILITY

To the degree that sex attaches one to the other, it also pulls the participants into highly vulnerable territory, to a place where feelings can get hurt and hearts can get broken. What sex binds together cannot be separated without some pain. After sex has done its bonding work, separation of any sort will incur significant tearing and psychological disruption, an experience that most adults will be all too familiar with. Repeated experiences of separation or rejection following the powerful attachments created by sex can create a vulnerability that is too much to bear. Such experiences induce emotional scarring and hardening.

Not surprisingly, the more sexually active our adolescents are, the harder they become emotionally. This desensitization may seem like a blessing, allowing them to play with fire and not get hurt. But as we have discussed in the previous chapters, the cost of the flight from vulnerability is the shortchanging of their potential as human beings and of the emotional freedom and depth that would make them truly alive.

Not even in the short term does engaging in sex leave the emotionally defended teenager unscathed. Just because the adolescent does not seem affected does not mean that she has not suffered consequences. The less consciously affected we are, the more wounded we may be on the unconscious level. Heather told me of having been raped on one of her dates, but she did so in a tone of unconcern and indicated that the event really had had no impact on her. It was not difficult to see the vulnerability this bravado was designed to cover or to predict that such surface hardening, unless reversed, would keep leading this girl into dangerous territory. Sexual contact that is not able to move the adolescent to greater vulnerability leads to intensifying the defenses against such vulnerability. When I asked one young client why she and her girlfriends drank so much at their parties, she replied without hesitation, "Then it doesn't hurt so much when you get banged."

One of the ultimate costs of emotional hardening is that sex loses its potency as a bonding agent. The long-term effect is soul-numbing, impairing young people's capacity to enter into relationships in which true contact and intimacy are possible. Sex eventually becomes a nonvulnerable attachment activity. It can even be addictive because it momentarily pacifies attachment hunger without ever fulfilling it. The divorce of sex from vulnerability may have a liberating effect on sexual behavior, but it derives from a dark place of emotional desensitization.

Although Heather was bright, attractive, engaging, and talkative, there was not a hint of vulnerability in anything she said or felt. She felt no fear, did not admit to missing anyone, was not in touch with her insecurity, and did not feel bad for anything she had done. Nicholas, too, was in a flight from vulnerability, leaving him bored, judgmental, arrogant, and contemptuous. He, too, was devoid of apprehension and free from feelings of insecurity. He despised the weak and had no stomach for losers. Neither Heather nor Nicholas was capable of being moved deeply. Both were immune to the attachment work of sex. Both had been inured against vulnerability before becoming sexually involved, but their sexual activity took their emotional hardening to another level.

Neither with their peers nor even with me were Heather and Nicholas particularly shy to talk about their sexual experiences. Such ease is an interesting but deceptive side effect of the flight from vulnerability—a loss of a sense of exposure when sharing personal information that would normally be considered intimate. Many adults are impressed with the apparent openness of today's youth regarding sexual matters, perceiving it as a sign of progress over the secrecy and timidity of yesteryear. "We would have never talked so candidly about such matters," applauded the mother of one highly peer-oriented fifteen-year-old. "When we were that age, we would have been too embarrassed to talk about sex." What this mother failed to see is that the brazen and shameless talk about sexual activity had nothing to do with courage or transparency but rather with the defense against vulnerability. It takes little courage to reveal something that is not the least bit intimate. There is nothing to be discreet about if one doesn't feel exposed. When sex is divorced from vulnerability, sex fails to touch us deeply enough to hurt. What should be highly personal and intimate can be broadcast to the world—and often is, on trashy TV programs.

For those kids who still feel deeply and vulnerably enough for sex to do its work, engaging in sex is like taking a plunge into emotions that are potent, into attachment that is inexplicable and often inextricable, into vulnerability so intense that it can hardly be touched. Although adolescents usually engage in sex to become closer, they do not count on getting stuck on each other in the process. The plunge into coupledom is likely to take them in over their heads. Some will find themselves attempting to avoid the inevitable pain of separation by clinging desperately to the other, pursuing the other relentlessly and holding on for dear life. Others will feel suffocated and trapped by a closeness they weren't prepared for and will seek to extricate themselves as soon as they can. If the coupling takes effect for both parties, some adolescents will find their tentative individuality strangled by the forces of fusion, their sense of emerging personhood swallowed up by couplehood. They will no longer be able to know their own preferences or make up their own minds without conferring first with their partner. "I don't know if we are girlfriend and boyfriend yet," one seventeen-year-old said, speaking of her latest sexual partner. "He hasn't told me yet."

Sex is being engaged in by kids who haven't the slightest inkling of what they are getting themselves into. The most defended among them appear to get away with it because they are no longer emotionally attachable, nor do they feel their pain. Their invulnerability makes sex look so casual and easy and fun. Those who do feel deeply and vulnerably are in for trouble: first getting stuck on the other, whether they want to be or not, and then feeling torn apart when the relationship no longer holds.

Given its cementing effect, the vulnerability required for it to work, and the vulnerability evoked if it indeed does work, it seems to me that we should be more concerned about safeguards for sex. Such caution is dictated not from moral considerations but directly from understanding the negative consequences of precocious sexuality on our children's healthy emotional development. Human superglue is not for kids to play with.

Viewed through the lens of vulnerability, the concept of safe sex takes on a completely different meaning—not safe from disease or unwanted babies, but safe from getting wounded and hardened. There is no guarantee of security in any attachment, of course, even attachments formed by mature adults. It is not so much that we can protect our children from getting hurt, but we can reduce their risk of becoming sexually involved in relationships that are not likely to satisfy or to hold. The sex of adolescence seldom comes with the protection of commitment, the promise of exclusivity, the tenderness of consideration, or the support of the community. It is sex that is unprotected in the deepest sense—psychologically. A person cannot keep on getting "married" and "divorced" without becoming hardened and desensitized, at least not without significant grieving taking place. Postcoital separation is too painful. Adolescents are no more immune from such natural dynamics than the rest of us. In fact, because of the tenderness of their years, their lack of perspective, and their natural immaturity, they are even more prone than adults to be wounded by their sexual experiences than we are.

## WHEN SEXUALITY LACKS MATURITY

The safest sex, from the perspective of attachment and vulnerability, would occur not as a way of forming a relationship, but in the context of a relationship that is already satisfying and secure. One would want to be as sure as possible that the relationship is exactly where one wants to be. Sex would be the final attachment act, the commencement exercise for exclusivity, creating closure as a couple. Sex can be only as safe as the individuals are wise. What is needed more than anything is exactly what peer-oriented adolescents lack: maturity. Immature adolescents who are adult-oriented are at least inclined to lean on their parents for their cues concerning sexual interaction. Peer-oriented kids are doubly cursed: they do not have the maturity required for healthy sexual interaction or decision making, nor are they adult-oriented enough to take advice from those of us who may have already learned some lessons the hard way.

Maturation is a prerequisite for sex in a number of ways.

The first fruit of maturation is separateness as an individual. A modicum of separateness is required to create a healthy union. One needs to know one's own mind enough to extend an invitation to another, or to turn down another's invitation. We need a self-preserving instinct to value autonomy, to experience personal boundaries, to be able to say no. For healthy sexuality we need the freedom not to become sexually involved or at least not to feel compelled to make things work at all costs. Not having reached the place where it is more important to be one's own person than to belong to someone or to possess someone, the adolescent is dangerously susceptible.

There is probably no more important arena for regard for another's separateness than in the sexual sphere. Consideration of the other person is essential to mature sexual interaction. For the psychologically immature, sex is not an interactive dance. In the premature leap into sexuality someone is bound to be hurt, to be taken advantage of.

As we discussed in the last chapter, peer orientation begets both bullies and those susceptible to being bullied. When it comes to sex, bullies once again demand what they do not freely command. Sex is rich in the symbolism that bullies are eager to collect: status, desirability, winning, scoring, deference, belonging, attractiveness, service, loyalty, and so on. Unfortunately, bullies are too psychologically shut down to realize the futility of demanding what is not freely given. The fantasies of bullies are not of invitation but domination, not of mutuality but superiority. Both Heather and Nicholas were essentially bullies regarding sex, in the sense of exploiting the weakness of others to meet their own needs. Their partners were hardly taken into consideration. In the case of Heather, her indiscriminate sexual acting-out also led her to being bullied herself, to the point of being subjected to date rape. Unfortunately, peer orientation creates an abundance of naive and needy subjects to prey on. It should come as no surprise that aggressive acts like date rape are escalating among teens.

Maturation is required for healthy sexual involvement in yet another way. The wisdom required for people to make good decisions requires the two-dimensional, integrative processing that only maturity can bestow. We have to be able to manage mixed feelings, thoughts, and impulses. The yearning to belong to another has to coexist with the desire to be one's own person; the maintaining of boundaries must mix with the passion to merge with another. Also required, of course, is the ability to consider both the present and the future. The psychologically immature are incapable of thinking of anything but the pleasure of the moment. To make good decisions, one must be capable of feeling both fear and desire simultaneously. If we appreciated the powerful feelings sexuality can unleash, we would be appropriately nervous at the outset. Sex should be both revered and feared, evoke both anticipation and apprehension, be a cause for both celebration and caution.

Adolescents lack the wisdom, insight, and impulse control to be safely entrusted with such decisions on their own. We could, of course, from our adult wisdom, impose structures and limitations on them that would keep their sexual behavior within safe bounds, and we could act as their consultants in decisions about sex, but with peer-oriented adolescents we lack the power and the connection to do so. If our young people were looking to us for counsel, we would undoubtedly inform them that they cannot really divorce decisions about sex from decisions about relationship. We would advise them to wait until they were confident that their relationship is emotionally sound, founded in genuine intimacy beyond the sexual interaction. The catch is that no matter how wise our counsel, the peer-oriented are not looking in our direction.

Many parents and educators today euphemize the sexual activity of adolescents as exploration and experimentation and see it as inherent to the nature of adolescence. The concept of an experiment suggests an air of discovery and the existence of questions. The teens who are most sexually active, however, are not the ones asking the questions. Adolescent sex is not so much a case of sexual experimentation as it is of emotional desperation and attachment hunger.

Adults typically attempt to deal with the hypersexuality of peer-oriented adolescents, as they do with bullying and aggression, by focusing on the interaction between the youngsters. We try to effect changes in behavior through admonishments, teaching, rewards and punishments. In this sphere, too, our efforts have been misdirected. There is little we can do to correct the aberrant sexuality of peer-oriented kids as long as they remain peer-oriented. There is much we can do, however, to address the aberrant orientation of kids who are precociously sexualized, at least when the children are our own. If we are to make a difference in their sexuality, we must first bring them back to the place where they truly belong—with us.

# UNTEACHABLE STUDENTS

E THAN HAD BEEN a good student in elementary school, even if he had never been a very interested one. He was quite bright. Although he seemed to lack a drive to excel, his parents and teachers were able to impress on him their agendas for learning and behavior. Teachers found him likable and engaging. By the time Ethan's parents came to see me, when their son was near the end of sixth grade, his compliance with adult expectations was history. Getting Ethan to do homework was a constant struggle. His teachers complained that he was not paying attention and was no longer receptive to being taught. Often argumentative and lippy, he did not perform at a level commensurate with his abilities. This change in teachability paralleled a newly found preoccupation with peers. In the previous several months Evan had latched on to one peer after another, copying their mannerisms and adopting their preoccupations. When things would start to fall apart with one schoolmate, he would become all the more desperate to make things work with another.

For Mia, the academic downturn came one grade earlier. Before fifth grade she had been thoroughly engaged in her learning, was full of interest, and asked many intelligent questions. Now she complained about being bored by her subjects. The parents learned, to their dismay, that she was not handing in some assignments and that the ones she was submitting were not up to her usual quality. Teachers were calling to report Mia's lack of attention and motivation as well as her incessant talking to friends in class, complaints her parents were unaccustomed to hearing. Confronted with their concerns, Mia appeared nonchalant. They also noticed that she rarely talked about her teachers anymore or, if she did, only in derogatory terms. Homework was no longer a priority to her; talking on the phone or connecting with her friends via the Internet were. When her parents attempted to curtail these activities, she defied them with an insolence and rancor they had never witnessed in the past.

These two cases represent a phenomenon endemic in our culture today: children capable yet unmotivated, intelligent but underachieving, bright but bored. On the other side of the same coin, education has become a much more stressful occupation than it used to be a generation or two ago. As many teachers nowadays attest, teaching seems to be getting harder, students less respectful and less receptive. Classrooms are increasingly unmanageable and academic performance appears to be slipping. The reading abilities of schoolchildren appear to have declined, despite the heavy emphasis many schools have placed on literary skills in recent years.[1] Yet our teachers have never been better trained than today, our curriculum never as developed, and our technology never as sophisticated.

What has changed? Once more we return to the pivotal influence of attachment. The shift in the attachment patterns of our children has had profoundly negative implications for education. Many parents and teachers still believe that we should be able to put a capable student together with a good teacher and get results. It never quite worked that way, but as long as learning happened, we got away with being naive. Until relatively recently teachers were able to ride on the coattails of the strong adult orientation engendered by culture and society. That time has passed. The problem we now face with regard to the education of our children is not something money can fix, curriculum can address, or information technology can remedy. It is bigger than all of this, yet simpler, too.

Knowledge, Goethe said, can't be put into a mind like coins into a bag. The teachability of any particular student is the outcome of many factors: a desire to learn and to understand, an interest in the unknown, a willingness to take some risks, and an openness to being influenced and corrected. It also requires a connection with the teacher, an inclination to pay attention, a willingness to ask for help, aspirations to measure up and achieve, and, not least, a propensity toward work. All these factors are rooted in or affected by attachment.

On close scrutiny, four essential qualities are primary in determining a child's teachability: a natural curiosity, an integrative mind, an ability to benefit from correction, and a relationship with the teacher. Healthy attachment enhances each of these; peer orientation undermines them all.

## PEER ORIENTATION EXTINGUISHES CURIOSITY

Ideally, what should lead a child into learning is an open-minded curiosity about the world. The child should ask questions before coming up with answers, explore before discovering truths, and experiment before reaching firm conclusions. Curiosity, however, is not an inherent part of a child's personality. It is the fruit of the emergent process — in other words, an outgrowth of the development responsible for making the child viable as a separate being, independent and capable of functioning apart from attachments.

Highly emergent children usually have areas of keen interest and are intrinsically motivated to learn. They derive great satisfaction from forming an insight or in understanding how something works. They create their own goals around learning. They like to be original and seek self-mastery. Emergent learners take delight in responsibility and spontaneously move to realize their own potential.

For teachers who value curiosity, invite questions, and give the child's interests the lead, emergent learners are a delight to teach. For such children, the best teachers are those who serve as mentors, fueling their interests, igniting their passions, putting them in charge of their own learning. If emergent learners don't always perform well in school it is probably because, having their own ideas for what they want to learn, they experience the curriculum imposed by the teacher as an unwelcome intrusion.

Curiosity is a luxury, developmentally speaking. Attachment is what matters most. Until some energy is released from having to pursue safe and secure attachments, venturing forth into the unknown is not on the developmental agenda. That is why peer orientation kills curiosity. Peer-oriented students are completely preoccupied with issues of attachment. Instead of being interested in the unknown, they become bored by anything that does not serve the purpose of peer attachment. Boredom is epidemic among the peer-oriented.

There is another problem regarding curiosity. Curiosity makes a person highly vulnerable in the peer world of "cool." The wide-eyed wonder, the enthusiasm about a subject, the questions about how things work, the originality of an idea — these all expose a child to the ridicule and shame of peers. The flight from vulnerability of peer-oriented children snuffs out their own curiosity, as well as inhibiting the curiosity of those around them. The peer orientation of our children is making curiosity an endangered concept.

## PEER ORIENTATION DULLS THE INTEGRATIVE MIND

For self-motivation, it helps to have an integrative mind—that is, a mind capable of processing contradictory impulses or thoughts. In a child with a well-developed integrative capacity, not wanting to go to school evokes concerns about missing school, not wanting to get up in the morning triggers an apprehension about being late. Lack of interest in paying attention to the teacher is tempered by an interest in doing well, resistance to doing what one is told mitigated by awareness that disobedience has unpleasant consequences.

For integrative learning, a child must be mature enough to tolerate being of two minds—of harboring mixed feelings, generating second thoughts, experiencing ambivalence. For the presence of the tempering element—the component that would counteract impulses that undermine learning—the child also needs to be attached appropriately. She must be able to feel deeply and vulnerably. For example, a child needs to be attached enough to care what adults—his parents and teachers—think, to care about their expectations, to care about not upsetting or alienating them. A student needs to be emotionally invested in learning, to be excited about figuring something out. Not being vulnerable—not caring—paralyzes learning and destroys teachability.

Students need an integrative intelligence for the kind of learning that is more than rote memory and regurgitation. To solve problems, a student needs to process more than one-dimensionally. Beyond mere facts he needs to discover themes, discern deeper meanings, understand metaphor, uncover underlying principle. A student has to know how to distill a body of material to the essence or to put the pieces together into a harmonious whole. Anything more than concrete thinking requires an integrative mind. Just as depth perception requires two eyes, depth learning requires the ability to see things from at least two points of view. If the mind's eye is singular, there is no depth or perspective, no synthesis or distillation, no penetration to deeper meaning and truth. Context is not taken into consideration; figure and background lack differentiation.

Unfortunately, a student's raw intelligence does not automatically translate into integrative intelligence. As I discussed in Chapter 9, integrative functioning is a fruit of maturation—the very process that peer orientation arrests. The immature fail to develop integrative abilities.

Our pedagogy and curriculum take the integrative abilities of children for granted. When we as educators fail to register what's missing, we also fail to realize what we're up against in trying to temper children's thinking or behavior. We try to get them to do something their minds are incapable of, and when we don't succeed, we punish them for that failure. Those with integrative minds assume that everyone else can think the same way. But this assumption no longer fits the kinds of learners we face in our classrooms today. Children who lack integrative intelligence are not amenable to this form of teaching and need to be approached differently. Peer-oriented students are more likely to be disabled learners—untempered in thought, feeling, and action.

## PEER ORIENTATION JEOPARDIZES ADAPTIVE TRIAL-AND-ERROR LEARNING

Most learning occurs by adaptation, by a process of trial and error. We attempt new tasks, make mistakes, encounter stumbling blocks, get things wrong—and then draw the appropriate conclusions, or have someone else draw them for us. Failure is an essential part of the learning process, and correction is the primary instrument of teaching. The flight from vulnerability evoked by peer orientation deals three devastating blows to this main pathway of learning.

The first blow strikes the trial part of the process. Trying new things involves taking a risk: reading out loud, offering an opinion, stepping into unfamiliar territory, experimenting with an idea. Such experimentation is a minefield of possible mistakes, unpredictable reactions, and negative responses. When vulnerability is already too much to bear, as it is for most peer-oriented children, these risks seem unacceptable.

The second blow hits the peer-oriented child's ability to benefit from error. Before we can learn from our mistakes, we have to recognize them and acknowledge our failure. We have to assume responsibility if we are to benefit from our errors and we need to welcome help, advice, and correction. Again, peer-oriented students are often too defended against vulnerability to become mindful of their mistakes or to take responsibility for their failures. If the mark on a test is too poor for such a student to tolerate, he will blame the failure on something—or someone—else. Or he will distract himself from facing the problem. The brains of children who are defended against vulnerability tune out anything that would give rise to feeling it, in this case the admission of mistakes and failure. Even being mildly corrected by a teacher or parent may threaten such a child with a sense of inadequacy and shame, the sense that "something is wrong with me." Pointing out what they did wrong will evoke from such children brazenly evasive or hostile reactions. Adults often interpret these responses as rudeness, but they really serve the function of keeping these kids from feeling their vulnerability.

The third strike against trial-and-error learning is that the futility of a course of action does not sink in when a child is too defended against vulnerability. As I pointed out earlier, frustration must turn into feelings of futility for the brain to figure out that something does not work (see Chapter 9). Registering futility is the essence of adaptive learning. When our emotions are too hardened to permit sadness or disappointment about something that didn't succeed, we respond not by learning from our mistake, but by venting frustration. In the case of students, the external target will be the "idiotic" teacher, the "boring" assignments, the lack of time. The internal target may be the self, as in "I'm so stupid." Either way, the mad doesn't turn to sad, the emotion associated with truly experiencing futility does not rise to the surface. Work habits are not changed, learning strategies are not modified, and handicaps are not overcome. Children stuck in this mode do not develop the resilience to handle failure and correction. They are locked into whatever doesn't work. In my practice I see increasing numbers of children who do the same things over and over and over again, despite repeated failure.

## PEER ORIENTATION MAKES STUDENTS INTO ATTACHMENT-BASED LEARNERS, EVEN AS IT ATTACHES THEM TO THE WRONG MENTORS

As I mentioned earlier in this chapter, from a developmental perspective there are only four basic learning processes. We have discussed how peer orientation undermines three of these—emergent learning, integrative learning, and adaptive learning. As long as children are emergent learners, they can be taught by teachers who allow their interests to take the lead. Children who are integrative can be brought face-to-face with the conflicting factors that need to be considered when solving a problem. Adaptive children can be taught through trial and error and correction. Such children are teachable by even those to whom they are not attached. When these crucial learning processes are suppressed, learning becomes dependent on one dynamic alone: attachment. Students hamstrung by their lack of emergence, integration, or adaptability can learn only when attachment is somehow involved. Their desire to learn may not be internal, but it can be potent if they are motivated by a strong urge to be close to the teaching adult—be it the teacher in the classroom or the homeschooling parent, or the family friend who may act as a mentor.

Attachment is by far the most powerful process in learning and is certainly sufficient for the task, even without the help of curiosity or the ability to benefit from correction. There have always been students who lacked adaptive, emergent, and integrative functioning. Although handicapped in terms of realizing their full potential, they can often perform well. Attachment-based learners are highly motivated in ways other students may not be. For example, they are more predisposed to learn via imitation, modeling, memorizing, and cue-taking. Attachment-based students also want to measure up and will be motivated to work for approval and for recognition and status. The problem arises not when children are restricted to attachment-based learning but when they become attached to peers rather than the mentoring adults.

Ethan, for instance, was almost exclusively an attachment-based learner to begin with. He possessed little emergent interest in things he was not familiar with. His adaptive functioning was minimal even before becoming peer-oriented. Thus Ethan was teachable only through attachment and only by teachers he felt close to. He had had a miserable experience in the second grade, a year when he had been unable to make a connection with his teacher. His newly found peer orientation was not what made him into an attachment-based learner, but what it did do was to completely destroy even his attachment-based ability to learn. A child who is used to learning only through attachment and whose instincts are misdirected by peer orientation will have his teachability greatly reduced, no matter how promising his innate potential may be.

Mia, on the other hand, had been very teachable prior to being peer-oriented, even by those she was not attached to. Peer orientation extinguished her curiosity, dulled her integrative mind, and sabotaged her ability to learn from trial and error. Peer orientation transformed her into an attachment-based learner by default. Mia's cleverness was now focused on one goal only: closeness with her friends.

For some kids, the decision to "dumb down" is fully conscious. "In the sixth and seventh grades I was always at the top of my class," recalls twenty-nine-year-old Ross, now a fitness instructor. "I got every award. In the eighth grade, when I was thirteen, other kids began to make fun of me. All of a sudden I wasn't smart—I was a nerd. That wasn't cool. I wanted to be with the jocks, the in-crowd. My choice was to fit in. I made sure I wasn't getting great marks. I deliberately made mistakes in math, just so I wouldn't have a perfect mark. Over the years, this led to bad study habits and, by the last two years of high school, my 'plan' had succeeded all too well. Even in college my bad study habits persisted and I never finished my degree. Now I wish I had been more self-adjusted as a teenager, less worried about what my friends thought."

## PEER ORIENTATION RENDERS STUDIES IRRELEVANT

For the peer-oriented, academic subjects become irrelevant. History, culture, the contradictions of society or the wonders of nature are of no interest to them. How is chemistry connected to being with friends? How does biology help to make things work with peers? Of what use are math, literature, social studies in matters of attachment? The words of the hit song from the late fifties capture it perfectly: "Don't know much about history, Don't know much biology . . . But I do know that I love you."

Formal education is not intrinsically valued by the young. It takes some maturity to realize that education can open minds and doors and that it can humanize and civilize. What students need is to value those who value education. At least that way they would follow our cues until they become mature enough to come to their own conclusions. Peer-oriented students know instinctively that friends matter most and that being together is all that counts. Arguing against someone's instinct, even skewed instinct, is impossible.

## PEER ORIENTATION ROBS
## STUDENTS OF THEIR TEACHERS

Immature young persons depend on attachment to help them learn. The less emergent, integrative, and adaptive the child, the more this will be true. In Chapter 5, I explained that attachment can be helpful to parents and teachers by commanding the child's attention, evoking her respect, and making the child amenable to being influenced—processes essential to the goal of educating the child. Adult-oriented children look to adults as the human compass points from whom to get their bearings and direction. They will be loyal to the teacher rather than the peer group and will see the teacher as a model, an authority, and a source of inspiration. When children attach to a teacher, that teacher has the natural power to script the child's behavior, to solicit good intentions, to inculcate societal values.

But who are the peer-oriented child's designated teachers? Not the teachers hired by the school board. Once a child is peer-oriented, learning peaks during recess, lunch hour, after school, and in the breaks between classes. What peer-oriented kids learn will not come from the school-teacher or from the curriculum. Nothing about a child's attachments will automatically dictate loyalty to government-certified, university-trained, institutionally appointed educators. When attachment is skewed, the school-teacher is rendered ineffectual, no matter how well trained, how dedicated, or revered by others.

We do not discount the value of a teacher's having a superior education, a wealth of experience, a deep commitment, a good curriculum, or access to technology. But these do not fundamentally empower a teacher to teach. Children learn best when they like their teacher and they think their teacher likes them. The way to children's minds has always been through their hearts.

Our postindustrial approach to education has tended to be idealistic, taking for granted that children can be taught by teachers they are not attached to. In the past several decades certain well-meant and even well-thought-out educational approaches have attempted to capitalize on the emergent, adaptive, and integrative factors in learning, making room for students' interests, individuality, interaction, and choices. If they have often failed, it is not because they are wrong in themselves but because peer orientation has made students impervious to them. Peer-oriented children are attachment-based learners by default, incapable of emergent, adaptive, integrative learning. The problem is that their misdirected attachments have them learning from the wrong teachers.

Conservative critics of education consider modern, "enlightened" approaches to teaching as failures, perceiving them as sowing anarchy, disrespect, and disobedience. Many look across the waters at the more authoritarian and structured approaches of continental Europe and Asia. What they do not realize is that these traditional educational systems exist in societies where, relatively speaking, adult attachments are still intact. That is what gives them validity and power. But even these educational systems are showing weaknesses as traditional hierarchical attachments break down. I had the opportunity to witness this personally in Japan and to participate as an invited scholar in an educational conference dedicated to exploring the problems of a system under strain. No postindustrialized society seems immune. Once a society begins valuing economics over culture, breakdown is inevitable and the attachment village begins to disintegrate. Teachers in authoritarian educational systems have not yet realized that it was connection, not coercion, that facilitated learning. Our educational system must be able to harness the emergent, integrative, and adaptive processes where they exist, but it must also create a safety net of connection and relationship to keep the attachment-based learners from slipping through the cracks. Authoritarian approaches looking back to the past can only make matters worse.

Given that peer orientation is devastating our educational system, one would think that we would be alarmed, seeking ways to reverse the trend or at least slow it down. On the contrary, we as educators and parents are actually aiding and abetting this phenomenon. Our "enlightened" child-centered approach to education has us studying children and confusing what is with what should be, their desires with their needs. A dangerous educational myth has arisen that children learn best from their peers. They do, partially because peers are easier to emulate than adults but mostly because children have become so peer-oriented. What they learn, however, is not the value of thinking, the importance of individuality, the mysteries of nature, the secrets of science, the themes of human existence, the lessons of history, the logic of mathematics, the essence of tragedy. Nor do they learn about what is distinctly human, how to become humane, why we have laws, or what it means to be noble. What children learn from their peers is how to talk like their peers, walk like their peers, dress like their peers, act like their peers, look like their peers. In short, what they learn is how to conform and imitate.[2]

Peer learning also makes students more independent of teachers, much to the relief, no doubt, of many overworked educators. Unfortunately, students then make no developmental headway. The root meaning of pedagogue is "leader"—specifically, one who leads children. Teachers can lead only if their students follow, and students will follow only those to whom they are attached. More and more, teachers, it would seem, are taking their cues from their students, thus putting the students in the lead and compromising the very spirit of pedagogy.

Peer orientation makes the already formidable task of educating the young all that much harder, taking a heavy toll on teachers in morale, stress levels, and even physical health. Peer orientation renders students resistant to the agendas of their teachers and committed to a perpetual campaign of working to rule. To encounter chronic resistance is a sure recipe for burning out. Teaching harder is not the answer. Getting into the attachment business is the only way teaching can be made easier. What fulfills a teacher is to open a student's mind. And to open our students' minds, we need first to win their hearts.

A final word on education. In this era of specialization and experts, we may think of teaching as the exclusive duty of teachers. Yet if we recognized the role of attachment in facilitating learning and in preventing peer orientation, we would see that the education of our young is a social responsibility shared equally by parents, teachers, and all the adults who come into contact with our young—and, too, of all those who shape the nature of the society and culture in which children develop and learn about life.

# PART FOUR

# HOW TO HOLD ON TO OUR KIDS

(or How to

Reclaim Them)

# COLLECTING OUR CHILDREN

So FAR IN this book we have shown that our society is out of touch with its parenting instincts. Our children are connecting with one another—with immature creatures who cannot possibly bring them to maturity. Now we look at solutions. How can we as parents and teachers reassume our nature-appointed roles as the mentors and nurturers of our young, as the models and leaders to whom they look for guidance?

I said in Chapter 1 that parenting requires a context to be effective, the attachment relationship. As a culture and as individuals we have, unwittingly, allowed peer orientation to erode that context. It is time to restore it. At the very top of our agenda we must place the task of collecting our children—of drawing them under our wing, making them want to belong to us and with us. We can no longer assume, as parents in older days could, that a strong early bond between ourselves and our children will endure for as long as we need it. No matter how great our love or how well intentioned our parenting, under present circumstances we have less margin for error than parents ever had before. We face too much competition. To compensate for the cultural chaos of our times, we need to make a habit of collecting our children daily and repeatedly until they are old enough to function as independent beings. The good news is that nature—our nature—tells us how to do that.

Like bees and birds and many other creatures, we human beings use instinctive behaviors to call forth one another's attachment responses. We also have a kind of courtship dance meant to attract other people and to form connections with them. Undoubtedly the most essential function of this dance, on par with procreation, is the collection of children. When adults are around infants, even if not their own, these wooing instincts come alive almost automatically—the smiles, nods, the big eyes, the cooing sounds. I like to call this kind of instinctive behavior the *attachment* or *collecting dance*.

You would think that if the attachment dance is a part of our nature, we should have no problem collecting our kids as long as we need to. Unfortunately, it doesn't work that way. Although the steps are innate to us all, we will not perform them if we have lost touch with our intuition. For many adults, child-collecting instincts are no longer triggered with children past infancy—and especially not with children who, unlike the cute infant, may no longer be trying actively to attach to us. If we are to gather our kids under our wings amid the many distractions and seductions of today's culture, we need to bring these collecting instincts into our awareness. We need to focus on them consciously. We need to use them in our parenting and our teaching just as purposefully as we might employ our wooing skills to attract some desirable adult partner with whom we want to be in a relationship.

When I observe adults interacting with infants, I can see that the attachment dance has four distinct steps. These steps progress in a specific order and, as they do, they form the basic model for all human courtship interaction. The four steps provide the sequence we need to follow in the task of collecting our children, from infancy and beyond through adolescence.

### Get in the Child's Face—or Space—in a Friendly Way

The objective of this first step is to attract the child's eyes, to evoke a smile, and, if possible, elicit a nod. With infants, our intentions are usually blatantly evident—we find ourselves going into contortions to get the desired effect. As children get older, our intentions should be less obvious so that we don't alienate them. Many of us have felt annoyed with salespeople, for example, who carry wooing behaviors too far and assume too easy a familiarity with a potential customer.

With infants, this courtship interaction is often an end in itself, intrinsically satisfying for the parent when successful and thoroughly frustrating when not. There is no agenda behind it; we are not trying to get the infant to "do" anything. Relationship building is an end in itself, and it ought to stay that way past infancy and throughout childhood. With today's emphasis on parenting strategy, we often focus on what to do instead of where to get to. The starting point and the primary goal in all our connections with children ought to be the relationship itself, not conduct or behavior.

The older children become, the more likely we are to get in their faces only when something goes wrong. This trend begins at the active toddler stage, when the parent has increasingly to protect the child from harm. According to one study, at the very beginning of this stage of mobile, restless exploration, 90 percent of maternal behavior consists of affection, play, and caregiving, with only 5 percent designed to prohibit the toddler from ongoing activity. In the following months, there is a radical shift. The aroused toddler's curiosity and impulsiveness lead him into many situations where the parent must act as an inhibiting influence. Between the ages of eleven and seventeen months, the average toddler experiences a prohibition every nine minutes.[1] The goal in such encounters is not to collect children emotionally but to correct or direct them. Somewhere around this time, or a little later, we put our collecting instincts to rest. In the same manner, adult courtship behavior often disappears once the relationship has been cemented. We begin to take the relationship for granted. Mistaken as this omission may be in adult attachment, it is disastrous with children. Even as we must be the guardians of our children's safety and well-being, we need to keep getting in their faces in ways that are warm and inviting, that keep enticing them to stay in relationship with us.

As children get older or become resistant to contact, the challenge changes from getting in their face in a friendly way to getting in their "space" in a friendly way. Although the task is more difficult, we must always focus on the objective of collecting the child. "It's true," admitted David, the father of a fourteen-year-old. "When I look at how I speak with my daughter, most of the time it's to get her to do something, or to teach her something, or somehow to change her behavior. It's rarely about just being together and enjoying her."

The collecting dance cannot evolve if we follow short-term behavioral goals. By turning our focus to the long-term objective of a nurturing relationship, we should discover from within the moves that can get us there. We can take heart from the knowledge that we have our instincts and intuitions on our side, even if they have been dormant for a while. Allow yourself to experiment and explore. It is a matter of trial and error, not a behavioral prescription. For every child, a different dance will emerge.

It is especially important to collect our children after any time of separation. Attachment rituals, fueled by this collecting instinct, exist in many cultures. The most common is the greeting, which is the prerequisite for all successful interactions. When fully consummated, a greeting should collect the eyes, a smile, and a nod. To ignore this step is a costly mistake. In some cultures, like in Provence and in some Latin countries, greeting children is still customary and expected. In our society, we often do not even greet our own child, never mind anyone else's. As children lose their own initiative to connect with us after times of separation, it may seem less important to us that we reach out to them. Nothing could be farther from the truth. We must compensate with our own enthusiasm and initiative.

The most obvious separations are caused by school and by work, but many other experiences can separate us as well. Sometimes the separation may be due to a child's being preoccupied with, say, television, play, reading, or homework. The first interaction should be to reestablish connection. Unless we can re-collect the child, not much will work. It is fruitless and frustrating, for example, to give a child directions when she is completely focused on the television set. At such a moment, before we call them to supper, we may wish to sit down beside them and, hand on their shoulder, engage them in interaction. We need to include some eye contact. "Hi. Good program? Looks interesting. Too bad, though—it's time to come to the table."

Collecting our children is also important after the separation caused by sleep. Morning would be a lot different in many families if the parent did not insist on parenting until the child had been properly collected. One of our own most fruitful customs when our boys were young was to create what we called a morning warm-up time. We designated two comfortable chairs in our den as warm-up chairs. Right after the boys woke up my wife, Joy, and I put them on our laps, held them, played and joked with them until the eyes were engaged, the smiles were forthcoming, and the nods were working. After that, everything went much more smoothly. It was well worth the investment of getting up ten minutes earlier to start the day with this collecting ritual instead of going directly into high-gear parenting. Children are designed to start in first gear, no matter how old they are and how mature they become.

In short, we need to build routines of collecting our children into our daily lives. In addition to that, it is especially important to reconnect with them after any sort of emotional separation. The sense of connection may be broken, say, after a fight or argument, whether by distancing, misunderstanding, or anger. The context for parenting is lost until we move to restore what psychologist Gershon Kaufman has called "the interpersonal bridge." And rebuilding that bridge is always our responsibility. We can't expect children to do it—they are not mature enough to understand the need for it.

For teachers and/or other adults who are in charge of children not their own, collecting them should always be the first item of business. If we try to take care of children or to instruct them without first having collected them, we run counter to their natural instinct to resist the demands and instructions of strangers.

It is undoubtedly this act of collecting a child that sets the master teacher apart from all the others. I will never forget my experience with my very first teacher, Mrs. Ackerberg. After my mother deposited me in the doorway of my first-grade class, and before I had a chance to be distracted by another child, this wonderful smiling woman came gliding across the room and engaged me in a most friendly way, greeting me by name, telling me how glad she was that I was in her class, and assuring me what a good year we were going to have. I am sure it took her very little time to collect me. After that, I was all hers and rather immune to other attachments. I didn't need them; I was already taken. I was not collected by a teacher again until fifth grade. The in-between years were a wilderness experience as far as my education was concerned.

### Provide Something for the Child to Hold On To

The principle behind the next step is simple: in order to engage children's attachment instincts, we must offer them something to attach to. With infants, this often involves placing a finger in the palm of their hand. If the child's attachment brain is receptive, she will grasp the finger; if not, she will pull her hand away. It is not an involuntary muscle reflex such as that elicited by tapping below the knee but an *attachment reflex*, one of many present from birth that enable such activities as feeding and cuddling. It indicates that the attachment instincts have been activated. The child is now ready to be taken care of.

Neither the adult nor the child knows or appreciates what is taking place. This simple finger grasp is an entirely unconscious interaction, the objective of which is to prime the attachment instincts, to get the child to hold on. In this case the infant is holding on physically, but the fundamental purpose includes emotional connection. By placing our finger into the child's palm, we are issuing an invitation to connection. Thus our part of the dance begins with an invitation.

As children get older, the point of the exercise is not holding on physically but holding on figuratively. We need to give children something to grasp, something to hold dear, something they can take to heart and not want to let go of. Whatever we provide must come from us or be ours to give. And whatever we give our children, the key is that in holding on to it, they will be holding on to us.

Attention and interest are powerful primers of connection. Signs of affection are potent. Researchers have identified emotional warmth, enjoyment, and delight at the top of the list as effective activators of attachment. If we have a twinkle in our eye and some warmth in our voice, we invite connection that most children will not turn down. When we give children signs that they matter to us, most children will want to hold on to the knowledge that they are special to us and appreciated in our life.

For our own children, the physical component is key. Hugs and embraces were designed for children to hold on to, and can warm up a child long after the hug is over. It is not surprising that many adults in counseling still grieve over the poverty of physical warmth their parents offered them in childhood.

I am often asked by teachers how they are to cultivate connection these days, now that physical contact is such a controversial issue. Touch is only one of the five senses and the senses are only one of six ways of connecting. (For the six modes of attachment, see Chapter 2.) Although touch is important, we need to keep in mind that it is certainly not the only way to connect with children.

For children who are emotionally defended against attaching in one of the more vulnerable ways, one may have to focus on less vulnerable offerings—like conveying a sense of sameness with a young person or finding an opportunity to demonstrate some loyalty by being on his side. In my work with young offenders, this was almost always where I started. Sometimes it would be as simple as noticing that we both had blue eyes or that we shared a similar interest and had something in common. Above all, an adult has to give something before the child will hold on.

The ultimate gift is to make a child feel invited to exist in our presence exactly as he is, to express our delight in his very being. There are thousands of ways this invitation can be conveyed: in gesture, in words, in symbols, and in actions. The child must know that she is wanted, special, significant, valued, appreciated, missed, and enjoyed. For children to fully receive this invitation—to believe it and to be able to hold on to it even when we are not with them physically—it needs to be genuine and unconditional. In Chapter 17, where I'll discuss effective discipline, we will see how damaging it is when separation from the parent is used punitively against the child. To engage in that oft-advised but damaging technique is to say, in effect, that the child is invited to exist in our presence only when he or she measures up to our values and expectations—in other words, that our relationship with them is conditional. Our challenge as parents is to provide an invitation that is too desirable and too important for a child to turn down, a loving acceptance that no peer can provide. In holding on to our gift of unconditional love, the child will be holding on to us emotionally—just as the infant held with closed fist the parent's finger.

The child must perceive our offering to be spontaneous for connection to work. It may seem counterintuitive to say this—and I'll explain my reasons shortly—but we cannot collect a child by giving what is expected, whether it be part of a ritual or as a birthday gift or as reward for some accomplishment. No matter how much fuss we may make, what we give under such circumstances will be associated with the situation or event, not with the relationship. Such giving never satisfies. A child may enjoy gifts, whether physical or emotional, that are expected, but her attachment needs cannot be satiated by them.

We cannot cultivate connection by indulging a child's demands, whether for attention, for affection, for recognition, or for significance. Although we can damage the relationship by withholding from a child when he is expressing a genuine need, meeting needs on demand must not be mistaken for enriching the relationship. In collecting a child, the element of initiative and surprise is vital. Providing something to hold on to is most effective when least expected. If what we have to offer can be earned or is seen to be some sort of reward, it will not serve as nurturing contact. Our offerings of connection must flow from the fundamental invitation we are extending to the child. This step in the dance is not a response to the child. It is the act of conceiving a relationship, many times over. It is an invitation to dance the mother of all dances—the dance of attachment. Again, it's a matter of conveying spontaneous delight in the child's very being—not when he is asking for anything, but when he is not. We show our pleasure in his existence by gestures, smiles, tone of voice, a hug, a playful smile, by the suggestion of a joint activity, or simply by a twinkle in our eyes.

It is widely believed, by the way, that to give in to a child's requests is to "spoil" the child. That fear contains no more than a grain of truth. Some parents compensate for the attuned attention, connection, and contact they are not providing by making indiscriminate concessions to a child's demands. When we spoil something, we deny it the conditions it requires. For example, we spoil meat by leaving it out of the fridge. The real spoiling of children is not in the indulging of demands or the giving of gifts but in the ignoring of their genuine needs. My cowriter's niece, a new mother, was told by a nurse at the maternity hospital not to hold her baby in her arms so long because "you will spoil her." On the contrary, the spoiling would be in the denial of closeness to the infant. Wisely, the mom ignored this "professional" advice. An infant and young child granted nongrudging parental contact will not be driven to excessive demanding when she gets older.

It is true that a highly insecure child can be exhaustingly demanding of time and attention. The parent may long for respite, not more engagement. The conundrum is that attention given at the request of the child is never satisfactory: it leaves an uncertainty that the parent is only responding to demands, not voluntarily giving of himself to the child. The demands only escalate, without the emotional need underlying them ever being filled. The solution is to seize the moment, to invite contact exactly when the child is *not* demanding it. Or, if responding to the child's request, the parent can take the initiative, expressing more interest and enthusiasm than the child anticipates: "Oh, that's a great idea. I was wondering how we could spend some time together! I'm so glad you thought of it." We take the child by surprise, making him feel that he is the one receiving the invitation.

Nor can one collect a child or offer him something to hold on to by showering him with praise. Praise is usually about something the child has done and, as such, is neither a gift nor spontaneous. Praise originates not in the adult but in the achievements of the child. A child cannot hold on to praise because it is subject to cancellation with every failure. Even if he could hold on to the praise, he wouldn't be holding on to the praise giver but the achievement that produced it. No wonder praise backfires in some children, producing behavior counter to what is praised, or causing the child to back out of the relationship in anticipation of falling short.

Are we saying that children should never be praised? On the contrary, it is helpful, compassionate, and good for the relationship—any relationship—when we acknowledge others for some special contribution they have made or for the effort or energy they have expended in making something happen. What we are saying is that praise should not be overdone, that we should be careful that the child's motivation does come to depend on the admiration or good opinion of others. The child's self-image should not rest on how well, or how poorly, she succeeds in gaining our approval by means of achievements or compliant behaviors. The foundation of a child's true self-esteem is the sense of being accepted, loved, and enjoyed by the parents exactly as he, the child, is.

### Invite Dependence

If the infant is old enough, we invite his dependence by extending our arms as if to pick him up, then waiting for a response before proceeding. If his attachment instincts are sufficiently engaged, he'll respond, lifting his arms, indicating a desire for proximity and a readiness to depend. The mutual roles of parent and child in this choreography of attachment are intuitive.

To invite dependence in the baby is to say, in effect, Here, let me carry you. I will be your legs. You can rely on me. I will keep you safe. To invite an older child to depend on us is to convey to the child that she can trust us, count on us, lean on us, be cared for by us. She can come to us for assistance and expect our help. We are saying to her that we are there for her and that it's okay for her to need us. But to proceed without first having gained the child's trust is asking for trouble. This is true for the parent as well as the day-care worker, the babysitter, the teacher, the foster parent, the stepparent, or the counselor.

Here our new-world preoccupation with independence gets in the way. We have no problem inviting the dependence of infants, but past that phase, independence becomes our primary agenda. Whether it is for our children to dress themselves, feed themselves, settle themselves, entertain themselves, think for themselves, solve their own problems, the story is the same: we champion independence—or what we believe is independence. We fear that to invite dependence is to invite regression instead of development, that if we give dependence an inch, it will take a mile. What we are really encouraging with this attitude is not true independence, only independence from us. Dependence is transferred to the peer group.

In thousands of little ways, we pull and push our children to grow up, hurrying them along instead of inviting them to rest. We are pushing them away from us rather than bringing them to us. We could never court each other as adults by resisting dependence. Can you imagine the effect on wooing if we conveyed the message "Don't expect me to help you with anything I think you could or should be able to do yourself"? It is doubtful that the relationship would ever be cemented. In courtship, we are full of "Here, let me give you a hand," "I'll help you with that," "It would be my pleasure," "Your problems are my problems." If we can do this with adults, should we not be able to invite the dependence of children who are truly in need of someone to lean on?

Perhaps we feel free to invite the dependence of adults because we're not responsible for their growth and maturity. We don't bear the burden of getting them to be independent. Here is the core of the problem: we are assuming too much responsibility for the maturation of our children. We have forgotten that we are not alone—we have nature as our ally. Independence is a fruit of maturation; our job in raising children is to look after their dependence needs. When we do our job of meeting genuine dependence needs, nature is free to do its job of promoting maturity. In the same way, we don't have to make our children grow taller; we just need to give them food. By forgetting that growth, development, and maturation are natural processes, we lose perspective. We become afraid our children will get stuck and never grow up. Perhaps we think that if we don't push a little, they will never leave the nest. Human beings are not like birds in this respect. The more children are pushed, the tighter they cling—or, failing that, they nest with someone else.

Life comes in seasons. We cannot get to spring by resisting winter; in winter plants are dormant—they will burst into bloom when spring comes. We cannot get to independence by resisting dependence. Only when the dependence needs are met does the quest for true independence begin. By resisting dependence, we thwart the movement to independence and postpone its realization. We seem to have lost touch with the most basic principles of growth. If we tried to pull our plants to make them mature, we would endanger their attachment roots and their fruitfulness. Disrupting children's attachment roots only causes them to transplant themselves into other relationships. Our refusal to invite them to depend on us drives them into the arms of each other.

To push children to handle separation before they are ready, whether it is at bedtime or outside the home, is to initially evoke panic and greater clinging, not less. Children who are unsuccessful in keeping the parent close may replace the parent with a substitute. This transference of dependence is often confused with true independence. By encouraging such false independence—or independence our children are not yet mature enough to handle—we are aiding and abetting peer orientation.

Teachers should be inviting dependence as well. In fact, it is usually those teachers who encourage their students to depend upon them who are more likely to be effective in fostering independence in the end. A master teacher, rather than pushing pupils toward independence, supplies them instead with generous offerings of assistance. A master teacher wants her students to think for themselves but knows the students cannot get there if she resists their dependence or chastises them for lacking maturity. Her students are free to lean on her without any sense of shame for their neediness.

There is no shortcut to true independence. The only way to become independent is through being dependent. Resting in the confidence that getting children to be viable as separate beings is not entirely up to us—it is nature's task—we will be free to get on with our part of the job, which is to invite their dependence.

### Act as the Child's Compass Point

A fourth way to engage the attachment instincts is to orient the child. This part of the dance begins when the baby is in our arms. Since children depend on us to get their bearings, we must assume the role of compass point and act as their guide. We adults take on this function automatically, without even being aware of it. We point out this and that, provide the names for things, and familiarize the growing infant with his environment.

In the school setting, at this part of the dance, the intuitive teacher moves to orient the child to where he is, who is who, what is what, and when this or that is going to happen: "This will be where you hang your coat," "This person's name is Dana," "Later on we will do some show-and-tell, and right now you can look at these books."

The variations on this collecting step are myriad and determined by the context and the needs of the child. While we are fairly intuitive with the young, many of us lose this orienting instinct with older children. We no longer assume the role of introducing them to those around them, of familiarizing them with their world, of informing them of what is going to happen, and of interpreting what things mean. In short, we fail to act as a guide to those who should still be depending upon us.

Children are automatically inclined to keep close to their working compass point. If we truly understood the potency of serving this function in children's lives, we would know it is much too significant a role to leave to others.

Intuitively we all experience the power of orienting as a primer for attachment. Imagine being in a foreign city, lost and confused, separated from your belongings, unable to speak or understand the language, and feeling helpless and hopeless about your circumstances. Imagine someone approaching you and offering her assistance in your own language. After she had helped orient you about the persons to contact and places to go, every instinct within you would be primed to maintain closeness with your guide. Once she turned to go, you would undoubtedly seek to prolong the conversation, grasping at straws to keep her close. This being true for adults, how much more so for immature creatures of attachment completely dependent on others to get their bearings.

Part of the problem of losing touch with this instinct to orient is that we no longer feel like experts in the world in which our children find themselves. Things have changed too much for us to act as their guides. It does not take children long to know more than we do about the world of computers and the Internet, about their games and their toys. Peer orientation has created a children's culture that is as foreign to many of us as our culture would be to new immigrants. Just like immigrants disoriented in a strange country, we lose our lead with our children. The language seems to be different, the music is certainly different, the school culture has changed, even the curriculum has changed. Each of these changes contributes to an erosion of confidence to the point that we perceive ourselves as the ones in need of orientation! We feel increasingly unable to orient our children to their world.

Another part of the problem is that peer orientation has robbed our children of the trigger that would, under more natural circumstances, activate our instinct to orient them—that look of being lost or confused. Those who wear this look, even as adults, can provoke orienting responses even from complete strangers. (My cowriter Gabor, a physician, claims he has honed this look of helpless disorientation to a fine art, especially around hospital nursing stations.) Although peer-oriented children have less of an idea than anyone of who they are or where they are going, the effect of peer orientation is to take away that sense of being lost or confused. The child embedded in the culture of cool does not look vulnerable, in need of orienting assistance. Proximity with her peers is all that counts. That is one of the reasons peer-oriented kids often appear to be so much more confident and sophisticated, when in reality they are the blind leading the blind. The net effect of not wearing their confusion on their faces is that our instincts to guide them remain dormant and our ability to collect them is diminished.

Despite the fact that our world has changed—or, more correctly, *because* of that fact—it is more important than ever to summon up our confidence and assume our position as the working compass point in our children's lives. The world may change but the attachment dance remains the same. We are pretty good at guiding our toddlers and preschoolers, probably because we assume that without us they would be lost. We are constantly informing them of what is going to happen, where we will be, what they will be doing, who this person is, what something means. It is after this phase that we seem to lose our confidence and this crucial collecting instinct becomes dulled.

We have to remember that children are in need of being oriented, and that we are their best resource for that, whether they know it or not. The more we orient them in terms of time and space, people and happenings, meanings and circumstances, the more inclined they are to keep us close. We must not wait for their confused look, but confidently assume our position in their life as guide and interpreter. Even a little bit of orienting at the beginning of the day can go a long way in keeping them close: "This is what we're doing today," "This is where I'll be, what is special about this day is . . . ," "What I have in mind for this evening is . . . ," "I would like you to meet so and so," "Let me show you how this works," "This is who will be taking care of you," "This is who to ask if you need help," "Only three more days until . . ." And of course, orienting them about their identity and significance: "You have a special way of . . . ," "You are the kind of girl who . . . ," "You've got the makings of an original thinker," "You have a real gift in . . . ," "You have what it takes to . . . ," "I can see you're going to go far with . . ." Acting as a child's compass point engages the attachment instincts and is an awesome responsibility.

With our own child, orienting reactivates the child's instincts to keep us close. When collecting another's child, orienting is an essential step to cultivating a connection. The secret is for the adult, be it teacher or stepparent, to take advantage of any orienting voids the child is experiencing by offering himself as a guide. If you can arrange situations that render the child or student dependent on you to get his bearings, so much the better for priming an attachment.

## RECLAIMING PEER-ORIENTED CHILDREN

These four steps of the attachment dance empower us to engage a child's attachment instincts and will bring most children into a working relationship with the caregiving adults. But there will be children too insulated by peer orientation for that basic attachment scenario to work. "What should I do if my child has already been 'lost' to the peer world?" some parents will ask. "Is there any way I can win him back?"

My closing message from Chapter 1 bears repeating here: there are always things we can do. While no one approach is foolproof in all situations, we may be confident of success in the long term if we understand where to direct our efforts. The very same steps and principles apply, even if the child's initial resistance to being courted may be quite entrenched and discouraging. Ultimately, a relationship is not something we can determine, only invite and entice. We can make it as easy as possible for "lost" children to return and as difficult as possible for the competition to hold on to them. So, how can we achieve this?

In many ways, peer orientation is like a cult, and the challenges of reclaiming children are much the same as if we were facing the seductions of a cult. The real challenge is to win back their hearts and minds, not just have their bodies under our roof and at our table.

When attempting to collect our children we must remember that they need us, even though they may not know it. Even the most alienated and hostile of teenagers needs a nurturing parent. Despite misdirected instincts and emotional shutdown, this knowledge is still embedded in their psyches and may slip out in the privacy of an interview with a concerned adult or counselor. "We always made sure that our kids' friends felt comfortable at our house," says Marion, the mother of two teenagers. "It seemed maybe they felt more comfortable here than in their own homes. These big 'tough' guys would sit around the kitchen table and have conversations with my husband and I that, later, they would confess to our boys, they would never have with their own parents."

We need to come at the task of collecting our children with an air of confidence and not let ourselves be put off or distracted from our mission. The more defiant and "impossible to be around" children are, the greater their need to be reclaimed.

Winning them back is important, not only to enable us to finish our job of parenting but to give them a chance to grow up. Children who have left the parental attachment womb prematurely must be enticed back in order to continue the process of maturation. "Regardless of age," writes the preeminent U.S. child psychiatrist Stanley Greenspan, "youngsters can begin working on developmental levels they have been unable to master, but they can do so only in the context of a close, personal relationship with a devoted adult."[2] Wooing the child back into a strong attachment bond and keeping him there is the basis for everything else we may try to do with and for the child.

The key to reclaiming a child is to reverse the conditions that cause peer orientation. We need to create an attachment void by separating the child from her peers, and then place ourselves in the void as substitutes. It is important to remember that peer-oriented children have high attachment needs, otherwise they would not be peer-oriented. The lack of proximity with peers is likely to be just as intolerable as the attachment voids were with the parents in the first place.

Frequently, especially if peer orientation is not too advanced, a gentle

reversal can be accomplished by imposing some restrictions on peer interaction while at the same time making it a priority to collect the child
whenever possible. It is important not to reveal one's agenda, as this can
easily backfire. The hardest part for many parents is the shift in focus
from *behavior* to *relationship*. Once the relationship has deteriorated, the
behavior can become increasingly offensive and alarming. Under such
circumstances we find it difficult to stop railing, cajoling, criticizing. To
change the focus, we must first come to terms with the futility of addressing behavior and redirect ourselves to the task of restoring the relationship.
Unless the shift is authentic, there will not be enough patience for the task
at hand. Most of us know intuitively how to court, we just need to know
that there is no other way to get where we want to go and that sooner is
better than later.

I'll address specific tactics like the creation of structures and the impo-
sition of restrictions in Chapter 17, but I will take a moment here to discuss grounding. Grounding continues to be a popular discipline for young
adolescents when some rule has been broken or violation has occurred. It's
a question of how we use it—as punishment or as an opportunity. Grounding usually restricts peer contact and so can actually serve to create an attachment void we can then take advantage of. If parents can see it as a time
to get in their child's face in a friendly way and provide something for the
child to hold on to, the result can be beneficial. Grounding by itself will
not do the trick. Thwarting peer interaction may only increase the child's
intensity in pursuing it. Grounding should also be avoided if the parent
lacks the natural attachment power and the inner confidence to pull it off.
Like most behavioral approaches, grounding works best with those who
need it least and is least effective with those who need it most. But under
any circumstances, grounding, if we are to employ it at all, works best if
parents seize it as an opportunity to reestablish the relationship with their
child. And that means taking all punitive tone and emotion out of the interaction.

Sometimes more radical measures are required, especially when attempts to collect the child have been fruitless and efforts to put even the
slightest wedge between a child and his peers have been in vain. There is
a broad range of interventions we can employ, depending on the family's
resources and the seriousness of the situation, from weekend excursions
alone with the child to extended travel as a family and everything in between. This is when a vacation home can come in handy, for those who
can afford one. Relatives in the country with an open heart and good collecting instincts are something money can't buy. Getting a child away for

the summer in the context of family, even if it isn't our own, is often an antidote to escalating peer involvement. Several families I know decided to move in order to create the attachment void with peers, and, fortunately, the results of this radical solution were successful. But creating such a void is only half of the solution. Collecting the child is the most important half.

One-on-one interaction is most effective in trying to collect a child. When there is more than one adult, the child can still escape from having personal encounters. And with other children present, the attachment void is never great enough to force the child into our arms.

It is impossible to dance with a peer-oriented child—we have to summon up every bit of initiative and ingenuity we can muster. For my teenage daughters Tamara and Tasha, the turning points in their own peer orientation came on trips planned for the purpose of winning them back. For Tasha, the bait was getting time off from school and going to a place I knew she loved. Even so, she became upset that she was going to miss school—not out of any academic concern but because school was where her friends were. Fortunately, by that time we were already on the ferry, past the point of no return. When we arrived at the seaside cottage I had rented, she announced that this was going to be boring because nobody was around. That is the thing about peer orientation; it demotes parents to the position of "nobody." "Everybody" is the name of those attached to and "nobody" is everyone else.

I had to remember not to let myself be alienated and not to battle against the symptoms. Things began rather slowly, but having booked several days off work, I was willing to wait until the attachment void became intolerable enough to impel Tasha to seek closeness with me. My task was to get in her space in a friendly way, without overdoing it. Her sullen expression was a far cry from the eyes that used to light up and the smile she used to flash in response to my presence. On this occasion, she first discovered me as a companion for walks and canoeing. Then came a few smiles; some warmth entered her voice. Finally came the talking and an openness to being hugged. With reconnection also came, interestingly enough, the desire to cook and eat together. When it came time to leave, neither of us was too eager to go back. On the way home, Tasha and I came up with some structures to preserve our relationship: a once-a-week walk together or a glass of hot chocolate in a cafe. I promised myself not to "ride" her during our special times. These specially arranged events were intended to preserve the attachment context—I could carry out my other parenting tasks of coaching and leading the rest of the time.

Tasha asked me why I had left her in the first place. I began by arguing that she had it all backward when, suddenly, I realized that she was right. It is the parent's responsibility to keep the child close. My daughter was certainly not to blame for the state our culture is in. In pursuing proximity with her peers, she was only following her skewed instincts. Although it was not my fault that our culture was failing us, it was still my parental responsibility to hold on to Tasha until she no longer needed me. I had unknowingly and unwittingly let her go before my parenting was done. I shudder to remember that, at the time, I was worried about taking a week off work. In retrospect, I know it was one of the best decisions I've ever made.

With Tamara, it was a few days of hiking and camping alone in the wilderness that restored our relationship. The bait was that she loved hiking and fishing and the outdoors. Her peer orientation was acted out at the beginning when she refused my help, walked ahead of me or behind me, and kept our interaction to a minimum. Her glum face was a reminder to me that I was not the company she wished for. I chose wilderness I was familiar with so I could be the compass point in every sense. It took a few days. Although, once more, I had to remind myself to be patient and to stay friendly, by the last day my daughter was walking by my side and welcoming my assistance. Like in the old days, she was full of show-and-tell and could talk my ear off. What took me by surprise was how quickly and how profoundly her warm smile could touch my heart. In the aftermath of her peer orientation, I had totally forgotten the joy that our relationship had once given me.

# PRESERVE THE TIES THAT EMPOWER

THE RELATIONSHIP BETWEEN child and parent is sacred. Faced with the challenge of the peer culture, we need to keep our children's attachments to us strong and to make these attachments last for as long as our children need to be parented. But how to achieve that?

## MAKE THE RELATIONSHIP THE PRIORITY

No matter what problem or issue we face in parenting, our relationship with our children should be the highest priority. Children do not experience our intentions, no matter how heartfelt. They experience what we manifest in tone and behavior. We cannot assume that children will know what our priorities are: we must live our priorities. Many a child for whom the parents feel unconditional love receives the message that this love is very conditional indeed. "The real challenge is keeping patient, holding the long-term view," says Joyce, mother of three young children. "When you are in a jam, it's hard to remember that you are in a relationship with a person, not just trying to get someone out the door in ten minutes. Problem is, we have our own agendas and sometimes we see the kid as an impediment."

Unconditional acceptance is the most difficult to convey exactly when it is most needed: when our children have disappointed us, violated our values, or made themselves odious to us. Precisely at such times we must indicate, in word or gesture, that the child is more important than what he does, that the relationship matters more than conduct or achievement. We make the relationship safe before we address behavior. It is when things are the roughest that we should be holding on to our children the most firmly. Then they, in turn, can hold on to us. Trying to parent, to "teach lessons" when we are upset or full of rage risks making the child anxious about the relationship. We can hardly expect a child to hold on to a connection that, in his eyes, we do not value. At such times the best thing to do is to collect ourselves, hold back our critical words, and forgo imposing any "consequences."

To some parents, such a way of relating feels unnatural. They fear that their children will perceive them as condoning misconduct. They believe that a failure to speak out immediately and consistently about inappropriate behavior will confuse the child and compromise their own values. Though understandable, that fear is misplaced. Confusion is rarely the issue: a child will usually know what is expected and is either unable or unwilling to deliver. The inability to deliver is usually a maturity problem; the unwillingness to deliver is usually an attachment problem. A child is much more likely to be confused not about what is valued but about his own worth and importance to the parent. This is exactly what requires clarification and affirmation. When we say to a child "That is unacceptable," unless the attachment is secure and the connection is sound, the child will likely hear "She doesn't like me" or "I'm not acceptable because . . . ," or "I am only acceptable when . . ." When a child hears such a message, whether we have actually said it or not, the relationship is damaged. The very basis on which a child wants to be good for us is undermined.

We do not compromise our values when we say that the child is more important than his conduct; rather, we affirm them at their deepest level. We dig down to bedrock and declare what is true. When challenged to clarify their values, parents, with very few exceptions, come out on the side of the child and the attachment. The problem is that we usually take the relationship for granted. We are conscious of other values—moral values, for example—but not of the most fundamental one to us all, attachment. When we interact with our children, it is these other values that we communicate. Only when attachment becomes conscious do we discover our deepest commitment—the child himself.

## PARENTING WITH ATTACHMENT IN MIND

If we took our cues from the natural sequence of development, our priorities would be clear. First would be *attachment,* second would be *maturation,* and third would be *socialization.* When encountering some turbulence with our child, first we would address the relationship, which is one and the same thing as preserving the context for maturation. Only afterward would we focus on societal fit—that is, on the child's behavior. Not before satisfying ourselves that the first two priorities were met would we proceed to the third. Accepting this discipline in our interactions with our children would keep us in harmony with developmental design and help us live in harmony with our most fundamental commitments. That's the thing about parenting: doing our best for our children works to bring out the best in us.

Parenting with attachment in mind means not allowing anything to separate the child from us, at least not psychologically. This challenge is much greater with a peer-oriented child because something already has come between parent and child: peers. Not only are peer-oriented children less inclined to attach to us, but they are driven to behaviors that may be hurtful and alienating. (For the negative energy of attachment that fuels such behaviors, see Chapter 2.) Our feelings as parents can be hurt even when a baby is unresponsive to our overtures. An older child caught up in peer orientation may not only be unresponsive but downright mean and nasty. It is painful to be dismissed, ignored, and disrespected. It is hard not to react to the rolling of eyes, the impatience in the voice, the uncaring demeanor, and the rude tone. The perceived arrogance and disloyalty of the peer-oriented child violates every attachment sensibility in the parent. It pushes all the wrong buttons. Such hurtful, insulting behavior pushes all our hot buttons—how can it not?

In Chapter 2, I called peer orientation an attachment affair. When our children abandon us for their peers, we feel just as violated, angry, and humiliated as we would in any other relationship we deeply cared about. It is natural, when wounded, to recoil defensively, withdrawing emotionally to avoid getting hurt even more. This is when the defensive part of our brain gives us the urge to back out of vulnerable territory to a place where insults no longer sting and the lack of connection does not turn the stomach. Parents are only human.

Withdrawing our attachment energy may defend us against further vulnerability, but the child experiences it as rejection. We need to recall that the child is not consciously setting out to hurt us, he is only following his skewed instincts. If, in response, we divest emotionally, we create an even greater attachment void that impels the child ever more powerfully into the arms of his peers. For the child, parental retreat almost always precipitates a downward spiral into peer attachments and dysfunction. Although it may seem to the parent that there is no connection to salvage, the relationship with mom, dad, and family still matter profoundly to even the most peer-oriented child. If we parents allow ourselves to become alienated, we will burn the only bridge by which the child can return. It takes a saint to not be alienated, but with our peer-oriented children, sainthood may be what we are called to. If that seems unnatural, it's because it is unnatural. Parenthood was never meant to be this way, was not designed by nature with the possibility that our children's hearts could be turned against us. Yet if we allow ourselves to be pushed away, there is nothing left for the child to hold on to. Keeping ourselves in the game, not allowing ourselves to become alienated is one of the most important things to do, for our children's sake and ours.

Truly, there is nothing more wounding than to feel continually rebuffed. It calls for drawing patiently and faithfully on our infinitely deep fount of unrequited love and hoping for a better day. Even if the situation leaves us feeling frustrated and hopeless, we must not abandon the field. As long as we stay open, there is a good chance that the wayward son or daughter will return.

Not infrequently, in an act of desperation, parents will deliver an ultimatum to their child. Usually it is some version of unless you shape up, you'll have to ship out. Whether formally used as a technique such as "tough love" or simply a gut-level response to bring the child in line, it rarely works with a peer-oriented child. Such an ultimatum assumes enough attachment to trade on. If the attachment is not strong enough, there will be no impulse in the child to stay close to the parent. Ultimatums make the child feel very keenly that her parents love and accept her only conditionally. They induce a peer-oriented child to detach even more from the parent and lead only to her deeper entrenchment in the world of peers.

Sometimes the ultimatum is not really an ultimatum at all but a way of relinquishing responsibility or calling it quits. The parent has had it. He lacks the hope that things will get better or the energy to make it so. If that be the case, it is better to find a way of parting that does not exacerbate the problem or make it more difficult to repair the relationship in the future. Rejection of this magnitude is difficult for any child to recover from. If holding on is no longer an option for the parents, I often suggest that they consider sending their child to a private residential school or lean on relatives or possibly find a family they're close to who'll lend a helping hand. The less overt the rejection, the more possible an eventual restoration. If the psychological connection has not been severed and the physical separation provides the parents with some relief, they may, perhaps, once again find the strength and the initiative to attempt to reclaim their child.

In some ways, less drastic but equally important to recognize, all parents may find themselves bailing out of the relationship from time to time, even if unwittingly. Making the relationship a priority involves doing some mending, especially when the emotional connection has been strained or severed. It is a rare parent who doesn't lose it sometimes. Perfect equanimity is beyond us. No matter how much insight we have or how straight our priorities may be, we are bound to be triggered into emotionally uncontrolled reactions by our children—all but the saints among us, that is. Temporary breaks in the relationship are inevitable and are not in themselves harmful, unless they are frequent and severe. The real harm is inflicted when we neglect to re-collect our child, thus conveying that the relationship is not important to us or, alternatively, if we leave the impression that it is the child's responsibility to restore the connection.

One way we can tell how dear something is to someone is by the obstacles they are willing to overcome in pursuing it. That is how our children know how dear the relationship is to us. When we make the effort to find our way back to our children's side, transcending our own feelings and containing theirs, we are delivering a powerful message that the relationship is our highest priority. When reactions are intense and feelings are frayed, it is time to reclaim our deepest priorities and to affirm our commitment to them. "I'm still your mom and always will be. I know it's hard to remember that I love you when I'm mad and sometimes I may even forget it myself for a moment or two, but I always come back to my senses. I'm glad our connection is strong. It needs to be at a time like this." The actual words aren't that important. It's the tone of your voice and the softness in your eyes and the gentleness of your touch that tell the story.

## HELP YOUR CHILD KEEP YOU CLOSE

I said in Chapter 2 that there are six ways of attaching, "each of them providing a clue to the behavior of our children—and, often, to our own behavior as well." What makes a child feel disconnected from us depends on which attachment dynamic happens to predominate in his emotional life.

Children attaching primarily through the senses are left with a feeling of separation when there is a lack of physical contact. Children who attach through loyalty are going to feel alienated if it seems to them that the parent is against them rather than for them. My cowriter Gabor recalls that his highly intelligent and sensitive son, then nine years old, felt so persistently nagged by his mom and dad that he imagined they took courses at night on how to make life difficult for children! Few kids would articulate their feelings so dramatically, but many children do feel that their parents are just not on their side.

Some children need to sense that they matter to the parents in order to feel close to them. If such a child perceives herself as not important to the parent, she will feel cut off—as, for example, if the child gets the impression that the parent considers work or other activities as being higher priorities than she, the child, in the parent's life. When he is connected at the heart, the lack of warmth and affection will make the child feel left out in the cold. If being known and understood is what creates a sense of intimacy, a sense of being misunderstood will create a wedge, as will a perception, even if unconscious, that the parents are harboring some essential secret. That is why parents should never lie to their children. Lies, however innocently intended, cannot protect a child from pain. There is something in us that knows when we are lied to, even if that awareness never reaches consciousness. Being excluded from a secret engenders a feeling of being cut off and gives rise to the anxiety of exclusion.

To summarize, whatever our children's main form of attaching, our primary goal is to help them stay connected enough to us so there is no need for them to replace us.

## STAYING CONNECTED WHEN PHYSICALLY APART

The greatest challenge exists with those children who are still primarily dependent on the senses for feeling close. Very young children are, of course, naturally like that, but many an older child, if peer-oriented, is also unable to keep his feelings of closeness to his parents in the foreground when he is physically away from them. We can recognize such children by their indifference and detachment from us after periods of physical separation, even if relatively brief, such as a day in elementary school. We could do well to borrow from the tricks that lovers use to bridge the gulf of physical separation. In fact, thinking in this way should generate a multitude of ideas. With lovers, the desire to preserve proximity is mutual, so both will usually apply themselves to the task. With children, the onus is on the parent to think of what the child requires. The challenge is the same regardless of the cause of separation: parents having to work, the child going to school, parents not living together, a hospitalization, going off to camp, or sleeping apart.

Some useful techniques for parents to help their children bridge unavoidable separation include giving the child pictures of themselves, special jewelry or lockets to wear, notes to read or have read, something of their own for the child to hold on to when apart, phone calls at appointed times, recordings of their voice with special songs or messages, something with their smell on it, gifts to be opened at special times. The list is potentially limitless. Everyone knows how to do this; it is a matter of recognizing that bridging physical separation is important and of assuming the responsibility. It is especially important to do so with those children who are not giving us the cues that this is what they need. Of course, we are talking about preadolescents here: such tricks will not go down very well with your teenager!

Another way of keeping connected is by giving your child a sense of where you are when you're not with her. Familiarizing her with your workplace can help. When you're away on a trip, set something up so she can follow your travels on a map. As with lovers, physical absence is much easier to endure when one is able to locate the other in time and place. To fail to provide a sense of continuity is to take the risk of being replaced.

We may need to enlist the help of others to keep us present in the child's mind when we are absent. We can ask friends, relatives, or other caregiving adults to talk to our child about us in a friendly way, to help him imagine what we are up to at certain times, to show him pictures that will evoke for him pleasant memories. Even if it may be initially upsetting for the child, such secondary contact with us serves the purpose of preserving the connection. With children who are at risk for replacing us with peers, other adults can play a significant role in keeping the child-parent relationship intact. This is especially true for children whose parents do not live together. If we are to act in the child's best interests, we need to do everything in our power to help our children keep the other parent close when we're apart. Given the increased risk for peer orientation in the wake of divorce, this should be one of our primary objectives and foremost responsibilities. Unfortunately, the consciousness of attachment is often not strong enough to overcome the personal conflicts that exist between the parents.

## INTIMACY: THE DEEPEST CONNECTION

The ultimate goal in helping our children keep us close is to cultivate a profound intimacy that our children's peers cannot compete with. No matter how close friends may be, it is rare for children to share their hearts with each other. Innermost feelings are typically guarded; the territory is usually too vulnerable to take the risk of being shamed or misunderstood. One mother recalls what happened when her teenage daughter's horse died in a riding accident. "I was shocked to find out," she says, "that Jenna's best friends knew absolutely nothing of her grief. When I asked why she hadn't told them, she replied matter-of-factly that those were not the kinds of things kids share with their friends!" Strange concept of friendship, but quite typical in the world of peer attachments.

The secrets that kids share with one another are often secrets about others or information about themselves that does not give too much away. The vulnerable stuff rarely gets said. That is fortunate for parents, since the sense of closeness that can come from feeling deeply known and understood is probably the deepest intimacy of all, creating a bond that can transcend the most difficult of physical separations. The power of such intimate parent-child connection cannot be overstated.

The first step in creating this kind of closeness is to draw the child out. Although many children need an invitation, asking them what they think and feel seldom works. Sometimes the trick is in finding the right kind of structure: regular outings together, shared tasks, walking the dog. With my mother, it was when we were washing the dishes or picking blueberries together that I would share the thoughts and feelings that hardly ever came out otherwise. The closeness I felt at those times was very special indeed and went a long way to create an enduring connection.

My coauthor's teenage daughter has a habit of coming into his study late at night, just when he's hoping for some privacy. At such times, however, she engages in personal sharing that she is hardly open to the rest of the day. He has learned to welcome and to appreciate these "intrusions," turns away from his reading or his e-mail to focus his attention on his child. We need to seize every opportunity.

Some children's feelings are shut down, for the defensive reasons I explained in Chapter 8. Getting them to divulge anything remotely vulnerable is daunting. We need to make it as easy as possible for them to share, and to remember that our primary objective is not to correct them or to teach them but to connect with them. Creating special one-on-one times and taking care not to be too direct are good beginnings. It is largely a matter of trial and error, but initiative and ingenuity will usually pay off. The more difficult such a connection is to form, the more important it is for us to pursue it. The more our children feel known and understood by us, the less risk we run of being replaced. This kind of connection is our best bet for immunizing our children against peer orientation.

Cultivating a sense of psychological intimacy is best done as a preventive measure. Once a child is intensely peer-oriented, we have probably lost the opportunity to develop such a connection. In such cases, we first need to collect the child in the ways I discussed in Chapter 14. To peer-oriented kids it is self-evident that talking to parents about anything that matters is out of order. A young caller on a radio program I was doing on this subject expressed with devastating clarity what parents of peer-oriented children are up against. In a tone oozing with the confidence of those in the know, this fifteen-year-old girl called to set me straight. "You're soooo weird. When you're a teenager, your friends are your family. Why would any teenager even want to talk to her parents? It's not right. It's not even normal." Given her peer orientation, she could not have seen it any other way. The malady is insidious—there is no sense in these kids that anything is awry. It is profoundly unhelpful to point out to a peer-oriented child that her instincts are leading her astray or that the intensity of her peer relationships does not serve her best interests. There is nothing rational about this aberration, and all the reason in the world cannot unbend instincts that are skewed. There is no other way but to win our children back, one by one.

Cultivating connections that are multifaceted and deeply rooted is the best prevention for peer orientation. (I will say much more in Chapter 17 about how to prevent peer orientation.) A child who feels known and understood is not likely to be satisfied with the poorer fare that peer orientation offers. In this way, we also provide our child with a model for future attachments as fulfilling as the kind experienced with his parents. Without such a template, his future relationships may be impoverished, based primarily on the one-dimensionality of peer interactions.

## CREATE STRUCTURES AND IMPOSE RESTRICTIONS

Necessary as we may consider it to impose order on a child's behavior, it is much more important to impose order on a child's attachments. We have two jobs here: establishing structures that cultivate connection, and restrictions that enfeeble the competition. And believe me, if we saw the situation clearly, we would realize that in our culture it's a knock-out-drag-out, no-holds-barred, no-quarter-given, winner-take-all and loser-gets-nuthin', devil-take-the-hindmost struggle for our kids hearts and minds!

Of course, there are limits to what we can do: we cannot *make* our children want to be with us, to orient by us, or love us. We cannot make them want to be good for us and we cannot decide who their friends are. With adult-connected kids we don't have to do any of these things—their attachment to us will do the work on our behalf. Equally, there are limitations on what we should do: we should not force ourselves on them, and we should not use force to hold them close. Holding on to our children is not about shaping their behavior but about engaging their attachment instincts and preserving the natural hierarchy. It is not enough—or even possible—to hold children close when their instincts are taking them away. We must work to preserve and restore the relationship so that being with us and depending on us feels right and natural to them. To this end we need to put structures and strictures in place. We should no more entrust our children's attachments to fate than we should leave to fate our health or our finances.

Structures and restrictions safeguard the sacred. Part of the role of culture is to protect values that we cherish but that, in our daily lives, we do not experience as urgent. We recognize, for example, that exercise and solitude are important for our physical and emotional well-being, yet seldom is our sense of urgency powerful enough to induce us to honor those needs consistently. Cultures in which exercise and meditative solitude are built-in practices protect their members from that lack of motivation. As our culture erodes, the structures and rituals that protect family life and the sacredness of the parent-child relationship—vitally important but not urgent in our consciousness—are also gradually eroded.

If Provençal culture were to succumb to economic pressures and to the culture du jour, the rituals that safeguard a child's attachments would likely disappear: the family sit-down meal, the collecting greetings at the school gate, the village festival, and the Sunday family walk. That is why today's parents need to take matters into their own hands to create a working miniculture of their own. We need some rites of attachment to safeguard the sacred, something that serves us in the long term so we don't have to be conscious of it in the short term. We cannot afford to let things slip so far that, like Humpty Dumpty, they cannot be put together again.

It is wise to use the attachment power we possess today to put structures in place that will enable us to preserve the power we will need for tomorrow. We need to build structures that restrict the things that would take our children away from us and, at the same time, allow us to collect our children. The rules and restrictions should apply to television, computer, telephone, Internet, electronic games, and extracurricular activities. The most obvious restrictions that need to be put in place are those that govern peer interaction, especially the free-style interaction that is not orchestrated by the adults in charge. Unless parents put some restrictions in place, the demand for play dates, get-togethers, sleepovers, and instant messaging time soon gets out of hand. It does not take long for the pursuit of contact with peers to take precedence over the desire for closeness with parents. Without rules and restrictions to give us the edge, it becomes increasingly difficult to compete. Note again that we are speaking here of prevention. Structures and strictures cannot be forcibly imposed on the peer-oriented child without doing further damage. Those situations call for different approaches.

Wise parents will not impose more restrictions than the attachment power they wield will bear. "When Lance was eleven, he went from being unpopular to suddenly being part of the in-group," recalls the mother of a teenager. "His father and I were very uncomfortable with his two new best friends. They didn't seem attached to parents, to be grounded in family. We were uncomfortable when these kids were over. It was a strong gut feeling. Both these kids put our nerves on edge.

"Suddenly Lance began to listen to their CD's; they were disgusting—and I'm a rock fan. Many f-words, full of violence. CD's I wouldn't now give a second thought to, but then, when my son was eleven . . . Anyway, this kid Josh, he was like a Pied Piper. It was like he had piped my son away. Lance changed. He became secretive with us, always demanding to be connected with these kids.

"We decided we had to break up that relationship. We failed miserably. We sat Lance down to have a talk with him. 'Your dad and I no longer want you to see Josh,' I told him. He cried at first, cried and cried. It became clear that he felt we had forced him to make a decision between us and Josh and that he had chosen Josh. He cried because he would miss me.

"He didn't speak to us. For three and a half months, we got nothing at all. He continued to see Josh, in school, after school, and on weekends. Finally we had to give in." What Lance's parents realized was that they could not confront the peer problem directly. They lacked the attachment power, which is why their attempt to limit their son's peer interaction was doomed to fail. They had to go back to basics and collect their son, woo him back into relationship with them.

Family outings and holidays need to be protected. If these times are to serve the purpose of collecting our children and preserving the ties, we can't afford to dilute the function by taking our children's friends along. Nor can we afford the kind of holiday that splits the family apart, as is becoming the fashion on both the ski slope and at the sun resort. It is an indication of how peer crazy we have become that even the family holiday has succumbed to the idea that children belong with children and adults with adults, or that holidays are to enable parents to get a break from their kids. The more breaks we take, the less attached children are to us. The irony is that they become more difficult to parent—and therefore the more breaks we need from them!

It gets harder to impose restrictions on adolescents, of course, especially those already highly peer-oriented. They demand the freedom to pursue their relationships with one another and heaven help anyone who obstructs them. To peer-oriented adolescents following their skewed instincts, it is vividly clear that they belong with one another and that parents are in the way of what really matters. As far as they are concerned, parents and teachers who don't understand these things are out of touch and just don't get it.

Hence the importance of putting structures in place while we still have the power to do so. If we leave it to fate, our families will gradually be torn asunder by individual pursuits, societal demands, economic pressures and, finally, the distorted instincts of our offspring. The structures that facilitate the parent-child relationship are key: family holidays, family celebrations, family games, family activities. Unless a time and place is set aside and rituals are created, pressures that are more urgent will inevitably prevail. For single-parent families, this task is even more crucial because the competing pressures are more intense. The cultural traditions that still exist in a marriage, even if weakened compared with those that prevailed in the past, often go by the wayside in the wake of family breakup.

Since our sojourn in Provence, I have come to consider the family sit-down meal as one of the most significant attachment rituals of all. Attachment and eating go together. One facilitates the other. It seems to me that the meal should be a time of unabashed dependency: where the attachment hierarchy is still preserved, where the dependable take care of the dependent, where experience still counts, where there is pleasure in nurturing and being nurtured and where food is the way to the heart. Studies of other mammals have shown that even digestion seems to function better in the context of attachment. Disturbed attachments probably explain the high incidence of abdominal pains of children in school and of their eating problems at lunchtime. They would also explain the resistance of many peer-oriented children to being fed by their parents and to sitting down at the table and partaking of the family meal.

Although the mere fact of eating together could facilitate some primitive connection, what is more likely to create genuine attachment has to do with the kind of interaction that takes place while eating. The family meal can be a potent collecting ritual. What other activity can provide such an opportunity to get in our children's faces in a friendly way, provide something for our children to hold on to, and invite our children to depend on us? What other activity provides us the opportunity to collect the eyes, coax the smiles, and get them nodding? No wonder the meal has been the pièce de résistance of human courting rituals for eons. It also explains why the family sit-down meal is the cornerstone of Provençal culture: tables are carefully set, courses are served one at a time, traditions are observed, meals are designed to take time, no interruptions are allowed. The sit-down family meal has a huge supporting cast, including the baker, the butcher, and the vendors at the village market. During the noon and evening meals, business ceases and stores lock their doors. Fast-food restaurants are rare, as are the habits of eating alone or standing up. Provence has been called a culture of food. It seems to me, however, that the consumption of food is only the most visible aspect. A more fundamental purpose is attachment. The family sit-down meal was certainly the centerpiece of our own family life while we stayed in Provence. It was what our children missed the most when we returned.

We are in deep trouble here in the New World. The sit-down family meal has become an endangered event. When it exists, it is more likely to be a perfunctory activity for the purpose of fueling up. There are places to go, work to be done, sports to be played, computers to sit at, stuff to buy, movies to take in, television to be watched. Eating is what one does to prepare for what comes next. Rarely do these other activities enable us to collect our children. Precisely now, when we need the family sit-down meal more than ever before, we're likely to eat on our own and allow our children to do the same. Of course, mealtimes that are tense, that end up in fights or set the stage for arguments about manners or who should clear the table will not serve a collecting function. Parents need to use meals to get into their children's space in a friendly way.

Personal structures are also important for collecting our children and preserving the ties. We have to create a time and place for an activity with a child where our real agenda is connection. Building relationships and maintaining attachments are much more effective one-on-one than in group settings. A limitless number of activities can provide the cover: working on a project, going for walks, playing a game, cooking together, reading. Bedtime rituals like stories and songs are hallowed attachment interactions with younger children. Again, most parents are more than capable of figuring these things out. What is lacking is the realization that our children's attachments to us need preserving if we are not going to lose them to the competition. Even a once-a-week activity can go a long way to meeting the goal of attachment.

## RESTRICTIONS ON PEER CONTACT

Although restrictions and structures work best when used preventively, they can also be used to temper the obsession with peers. It is always best to be as indirect as possible. Telling a child that their friends matter too much only reveals how weird we are and how little we understand. We need to create events and structures that do the job without disclosing our underlying agenda. If lunch hour is the peer-bonding time, then, when the parents or other caregivers are in a position to do so, seeking alternatives would be a priority. If after school is the prime time for peer attachment, after school should be the target for activities that compete. If sleepovers are a problem, imposing some restrictions on their frequency would be in order. Our own policy of once-a-month sleepovers for our daughter Bria met with considerable protest at times. One day, in frustration, she burst out with "But it's not fair—you're interfering with our bonding time." She couldn't have said it more succinctly or reinforced our concerns more thoroughly. If the attachment technologies in one's home—cell phones, Internet, Microsoft Messenger—serve the purposes of children consorting with the competition, then we need to find some way to reduce access to this technology or to create competing structures. Once a child is truly peer-oriented, however, the instincts to pursue proximity with her peers can be so powerful that rules may no longer be sufficient to control behavior. In these cases, the technological paraphernalia that serve peer attachments may need to be sacrificed, just as alcohol would be barred from the home if a family member had a drinking problem or the television would be disconnected if the limits you imposed were being ignored.

Sometimes a parent can successfully compete with the child's peers by being one step ahead of them. Peer-oriented children often have difficulty planning ahead. They want to be together, yet if they take too much initiative, they will appear too needy and thereby set themselves up for possible rejection. They learn to master the indirect: "Hi, whatcha wanna do?" "I dunno, whatcha wanna do?" "I dunno." "Well, maybe we could just hang or sumthin." "I don't care, whatever"—and round and round it goes. Peer-oriented kids somehow drift together without ever putting themselves or the other into a place of vulnerability. Attachment provides the impetus for getting together but the fear of vulnerability prevents them from being too openly forward about it. The silver lining in this situation is that it provides parents with opportunity for a preemptive strike. Planning something a day or sometimes only hours in advance of the predictable times of peer socializing—a special meal, a shopping trip, a family outing, a favorite activity—can keep the child from being sucked into the spiraling vortex of peer interaction. Being creative in heading off the peer bonding time is much better than reacting to the symptoms of peer orientation.

Often, if we can slow the peer interaction sufficiently, an automatic self-selection process will take place. The more intensely peer-oriented among our children's friends will move on to others who also seek to connect primarily with other kids. And, because we all want to attach to people who share our interests and values, those children who are well-connected with their parents are likely to find friends whose families are also more important to them. This is exactly what happened to Bria in the sixth and seventh grades. Her more peer-oriented friends had gone off to seek others of the same kind and the friends she was left with had families to whom they were very attached and wanted to remain close to. Friends that don't compete with family are exactly what we want, for our children and for ourselves.

Of course, the process of getting there may take our children, if already peer-oriented, through some distressing times. It is hard to do things that distress our children, even when we know it is best for them in the long run. By imposing restrictions on children intent on pursuing their peers, we put them in a terrible predicament. Their ability to stay close to one another depends on seizing every opportunity for contact and connection. To miss an MSN exchange with a buddy, Internet chat room event, a phone opportunity, a get-together, a sleepover, or a party is to endanger the relationship. This obsessive insecurity is usually well founded. The more intensely peer-oriented will not tolerate those who fail to pursue proximity as intently as they do or whose parents are getting in the way. As cruel as it may seem, it is, nevertheless, often in the child's best interests to get in the way. None of us want to see our children left out in the cold, but it is by far the lesser of two evils when peer relationships threaten closeness with parents. There is no way of saving a peer-oriented child from distress. The only choice is whether the distress is now or later. The distress we create in the short term prevents far greater problems in the future.

Because of the distress our restrictions will create for our children, we should be prepared for a rough ride. When we impose restrictions on children intent on making it work with peers, they will, most likely, be intensely frustrated. If there were any question about the fact that the child was in over his head, his rude and loud expressions of deep frustration should put all doubts to rest. In his current medical work with drug addicts, my coauthor, Gabor, frequently witnesses similar outbursts of desperation and unmitigated rage when he, say, refuses to prescribe a narcotic an addicted person is demanding. The wise approach is not to take such attacks personally. Always keep in mind that for the peer-oriented child, the answer to life is proximity with peers. To interfere with that quest is to evoke tremendous attachment frustration, so parents had better be prepared to encounter hostility and aggression. Furthermore, remember that peer-oriented kids get stuck in their agendas and cannot let go. Since the futility of a course of action does not sink in for them, they become persistent to the point of obnoxiousness. It is a mistake to think of this as headstrong or strong-willed; stuck and desperate is how it really is. The more intensely peer-oriented kids cannot imagine life outside peer attachments. We therefore need to be prepared to endure and contain the reactions that our rules and restrictions provoke. Our task here is to hold on to ourselves—that is, not to get triggered and overwhelmed by our own out-of-control reactions. That will help us to hold on to our children in such situations until we can get through to the other side.

In setting up restrictions we need to combine an optimistic sense of what our children need with a realistic view of what is possible—that is, of how much attachment power we actually possess. The more indirect we can be in imposing restrictions and the more proactive we can be in putting structures in place that do the job, the more likely we can avoid the head-on collisions. Attempting to enforce rules when we lack the attachment power only sets the stage for revealing our impotence. Impotence is not something we ever want to show. Once our lack of power is revealed, even our most ominous threats will be unmasked as the bluffs they are—unless we are prepared to up the ante and use force in ways that will severely damage the relationship. Without attachment power we have no genuine power at all.

Also important to remember when imposing limitations on peer interaction is that this is only half of the solution. With peer-oriented children, the challenge is not just to separate them from their peers, but to reverse the process that took them away from us in the first place. We have to replace their peers with ourselves, their parents. If we create an attachment void through our restrictions, we need to be prepared to fill it with ourselves. I have already pointed out that grounding should not be used as a punishment but as an opportunity (see Chapter 14). The real benefit is not in the lesson learned—as we will see in the next chapter, punishments designed to "teach a lesson" seldom do. Discouraging peer interaction through grounding, however, can create room for substituting time with us in place of the peer interaction.

As parents, we need a lot of confidence to stand against the prevailing current, to impose limits on peer interaction, and to set structures to preserve our children's attachments to us. It may require some courage to withstand the incredulous and critical responses of our friends who do not understand why we don't value peer contacts as they do and why we would seek to keep them within narrow bounds. "Even with friends we are close to, people lovely and with great integrity, we are still finding the same bugaboos, the same pressures to allow unrestricted playtime with peers for our kids, regular sleepovers and so on," says a young father. "Every time we answer the question why we don't, we are unintentionally insulting them, because they have made the opposite choice."

We need strength to withstand the desperate pleadings of a peer-oriented child, to endure the inevitable upset and the storm of protest. Above all, we need faith in ourselves as our child's best bet. It helps to have some conceptual support for your own parental intuition—and this book is meant to provide that—but it still requires courage to go against the flow. *We do not recommend that parents accept our suggestions until they have the confidence, the patience, and the warmth to follow through with them. One must not parent a child from a book—not even this one!*

Our actions and attitudes must come from a deep self-assurance that what we are doing is in our child's best interests—and that takes the full confidence of one's own insights and a steadfast commitment to one's convictions.

# DISCIPLINE THAT
# DOES NOT DIVIDE

IMPOSING ORDER ON a child's behavior is one of the greatest challenges of parenting. How do we control a child who can't control himself?
How do we get a child to do something she does not want to do? How do
we stop a child from attacking a sibling? How do we handle a child who
resists our directions?

In our quick-fix culture with its focus on short-term results, the be-
all and the end-all is the behavior itself. If we gain compliance, even if
only temporarily, we deem the method successful. Yet once we factor in attachment and vulnerability, we see that behavioral approaches—imposed
sanctions, artificial consequences, and the withdrawal of privileges—are
self-defeating. Punishment creates an adversarial relationship and incurs
emotional hardening. Time-outs to teach a lesson, "tough love" to bring
behavior into line, and "1-2-3 Magic"* to make kids comply are tactics
that strain the relationship. When we ignore a child in response to a
tantrum, isolate the misbehaving child, or withdraw our affection, we undermine a child's sense of security. Ordering children around provokes
counterwill—as, for that matter, does bribing them with rewards. All such
techniques place the child at risk of being drawn into the peer vortex.

What approaches, then, are left for the parent to use?

There remain plenty of safe, natural, and effective ways of changing be-

---

*"1-2-3 Magic" is a popular "three strikes, you're out" method for toddlers and young
children, from a best-selling book by that name.

havior. Some of these methods arise spontaneously if we are concerned less with what to do than with what is important in the parenting process— in other words, if at all times we remain conscious of attachment. When, instead, the focus is on behavior, we take risks that threaten the very basis of our power to parent: our relationship with our children.

This chapter is not a comprehensive guide for handling problem behavior. It does, however, offer alternatives to methods that run roughshod over relationship and emotion and introduces the basic principles of a discipline that doesn't divide. These guidelines represent, for the most part, a one-hundred-eighty-degree turn from prevailing practices. They may take some time to assimilate and incorporate. For some parents this approach requires a significant change in thinking and focus, while to others it validates what they have been practicing all along.

## WHAT IS TRUE DISCIPLINE?

To begin, let us expand our concept of discipline. In the context of parenting, discipline is typically thought of as punishment. On a closer look, however, we see that discipline is actually a rich word with a number of related meanings. It can also refer to a teaching, a field of study, a system of rules, and self-control. In that sense, it is parents who first need to acquire discipline. When it comes to children, we use the term *discipline* not in the narrow sense of punishment but in its deeper meanings of training, bringing under control, imposing order on. There is no question that children require discipline. We need to ensure discipline in ways that do not damage the relationship, trigger crippling emotional defenses, or foster peer orientation.

Over many years of parent consulting, I have gradually organized my thoughts around this matter into *seven principles of natural discipline.* By natural, I mean developmentally safe and attachment-friendly—that is, respectful of both the parent-child relationship and the child's long-term maturation. These are principles, not formulas. How they translate into action will vary from situation to situation, child to child, parent to parent, personality to personality and will depend on the needs and agendas of both child and parent.

The current tendency in the parenting literature is to cater to the demand for parenting skills or parenting strategies. That is not what parents need. Strategies are far too definitive and limiting for a task as complex and subtle as parenting. They insult the intelligence of the parent and usually the intelligence of the child as well. Strategies make us depend on the experts who promote them. Parenting is above all a relationship, and relationships don't lend themselves to strategies. They are based on intuition. These seven principles are designed to awaken or support the parenting intuition we all possess. We do not require skills or strategies but compassion, principles, and insight. The rest will come naturally—although I'm not saying it will come easily.

As we work to bring attachment values into action, most of us may have to struggle with our own impulsive reactions and our own immaturity, with our own inner conflict. Above all, we may have to struggle with feelings of futility. Very few parents come ready-made. Parents are begotten out of attachment and adaptation. The attachment, of course, is the child's attachment to us, enabling and empowering us as parents. The adaptation part has to do with our ongoing personal evolution as the futility sinks in when the things we try don't work. There is no shortcut to this trial-and-error process. We must, however, let ourselves feel the sadness and disappointment when we have a sense of failure. Emotional hardening will only truncate our development as parents, leaving us rigid and ineffective.

In short, these seven principles of natural discipline could just as well be entitled *seven disciplines for parents*. They involve bringing oneself under control and working systematically toward a goal. Our ability to manage a child effectively is very much an outcome of our capacity to manage ourselves. We need to find the same compassion for ourselves that we wish to extend to our child. For example, the answer to a lack of self-control on our part is not to punish ourselves or to exhort ourselves to be good. Such methods do not work for us any more than they do for our children. The answer lies in accepting that, we, too, are fallible and our darker emotions may get the better of us. At times, our rage can arise despite our love for our child and our commitment to her welfare. In some situations, if it's possible to do so without being negligent, we may have to put ourselves on hold as parents until loving impulses once more come to the surface. For example, we may hand the parenting duty to our partner or other trusted adult while we take a time-out—not to punish the child but, amid our own mixed feelings, to find the accepting and nurturing ones toward our child. In the midst of such conflicting elements we find control, balance, perspective, and wisdom.

Discipline should not and need not be adversarial. It is not our children's fault that they are born uncivilized, immature; that their impulses rule them or that they fall short of our expectations. The discipline for parents is to work only in the context of connection. Sometimes when, in the safety of my office, a frustrated parent is trashing her child, I will suggest she stop a minute to feel her emotional connection with the child and then to talk to me again about her concerns. It is amazing how differently things occur to us when we have found our way to the child's side.

Just as we found with the maturation process, we have an ally in nature. We don't have to do it all: discipline is built into the developmental design. There are natural processes by which a child is spontaneously corrected. Part of the task parents face is to work *with* nature, not against it. The most significant of these dynamics is, of course, attachment, but there are also the emergent process—the child's innate drive for self-mastery; the adaptive process—the capacity to learn from what doesn't work; and the integrative process—the ability to endure mixed feelings and ideas. Each of these mechanisms of natural development brings order to behavior and renders the child more fit for society. The difficulty arises when these processes are stuck or skewed—and, for reasons I explained in Chapters 9 and 13 especially, they do become stuck in the peer-oriented child. There is very little to work with when the dynamics that should naturally and spontaneously give rise to discipline are impaired or distorted.

As we come to the seven principles, we will first consider approaches to discipline that are piggybacked onto natural development. These principles should not be taken as immutable prescriptions. They are values to aim for, core ideas to return to when the inevitable frustrations of parenting tempt us to adopt the self-defeating techniques of "good old-fashioned discipline."

## THE SEVEN PRINCIPLES OF NATURAL DISCIPLINE

### Use Connection, Not Separation, to Bring a Child into Line

Separation has always been the trump card in parenting. Today it has been elevated to a fad in the guise of time-out's. Stripped of euphemistic labels, these tools of behavior modification are recycled forms of shunning—isolation, ignoring, cold shoulder, the withholding of affection. They have always engendered more problems than they solved. Today they bring an added disadvantage: they help create conditions that increase children's susceptibility to peer orientation.

The withdrawal of closeness (or threatening its loss) is such an effective means of behavior control because it triggers the child's worst fear—that of being abandoned. If contact and closeness were not important to the toddler or older child, separation from us would have very little impact.

When we disrupt the contact or rupture the connection (or when the child anticipates that this may happen), we bring the child's attachment brain to high alert. In all cases, the child's response will come from a state of anxiety, but how the child shows that will depend on his particular way of attaching. A child who is used to preserving contact with the parent by being "good" will desperately promise never to transgress again. His attempt to regain connection will bring a stream of "I'm sorry's." The child whose way of staying close is through affectionate gestures and words will, when he feels his attachment threatened by the parent, become full of "I love you's"—that will be her mode of restoring proximity. If physical contact is paramount, the child may become clingy for a few hours, not wanting to let you out of her sight. The point for parents to understand is that these manifestations do not represent genuine understanding or contrition, *only the anxiety of the child trying to reestablish the relationship with the parent.* It is naive to think that by such methods we are teaching children a lesson or making them consider the error of their ways.

There is a high cost to playing the separation card: insecurity. The child disciplined by means of separation can count on closeness and contact with the parent only when measuring up to the parent's expectations. Under such conditions the child experiences no release, no rest from the drive to attach, and, therefore, no freedom for the emergence of his individuality and independence. The child may become very "good," but will also be devoid of emergent energy. His development is sabotaged.

The threat of separation works only because the child is attached to us, craves closeness with us, and is not yet emotionally defended against vulnerability. He is, in other words, still capable of experiencing his yearning for attachment and his hurt at separation. If these conditions do not exist, separation is ineffective as an instrument of compliance. On the other hand, any "success" will be only temporary. Whether it is physical separation or emotional withdrawal, the child's sensitivities are likely to be overwhelmed. If we as adults feel hurt when ignored or when shunned, how much more do our children. It may be difficult for parents who use time-outs with nothing but good intentions to accept this, but the ultimate consequences of that separation technique are very negative for the sensitive young child. It attacks the child at his most vulnerable point—his need to stay attached to the parents. Sooner or later the child will be forced to protect himself against the pain of being wounded in this way. He will shut down emotionally—or, more correctly, his attachment brain will. (See Chapter 8 for a discussion of defensive shutdown.)

By using the relationship against the child, we provoke the attachment brain into shutting us out, creating a gaping void of connection. In effect, we are inducing the child to seek his attachment needs elsewhere and by now it is clear with what result. By using time-outs and reacting in ways that break the connection, we are effectively throwing our children to their peers.

The child's brain can also defend against the vulnerability of separation by resisting contact with the parent. Such a child may hide under the bed or in the closet and rebuff overtures by the parents for reconciliation. Or, in anticipation of trouble, she may run to her room or demand to be left alone. In one way or another, the experience of separation will trigger a child's instinct to detach from us.

Separation is especially harmful when used punitively as discipline for aggression. As I explained in Chapter 10, the fuel of aggression is frustration. The end result of employing separation is more aggression, not less. Any compliance we may achieve with an aggressive child by using time-outs, tough love, and other techniques of separation will be short-lived, since it's based on nothing more than the child's temporary alarm about the relationship. As soon as proximity with the parent is restored, the aggression will return with greater force, the added fuel coming from the attachment frustration we have just provoked. Our inept attempts at nipping aggression in the bud only promote its growth.

Subjecting a child to unnecessary experiences of separation, even if from the best of intentions, is shortsighted, and a mistake that nature does not easily forgive. It is foolish to risk our power to parent tomorrow for a little extra clout today.

The positive and natural alternative to separation is *connection.* Connection is the source of our parenting power and influence and of the child's desire to be good for us. Connection should be both our short-term objective and our long-term goal. The trick is to be mindful of connection before a problem occurs instead of imposing separation afterward, to head off future problems rather than reacting punitively after our child's behavior gets out of line.

The basic parenting practice that derives from this shift in thinking is what I call "connection before direction." The idea is to collect the child—engaging the child's attachment instincts along the lines discussed in Chapter 14—in order to give guidance and to provide direction. By cultivating the connection first we minimize the risk of resistance and lessen the chances of setting ourselves up for our own negative reactions. Whether with the uncooperative toddler or the recalcitrant adolescent, the parent first needs to draw near the child, reestablishing emotional closeness before expecting compliance.

A single example illustrates this simple principle. Eleven-year-old Tyler was in the backyard pool with his sister and a few friends. They were having a good time until Tyler got carried away and started hitting his playmates with a plastic noodle. The mother told him to stop, but he didn't. The father became angry, yelled at Tyler for disobeying his mother, and ordered him out of the pool. He refused to obey. The father finally jumped in, dragged him out, and, thinking to teach his son a lesson, sent him off to his room to think about what he had done. Tyler's behavior, the parents explained to me, was completely intolerable and must not happen again. They had, however, heard me speak about the risks of using separation to bring a child into line and wanted to know what they could have done differently.

Once the situation unraveled as it did, the parents probably needed to take a breather before proceeding. When in trouble, it is better to increase proximity rather than to decrease it. *The will to connect must be in the parent before there is anything positive for the child to respond to.* When the will to connect resurfaces in the parent, the first step is to restore the connection. Taking a walk together, going for a ride together, throwing a ball — the human connection must be intact before we are likely to get points across. In this case, what got the parents off on the wrong foot was what was missing at the beginning of their interaction. Tyler was completely engaged in what he was doing. In that mind-set, he was not orienting by his parents or tuned in to any desire to follow their bidding. Under such circumstances, reconnecting with the child is imperative before proceeding. Attempts to connect might have included, "Wow, Tyler, are you ever having fun." With that, one would likely get a grin and a nod in agreement. Having the eyes, the smile, and the nod, the next direction from the parents would have been to bring the child near. "Tyler, I need to talk to you for a minute in private. Come here to the side." Once the child is collected, the parent would be in a position of power and influence. He could provide some direction to calm things down and preserve the fun for all. Furthermore, the wear and the tear on Tyler's attachments would have been prevented, a point that is of greater concern developmentally than teaching Tyler a lesson. Instead of using separation at the tail end, Tyler's parents needed to use connection at the front end.

It's not a complicated dance; in fact, it is surprisingly simple. The trick is the little attachment step at the beginning. The principle of *connection before direction* applies to almost anything, whether asking about home-work, requesting help with setting the table, reminding the child about clothes to be hung up, informing that it is time to switch off the television, or confronting on some sibling interaction. If the basic relationship is good, this process should only take a few seconds. If the attachment is weak or defended against, the attempt to collect the child should reveal this to us. It is very difficult to impose order on the behavior of a child when there is underlying disorder in attachment. A failure to collect the child should be a reminder for us to back off a preoccupation with conduct and to focus our effort and attention on building the relationship.

When we first employ this practice of *connection before direction*, it may strike us as a little awkward and self-conscious. Once it becomes habit, however, the wear and tear on the relationship should decrease signifi-cantly. Parents who get good at this will often solicit the smile and the nod before placing their request or making their demand. The results can be astounding.

### When Problems Occur, Work the Relationship, Not the Incident

When something goes wrong, the usual response is to confront the behav-ior in question as soon as possible. In psychology this is referred to as the *immediacy principle* and is based on the notion that if the behavior is not addressed forthwith, the opportunity for learning will be lost. The child will have "gotten away" with misbehaving. This concern is unfounded.

The immediacy principle has its roots in the study of animal learning where there is no consciousness to work with, nor any ability to communi-cate with the subjects. Working with our children as if they were creatures without consciousness conveys a deep distrust and discounts their hu-manity. Like adults, children are disinclined to hold dear those who mis-judge their intentions and insult their abilities, especially when substitute attachments are readily available.

Trying to make headway in the midst of an upsetting incident fails to make sense for other reasons as well. During an upset the child is likely to be out of control. Choosing such a moment to correct, direct, or to teach "lessons" is a waste of time. As for us, the inappropriate behavior of our child often catches us by surprise, evoking intense emotional reactions. So our behavior—just like that of our kids—is also more likely to be urgent and untempered. Addressing problems requires thoughtful preparation. The midst of an incident is rarely when the child will be at his most recep-tive or we at our most mindful and creative.

With the relationship in mind, the immediate objectives are to stop the behavior if need be and to preserve a working attachment. We can always revisit the incident and the behavior later, once we have calmed the intense feelings and reestablished the connection.

Some behaviors push our buttons and sorely test our ability to stay attached to our child. At the top of the list are aggression and counterwill. If we are at the receiving end of insults, "I hate you's," or even physical aggression, the immediate challenge is to survive the attack without inflicting damage on the relationship. Now is not the time to comment on the nature of the behavior or its hurtful impact. Nor is this the time to issue threats and sanctions or send the child into isolation. To prepare for the intervention that is to come, parents must preserve their dignity. We have to avoid exacerbating the situation by uncontrolled emotional displays. If we allow our feelings of victimization to dominate, we cannot maintain the role of the adult in charge.

Focusing on the frustration instead of taking the attack personally will often help: "You're upset with me," "You're really frustrated," "This wasn't working for you," "You wanted me to say yes and I said no," "You're thinking of all the bad words you can call me," "Those feelings have got away with you again." It's not the words that are critical, but the acknowledgment of the frustration that exists in the child and a tone of voice that indicates that what has just happened has not broken the union. In order to preserve our working relationship with a child, we need to indicate somehow that the relationship is not in danger.

Sometimes it helps to throw an infraction flag. "This is not good. We'll talk about this later." The words, again, are less important than the tone, which should be friendly and warm, not threatening. The primary connection that needs preserving is the human one. We need to restore calm, in ourselves and in the child. At the appropriate time, we make good our date to sort things out. First we collect the child and only then do we attempt to draw lessons from what happened.

### When Things Aren't Working for the Child, Draw Out the Tears
### Instead of Trying to Teach a Lesson

A child has much to learn: to share mommy, to make room for a sibling, to handle frustration and disappointment, to live with imperfection, to let go of demands, to forgo having to be the center of attention, to take a no. Remember, one of the root meanings of discipline is "to teach." A large part of our job as parents is therefore to teach our children what they need to know. But how?

These life lessons are much less a result of correct thinking than of adaptation. The key to adaptation is for futility to sink in whenever we are up against something that won't work and we can't change. When the adaptive process is unfolding as it should, the lessons are learned spontaneously. Parents are not working alone.

The adaptive process accomplishes its task of "disciplining" our children in a number of natural ways: by bringing to an end a course of action that does not work; by enabling the child to accept limitations and restrictions; by facilitating the letting-go of futile demands. Only through such adaptation can a child adjust to circumstances that cannot be changed. Through this process a child also discovers that she can live with unfulfilled desires. Adaptation enables a child to recover from trauma and transcend loss. These lessons cannot be taught directly either through reason or through consequences. They are truly teachings of the heart, learned only as futility sinks in.

The parent needs to be both an agent of futility and an angel of comfort. It is human counterpoint at its finest and most challenging. To facilitate adaptation, a parent must dance the child to his tears, to letting go, and to the sense of rest that comes in the wake of letting go.

The first part of this dance of adaptation is to represent to the child a "wall of futility." Sometimes this will be of our making, but most often it is made of the realities and limitations of everyday life: "Your sister said no," "This won't work," "I can't let you do that," "There isn't enough," "That's all for today," "He didn't invite you," "She wasn't interested in listening to you," "Sally won the game," "Grandma can't come." These realities need to be presented firmly so they do not become the issue. To equivocate—to reason, to explain, to justify—is to fail to give the child something to adapt to. If there is any chance for the situation to be changed, there will be no priming adaptation. It's a matter of getting the child adjusted to exactly how things are, not as he—or even you—would wish them to be.

The failure to stand firm when something is immutable provokes the child to seek escape routes from reality, and thus foils the adaptive process. There will be plenty of time to convey your reasons, but only after the futility of changing things has been accepted.

The second part of the adaptation dance is to come alongside the child's experience of frustration and to provide comfort. Once the wall of futility has been established—in a way that is firm without being harsh—it is time to help the child find the tears beneath the frustration. *The agenda should not be to teach a lesson but to move frustration to sadness.* The lesson will be learned spontaneously once this task is accomplished. We can say things like "It's so hard when things don't work," "I know you really wanted this to happen," "You were hoping I'd have a different answer," "This isn't what you expected," "I wish things could have been different." Again, much more important than our words is the child's sense that we are with her, not against her. When the time is right, putting some sadness in our voice can prime the movement to tears and disappointment. It might take some practice to feel this point; to go too quickly or to be too wordy can backfire. This dance cannot be choreographed; the parent has to feel his way along. Here, too, we learn by trial and error.

At times the parent can make all the right moves and still fail miserably in priming the adaptive process. The problem might be that the child does not perceive the parent as a safe source of attachment comfort. More often, the tears do not flow because the adaptive process is stuck: a casualty of the child's having become too defended against vulnerability. Futility does not sink in.

Adaptation works both ways. Sometimes we parents may need to adapt to our children's lack of adaptiveness. When the process that promotes natural discipline is not active in our child, we need to retreat from our attempts to press forward. At such times we need to find our own sadness and let go of our futile expectations. Letting go of what doesn't work, we are more likely to stumble upon what does. If the telltale signs of adaptation are lacking—if the child's eyes don't water when agendas are foiled, if loss does not evoke sadness, if mad does not move to sad—the parent will need to find another way to create order out of chaos. Fortunately, other ways do exist.

### Solicit Good Intentions Instead of Demanding Good Behavior

The fourth shift in thinking calls for a change of focus from behavior to intention. Intentions are greatly undervalued. The prevailing sentiment in our society is that intentions are not good enough, that only appropriate behavior is to be accepted and applauded. Is not the road to hell paved with good intentions? From a developmental perspective, nothing could be farther from the truth. Good intentions are like gold: intention is the seed of values and the precursor of a sense of responsibility. It sets the stage for mixed feelings. To neglect intention is to overlook one of the most valuable resources in a child's experience.

Our objective, whenever possible, should be to solicit good intentions in the child. Success requires, once again, that the child should want to be good for us, to be open to being influenced by us. The first step, as always, must be to collect the child, to cultivate the connection that empowers us.

Next we use our influence to coax the child in the right direction—or at least in a direction incompatible with trouble. It isn't enough for children to know what we want. The intention to comply must be their own. For a toddler not wanting to go with mommy, it would involve collecting him and then priming an intention that would get him going in the direction you desired. "Do you think you could give a hug to grandma now and say good-bye?" "I need some help carrying this to the car. Do you think you can carry it for me?" The trick is to get the child's hands on his own steering wheel — just as at an amusement park many rides will have little steering wheels that do not actually direct the train or vehicle but allow the small driver to believe that he is in charge. Better yet is to anticipate problems before they occur by appealing to the child's own sense of mastery. For example, if you know you are going to meet resistance when it is time to leave, collect the child beforehand and solicit an intention to come when you say it is time to leave. "Will you be ready to get your shoes on when we need to go?" Acknowledging that it may be hard for the child but asking her if she thinks she can do it should bring her onside.

Soliciting good intentions in older children involves sharing with them your own values or finding within them the seeds of your values. For example, a parent might share his own goals regarding the handling of frustration: "I'm always proud of myself when I can feel frustrated without insulting anyone. I think you're old enough now to give it a try. What do you think? Are you willing to work on it?" For children who tend to get caught up in their own intensity, it might involve a little preventive huddle before the child is about to engage in an activity where problems are likely to occur. "I know when you're having fun, sometimes you get carried away and forget to stop when somebody is asking you to. Could I count on you to give it a try? I know you love it when the other kids are here to play and would like it to last as long as possible."

We are not saying that soliciting a good intention will automatically result in the desired behavior. Even for adults, good intentions don't always translate into action. But the child has to start somewhere, and aiming in the right direction is where to begin.

In soliciting a good intention, we are trying to draw attention not to our will but to the child's. Instead of "I want you to . . . ," "You need to . . . ," "You have to . . . ," "I told you to . . . ," "You must . . ." elicit a declaration of intention or at least a nod affirming it: "Can I count on you to . . . ?" "Are you willing to give it a try?" "Do you think you could?" "Are you ready to . . . ?" "Do you think you can handle it now?" "Will you try to remember?" There are, of course, times when we need to impose our will. Necessary as that may be, it does not by itself lead to good intentions on the child's part. And imposing our will is always counterproductive if done too coercively or outside a good connection.

Soliciting good intentions is a safe and highly effective parenting practice. It transforms kids from the inside out. What cannot be accomplished through soliciting good intentions is not likely to be achieved by other means.

It is essential to acknowledge a child's positive intentions instead of identifying him with his impulses, actions, or failures. The parent needs to be as supportive and encouraging as possible: "I know this isn't what you wanted to happen," "It's okay, you'll get there," "I'm glad you didn't mean to, that's important." Unless we take the sting out of the inevitable failures, the child will be tempted to give up. Intentions need to be carefully nurtured to bring them to fruition.

If we can't get to first base in soliciting good intentions, either the child isn't mature enough or we aren't persuasive enough—or there are problems in the attachment relationship. The child's attachment to us may be shut down—defended against—or insufficiently developed. Our inability to solicit good intentions in the child should alert us to these underlying problems and move us to take remedial action. Even our short-term failures can, in this way, serve a positive long-term purpose. To harp on the child's "bad" behavior when we can't even solicit an intention to be good is putting the cart before the horse.

### Draw Out the Mixed Feelings Instead of Trying to Stop Impulsive Behavior

"Stop hitting," "Don't interrupt," "Cut that out," "Leave me alone," "Stop acting like a baby," "Don't be so rude," "Get ahold of yourself," "Stop being so hyper," "Don't be silly," "Stop bugging her," "Don't be so mean." Trying to stop impulsive behavior is like standing in front of a freight train and commanding it to stop. When a child's behavior is driven by instinct and emotion, there is little chance of imposing order through confrontation and barking commands.

There was a time in the history of psychology when the brain of the child was perceived to be a tabula rasa, a blank slate, free of internal forces compelling the child to act one way or another. Were that the case, a child's behavior would be relatively easy to bring under control, either through direction or through consequences. Though many parents and educators still operate under this illusion, modern science has established a completely different perspective. Neuropsychologists who study the human brain are uncovering the instinctual roots of behavior. Many of a child's responses are driven by instincts and emotions that arise spontaneously and automatically, not from conscious decisions. In most circumstances, children (and other immature human beings) are already under internal orders to behave in a certain way. The fearful child is following instinctual orders to avoid. The insecure child may be compelled to cling and hold on. Frustration often induces a child to demand or to cry or to attack. The shamed child is under orders to hide or conceal. The resistant child automatically counters the will of another. When a child is impulsive, impulses rule. There is order in this universe, just not the kind of order we would like to see. The brain is only doing its job in moving the child according to the emotions and instincts activated.

There is an alternative to confrontation. The key to self-control is not willpower, as we once thought, but mixed feelings. It is when conflicting impulses mix together that the orders cancel each other out, putting the child in the driver's seat, as it were. A new order emerges where behavior is rooted in intention rather than impulse. Such behavior is much less driven and therefore much easier to work with. Our job is to help bring the conflicting feelings and thoughts that exist in the child into his consciousness. Remember, from Chapter 9, that the root meaning of temper was to mix together different elements—and that's precisely what we need to do! Rather than trying to address the behavior, we draw out *the tempering element* to moderate the impulse that gets the child into trouble.

In a child full of attacking feelings, for example, we want to draw into his consciousness the feelings, thoughts, and impulses that would conflict with attacking. This goal cannot be achieved by means of confrontation. Confrontation leads, at best, to an empty compliance or, on the other hand, to defensiveness. It does nothing to develop impulse control from within. The moderating elements could be feelings of affection, of caring, or of alarm. The child could feel a concern about hurting or anxiety about getting into trouble. If the child is driven by counterwill impulses, we would want to pull into awareness strong feelings of attachment, of wanting to please, of desire to measure up. The trick is to draw the mixed feelings into consciousness at the same time.

When coaxing conflicting feelings into consciousness, we need to get outside the incident in which the problem occurs and inside the relationship where we can take the lead. That task should be attempted only when the intensity of the feelings has eased somewhat.

It is always wiser to remind the child first of the moderating impulses than the uncontrolled emotions that got him into trouble. Once the child is feeling friendly and affectionate we can recount the frustration that went before. "We are having such a good time together right now. I remember this morning when you weren't too happy with me. In fact, you were so angry, you really let me have it." We need to build some room for these mixed feelings. "Isn't it funny the way we can get so mad at the ones we love." Likewise with feelings of counterwill. "It seems right now that it is easy for you to do what I ask. A couple of hours ago, you felt I was bossing you around."

Approaching problem behavior by drawing out the tempering element is attachment-friendly. We as parents take the lead in seeing both "this" and "that" in the child. We invite conflicting elements to exist and communicate acceptance of what is within the child. Discipline of this kind draws our children to us instead of pushing them away.

We often tell our children to cut it out—as if they could perform psychic surgery on themselves! We cannot cut out of a child's repertoire behavior that is deeply rooted in instinct and emotion. The impulses are with us as long as we live. Unless we have become numbed, we should all feel the impulses associated with shame, with insecurity, jealousy, possessiveness, fear, frustration, guilt, counterwill, dread, and anger. Nature's answer is not to cut something out, but to add something to consciousness that would, if necessary, check the impulse in question.

### When Dealing with an Impulsive Child, Try Scripting the Desired Behavior Instead of Demanding Maturity

Not all children are ready for the more advanced ways of encouraging and teaching discipline we have so far discussed. Those, for example, who have not yet developed mixed feelings are incapable of tempered experience, no matter how skilled or how diligent we may be.

Children who have trouble with self-control also lack the ability to recognize the impact of their behavior or to anticipate consequences. They are incapable of thinking twice before acting or of appreciating how their actions affect other people. They lack the capacity to consider anyone else's point of view simultaneously with their own. These children are often judged to be insensitive, selfish, uncooperative, uncivilized, and even uncaring. To perceive them in such a way, however, is only to set ourselves up for becoming incensed at their conduct and for making demands they cannot possibly fulfill. Children limited to a one-dimensional awareness cannot execute even such simple demands as be good, don't be rude, don't interrupt, be nice, be fair, don't be mean, be patient, don't make a scene, try to get along—or myriad other orders we may bark at them. We cannot get our children to be more mature than they are, no matter how much we insist they "grow up." Expecting them to do the impossible is frustrating and, worse, suggests that there is something wrong with them. Children cannot endure such a sense of shame without becoming defensive. To preserve our relationship with a child not yet capable of mature functioning, we have to jettison unrealistic demands and expectations.

There is another way to deal with immature children: rather than demanding that they spontaneously exhibit mature behavior, we could script the desired behavior. Following our directions will not make the child more mature, but it will enable him to function in social situations that otherwise she is not yet developmentally ready for.

To script a child's behavior is to provide the cues for what to do and how to do it. When children are not yet capable of getting along spontaneously, their actions need to be orchestrated or choreographed by someone the child is taking the cues from: "This is how you hold the baby," "Let's give Matthew a turn now," "If there is a hug in you for grandma, this would be the time to give it," "We pet the cat like this," "It's daddy's turn to talk now," "This is the time to use your quiet voice."

Successful scripting requires the adult to position himself as a cue-giver for the child. Again, we begin with the basics: we collect the child first in order to be able to work from within the relationship. It is very much like the mother goose with goslings; getting the offspring into line before bringing the behavior into line. Once a child is following us, we are free to take the lead. Of course, our ability to prescribe a child's behavior will be only as good as the child's attachment to us. It doesn't have to be particularly deep or vulnerable, only strong enough to evoke the instincts to emulate and to imitate.

For successful directing, the cues for what to do and how to be must be given in ways the child can follow. It doesn't work to give negative instructions because that does not actually tell the child what to do. In fact, for the immature and severely stuck, all that registers is often the action part of the command! The "don't" is often deleted from awareness, leading to the opposite behavior of what was desired. Our focus must be diverted away from the behavior that causes trouble and focus on the actions that are desirable. Modeling the behavior you want the child to follow is even more effective. Like a director working with actors or a choreographer with dancers, the end result is created first in the adult's mind.

An example of scripting to get the desired behavior—one that we are much more likely to be intuitive about—is teaching a child to ski. In this case, we are quite cognizant of the fact that it is useless to say to a child,

"Get your balance," "Don't fall," "Slow down," "Ski in control," "Make your turns." These will be the outcomes of properly scripted behavior, but they cannot be what we demand, at least not until the child learns to ski. Instead, we may show a child how to make a pizza wedge with his skis and then proceed to give cues that the child can follow—like "Make a pizza," "Step down on your right," "Touch your knees," and so on. The end result will be balance, breaks, and turns. It looks as if the novice skier knows how to ski; in reality the child is only following the cues until the actions become ingrained and, finally, self-generated. Unlike in skiing, in human interaction we do not gain the capacity to generate from within the appropriate actions and responses until maturity.

When it comes to social behavior, we must not focus on the relationships between children. This process of directing is one of the child following the adult. Scripting is not designed to teach a child social skills—generally an exercise in futility—but to orchestrate the social interaction until maturation and genuine socialization emerge. That is why the focus is not on the relationship between the children but on following the cues of the adult.

The following story was told to me by a close friend whose job involved supervising teachers. This incident happened when she was observing a second-grade teacher who had an outstanding reputation for her inspiring ways with students. A special-needs student had asked to leave the room to go to the bathroom. On his reentry into class, he exclaimed that this time he had been able to do it himself. He was quite unaware that his pants and underwear were still at his ankles. What happened next was amazing. Instead of the shaming laughter that one would expect on such an occasion, these students whirled around to look at their teacher. She applauded appreciatively and all the students followed suit.

The interaction was wonderfully civilized and amazingly gracious. To sense another's vulnerability and move to protect it takes both maturity and skill. The maturity and skill, however, were in the teacher, not in the students. In their case what looked like social competence was simply following cues. The answer was not in the relationships between the students but in the relationship of each student with his or her teacher. Immature beings should not be left to their own devices in social interaction.

Many kinds of behavior can be scripted: fairness, helping, sharing, cooperation, conversation, gentleness, consideration, getting along. Although getting children to act mature will not make them more mature, it will keep them out of trouble until the underlying impediments to maturation can be addressed and their maturity catches up. Helping children keep out of trouble by scripting safeguards attachment and works both ways— helping their attachment to us and our attachment to them.

### When Unable to Change the Child, Try Changing the Child's World

The less children are in need of discipline, the more effective any method will be. The obverse is also true: the more a child is in need of discipline, the less effective the commonly taught disciplining techniques will be.

What makes any child difficult to discipline is the absence of the factors that provide the basis for our natural principles of imposing order on behavior. It is difficult to discipline a child who is not easily induced to consider the thoughts and feelings that would keep the troubling impulses in check, who cannot be brought to form good intentions, is unable to feel the futility of a course of action, and lacks the motivation to be good for those in charge. With such children the temptation for us is to become more heavy-handed. Unfortunately, adding force usually backfires for the very same reasons that this child is more difficult to discipline in the first place: coercion elicits counterwill, punishment provokes retaliation, yelling leads to tuning out, sanctions evoke aggression, time-outs lead to emotional detachment. When reasonable attempts to discipline do not work, the answer is not to discipline harder but to discipline differently.

Given that coercive techniques are ultimately self-defeating, we come now to the last but by no means least important instrument in the tool kit of natural discipline techniques: imposing order on the child's environment. The intent here is not to change or extirpate "bad" behavior but to alter the experiences that give rise to the behavior. Instead of trying to change the child in these cases, it would be more fruitful, if we can, to alter the situations and circumstances that trigger the problem behavior.

This approach to discipline requires three things of the parent: (1) the ability to feel the futility of other disciplinary modes and to let go of what does not work, (2) insight about what factors in the child's environment trigger the troublesome behavior, and (3) some ability to change or control these adverse factors. It takes a truly adaptive parent to sense the futility of harping on behavior and to stop railing against what the parent cannot change: in this case, the child's impulsive behavior. It takes a wise parent to focus on what the child is reacting to: the circumstances and situations surrounding the child. In other words, a parent must first let go of trying to change the child.

Insight is key. One needs to get past the problem behavior to see what the child is reacting to. How we see the problem will ultimately determine what we do about it. If what we perceive is that a child is being willful, we are inclined to focus narrowly on trying to fix his behavior, which we dislike and resent. If, instead, we recognized that a child is simply getting carried away by his impulses, we would be more apt to alter the situation that evoked those impulses in the first place. If all we see is that a child is throwing a tantrum or is striking out at someone, we are likely to focus on the aggression. If, on the other hand, we recognized that a child is unable to handle the frustration he is experiencing, we would try to change the circumstances that frustrate him. If what we see is a child defying our demands to stay in his room at bedtime, we might treat it as a case of disobedience. But if we perceive, instead, a young child overcome by fears of separation or of darkness, we would do what we could to make bedtime less threatening. If we see a child resisting doing what he is told, we want to root out the noncompliance. If, instead, we see that a child's counterwill buttons are being pushed by the pressure he feels, we would reduce the pressure we are applying. We might confront a child about his "bad" manners if we see him simply as being rude to an adult in refusing to communicate. If we recognized that only the child's inherent shyness inhibits him from interacting with people he doesn't know, we would do what we could to put him at ease. If we see a child as a liar, we are likely to confront his untruths in a judgmental and stern manner; if we had the wisdom to know that a child conceals the truth only because he is too insecure in our love to risk our wrath or disappointment, we would do everything in our power to restore his sense of absolute security. "Who alone has good reason to lie his way out of reality?" wrote Friedrich Nietzsche. "He who suffers from it."

In all these situations, our intervention will be only as effective as our insight is sound. But when the child's environment is affecting her behavior and that behavior is out of both her and our control, it only makes sense to shift our focus from the child's behavior to what provokes it.

But if we continually alter the child's situation to reduce the frustration or pressure she experiences, do we not risk undermining the child's adaptation to her world? Do we not foster unhealthy dependence on us? That is very true. In my consulting practice with parents, I encounter many sensitive and caring parents who unwittingly interfere with their child's adaptation by using this approach to the extreme. It should never be employed to the exclusion of other methods of discipline, such as drawing out feelings of futility when up against things that can't or shouldn't be changed. We must never fail to help a child move from frustration to futility, whenever that is possible, to cultivate mixed feelings or to solicit good intentions. If we are able to encourage a positive change in the child, we should not be trying to change the child's world instead.

We return briefly to the subject of structure, which I touched on in the last chapter. The use of structure and routine is a powerful way of imposing order on a child's world, and thus on the child's behavior. The less receptive a child is to other modes of discipline, the more we need to compensate by structuring the child's life. Structures create a child's environment in a predictable fashion, imposing some needed ritual and routine. That has been one of the traditional functions of culture, but as customs and traditions are eroded, life becomes less structured, more chaotic. In such an atmosphere, children who are developmentally immature become unglued. Parents react by becoming more prescriptive and coercive. The combination is disastrous.

Structures need to be created for meals and for bedtimes, for separations and for reunions, for hygiene and for putting things away, for family interaction and closeness, for practice and for homework, for emergent, self-directed play and for creative solitude. Good structures do not draw attention to themselves or the underlying agenda, and they minimize bossing and coercion. Good structures are not only restrictions, they are creative. For example, a very important routine is to have a time and place to read to a child. The primary purpose of this structure is to create opportunity for one-on-one closeness and connection and also to get the child engaged in good literature without using coercion.

The more a child is stuck, the more important structures are. Structures provide familiarity, something stuck kids instinctively yearn for. They create good habits. Most important, structures decrease the need for bossing and coercion on the part of adults, preventing needless conflict.

In this chapter we have avoided methods that would push the child away from us. Parents in days gone by may have gotten away with such techniques, but if they did, it was only because they had no reason to fear the competing attachments with which today's parents are confronted. There was no peer orientation to draw children outside the family circle. Today we have no reasonable choice but to employ a discipline that preserves our connection with the child and promotes maturation. Maturation—the ultimate solution to discipline problems—cannot be achieved overnight, but our patience will be well rewarded. And even in the short term we parents surely have enough to deal with without provoking our children.

# PART FIVE

# PREVENTING PEER ORIENTATION

# DON'T COURT THE COMPETITION

W̲E HAVE TO stop setting up our children's peers to replace us—keeping in mind, of course, that the enemy is not our children's peers but peer orientation.

We have been taken in by peer orientation, much like the ancient people of Troy were fooled by the Trojan Horse. Perceiving this large wooden horse to be a gift from the gods, the Trojans brought it within the walls of their city and set the stage for their destruction. In the same way, today's parents and teachers view early and extensive peer interaction in a positive light. We encourage it, unaware of the risks that arise when such interaction occurs without adult leadership and input. We fail to distinguish between peer relationships formed under the conscious and benign guidance of adults and peer contacts occurring in attachment voids. Unwittingly, we encourage peer orientation to sabotage our children's attachments to us. If the Trojans could have seen their Greek enemies lurking within that deceptive contraption they would not have been hoodwinked. That is our problem today. The Trojan Horse of peer orientation is perceived as a gift rather than the threat it is.

Our failure to foresee the ill effects is understandable, since the early fruits are appealing and enticing. At first glance peer-oriented children appear to be more independent, less clingy, more schoolable, more sociable and sophisticated. No wonder we are taken in, given our lack of awareness of the mechanisms involved and of the costs to follow in the long term. How, then, to avoid the trap?

## DON'T BE FOOLED BY THE
## FIRST FRUITS OF PEER ORIENTATION

For many adults, children's ability to hang out together and entertain one another feels like emancipation. Peers appear to be a kid's best babysitters. Especially since parents can no longer rely on grandparents, extended family, and the community around us to share in child-care tasks, peers can seem like a godsend, giving a break to weary and worn parents and teachers. How many of us have not felt grateful when the invitation from our child's friend has liberated us for a weekend day of relaxation or has granted us much needed time and space to work on necessary projects? The children seem happy and our workload is lightened. Little can we imagine just how much more time, energy, cost, and remedial parenting these experiences will exact in later years should peer orientation take hold.

Compared with adult-oriented kids, peer-oriented children come across as less needy and more mature. Peer-oriented kids no longer put pressure on us to do things together, to be involved in their lives, to listen to their concerns, to help them with their problems. With the high premium we in our society place on independence—our own and our children's—peer orientation looks good. We forget that growing up takes time. In our postindustrial culture we are in too much of a hurry for everything. We probably would not be taken in by false impressions if we weren't so impatient for our children to grow up.

These children are able to let go of us earlier only because they are holding on to each other. In the long term they are more likely to be stuck in psychological immaturity. They are much less likely to think for themselves, chart their own course, make their own decisions, find their own meanings, and be their own persons.

Helping to lull us into complacency is the fact that, at least initially, peer-oriented children also tend be more schoolable. The cost of that mistaken impression, the loss of teachability, was discussed in Chapter 13. Peer orientation can make a child temporarily more school-friendly, owing to the effects of separation on learning. School takes children out of the home, separating parent-oriented children from the adults to whom they are attached. For such children the separation anxiety will be intense and the sense of disorientation at school will be acute. Many of us are able to remember our own first days in a new school situation—the tightness in the stomach, feeling lost and confused, scanning desperately for someone or something familiar. For young children this disorientation is often unbearable and the elevated anxiety it provokes interferes with learning. Anxiety dumbs us down, lowering our functional I.Q. Being alarmed affects our ability to focus and to remember. Anxiety makes it difficult to read the cues and follow directions. A child simply cannot learn well when feeling lost and alarmed.

Children already peer-oriented by the time they enter school do not face such a dilemma. In the first days of school in kindergarten, a peer-oriented child would appear smarter, more confident, and better able to benefit from the school experience. The parent-oriented child, impaired by separation anxiety would, by contrast, appear to be less adept and capable — at least until he can form a good attachment with a teacher. Peer-oriented kids have all the advantages in situations that are adult poor and peer rich. Because peers are plentiful and easy to spot, the child need never feel lost or without cues to follow. Thus, in the short term, peer orientation appears to be a godsend. And it is undoubtedly this dynamic that research taps into when discovering benefits to early education.

In the long term, of course, the positive effects on learning of reduced anxiety and disorientation will gradually be canceled by the negative effects of peer orientation. Thus follows the research evidence that early advantages of preschool education are not sustainable over time.[1] Peer-oriented kids go to school to be with their friends, not to learn. If these friends are also not into learning, academic performance will slip. When children go to school to be with one another, they are primed only to learn enough to not stand out, to remain with those their own age. Other than that, learning is irrelevant and can even be a liability to peer relationships.

Anxiety also comes back to haunt peer-oriented learners. Because peer attachments are inherently insecure, anxiety often becomes a chronic condition. Peer-oriented kids are among the most agitated, perpetually restless, and chronically alarmed. When around groups of peer-oriented kids, one can almost sense the hyperness in the air. Numb to the vulnerable feelings of anxiety, peer-oriented children are left only with its physiological aspects: agitation and restlessness. Whether consciously felt or not, being alarmed incapacitates learning. Peer orientation may initially enhance performance but ultimately sabotages academic achievement. As a child's attachment to his peers intensifies, the gap between his intelligence and achievement will grow. The very condition that usually creates the head start will ultimately trip these kids up.

Interestingly, home-schoolers are now the favored applicants of some big-name universities.[2] According to Jon Reider, admissions official at Stanford University in California, they are desirable applicants because "home-schoolers bring certain skills—motivation, curiosity, the capacity to be responsible for their education—that high schools don't induce very well."[3] In other words, preschooled kids may have the best head start, but homeschooled kids have the best finish, because in our educational system we have neglected the crucial role of attachment.

Preschool is not the primary problem and home school is not the ultimate answer. The key factor is the dynamic of attachment. Subjecting children to experiences that make a child dependent on peers does not work. We need to ground children's experience of schooling in adult attachments.

## SHYNESS IS NOT THE PROBLEM WE THINK IT IS

We usually think of shyness as a negative quality, something we would want children to overcome. Yet developmentally, even this apparent handicap has a useful function. Shyness is an attachment force, designed to shut the child down socially, discouraging any interaction with those outside her nexus of safe connections.

The shy child is timid around people she is not attached to. It is only to be expected that adult-oriented children are often socially naive and awkward around their peers, at least in the earlier grades. Peer-oriented kids, by contrast, appear to be socially successful. This is their forte. They should know what is cool and what is not, what to wear and how to talk—they are applying most of their intelligence to reading from one another the cues on how to be and how to act.

Much of the sociability of peer-oriented children is the result of a loss of shyness. When peers replace adults, shyness is reversed. The child becomes shy with adults but gregarious in the company of peers. We see the child around her peers coming out of her shell, finding her tongue, presenting herself more confidently. The change in personality is impressive, and we are apt to give credit to the peer interaction. Surely, we tell ourselves, such a highly desirable outcome could not emanate from something problematic! Yet true social integration and real social ability—caring about others and considering the feelings of people they do not know—will not, in the long term, be the attributes of the peer-oriented child.

Adult-oriented children are much slower to lose their shyness around their peers. What should eventually temper this shyness is not peer orientation but the psychological maturity that engenders a strong sense of self and the capacity for mixed feelings. The best way to deal with shyness is to promote warm relationships with the adults who care for and teach the child. With attachment in mind, it's not shyness we ought to be so concerned about but the lack of shyness of many of today's children.

## THE STRESS OF DAY CARE IN
## THE ABSENCE OF ATTACHMENT

The current day-care situation illustrates how, unwittingly, we court the competition. Millions of children throughout the world today spend some if not most of their waking hours in out-of-home care. According to recent statistics, the majority of working mothers in the United States return to work before the child's first birthday.[4] Day care, especially the way it is being approached in America, is risky business. Children find day care stressful, as recent studies have shown. The level of the stress hormone cortisol is higher in children at day care than at home.[5] The stressful effects of day care increase with the shyness of the child. As we have seen, shyness reflects a lack of emotional connection. A child would not come across as shy if she felt at home with the caregiver in charge. In the absence of a warm connection, she faces the double stress of separation from the parent and of having people imposed upon her whom her natural instinct is to repel.

Another line of research has shown that the more time preschoolers spend with one another, the more they are influenced by their peers.[6] That influence is measurable within a period of only several months. Boys are much more susceptible to becoming peer-oriented than girls, a finding consistent with the observation that boys' attachments to their parents are often less developed. Thus, they are more prone to replacing their parents with their peers. Most significant is the finding that the more the boys identify with their peers, the more resistant they are to contact with the adults in charge.

Not only are the seeds of peer orientation sown in day care and preschool, but the fruit is already in evidence by the fifth year of life. One of the largest studies ever done on this subject followed more than a thousand children from birth to kindergarten.[7] The more time a child had spent in day care, the more likely she was to manifest aggression and disobedience, both at home and in kindergarten. As discussed in previous chapters, aggression and disobedience are the legacy of peer orientation.

The more they had been in day care, the more these children exhibited counterwill as indicated by arguing, sneakiness, talking back to staff, and failure to take direction. Their elevated frustration was indicated by temper tantrums, fighting, hitting, cruelty to others, and the destruction of their own things. These children were also more desperate in their attachment behavior: given to boasting, bragging, incessant talking, and striving for attention, as we would expect when attachments are not working.

Peer orientation is not the only cause of disturbed attachments, but in our children's world it is the major one. Viewed through the lens of attachment, the findings of the three lines of research could not be clearer in pointing to the risk of our young of becoming peer-oriented in our day cares and our preschools. The most obvious solution would be to keep them home, especially the most shy and vulnerable ones, until they're mature enough to handle the stress of separation from parents. In response to these research findings, a number of experts, including Stanley Greenspan[8] and Eleanor Maccoby,[9] have advised parents to do just that, if they have the financial resources to do so. While this advice makes sense in light of the data, it misses the point. Children don't need to be at home but they most certainly need to feel at home with those who are responsible for them. *Home* is a matter of attachment and attachment is something we can create. Being *related* is not the issue in child care; being *connected* most certainly is.

The shyness of a child in a particular setting should be a sign to us that the context is not present yet where that child is ready to be taken care of. We create that context by connecting with him. I find this true, even with my own grandchildren. My challenge is first to collect them. Once I have, the shyness melts away and they become receptive to my grandparenting.

Day care and preschool do not have to be risky, but to reduce the risk, we need to be aware of attachment. The adults involved need to be willing to create a context of connection with our children. Meanwhile, there are things we can do as parents, both in selecting the settings our children are involved in, as well as fostering connections between our children and the adults in charge whenever possible. Yes, one solution may be to keep children at home until they can hold us emotionally close even when physically apart from us—or until they are mature enough to function independently, apart from attachments. The other solution is for them to become attached to their caregivers and teachers. That will protect our children (and these adults) from being stressed and will keep us from being prematurely replaced. More on how we can do this will follow in our next and final chapter.

## GETTING ALONG WITH OTHERS DOES NOT ARISE FROM PEER CONTACT

"When my son was three years old I felt it very important to enroll him in groups and circumstances where he could be with other kids," a father recalls. "The less successful he was at making friends, the more frantic I became to encourage his interactions with other children, to set up situations where he would have the opportunity to play with his peers and to form relationships with them." Many parents experience a similar drive to induct their children early into the peer world. Even those parents whose instincts are to hold on to their children longer before exposing them to peer influences may feel themselves under tremendous pressure from family or friends or parenting professionals to "loosen the apron strings."

The conviction is almost universal that children must be exposed to interaction with peers early so that they may learn to get along with one another and to fit in. Many parents seek playgroups for their toddlers. By the preschool age, arranging peer contacts for our children has often become an obsession. "Learning how to be a friend is more important than anything. It's essential to learn this before school starts," typifies the comments I have heard from many parents of preschoolers. "As parents, we need to force our children to socialize," the father of a four-year-old asserted. "Without preschool our son wouldn't be mixing with other kids enough to learn how to get along with people." One early childhood educator informed me that "the whole basis of preschool is to help children learn social skills. If children don't have friends by the time they enter kindergarten they will have all kinds of trouble later on, not only socially but with self-esteem and learning." The less children are able to get along and fit in, the more likely it is that interaction with their peers is prescribed to fix the problem. Commonly in our society parents and teachers go out of their way to enable their children and students to socialize with one another.

The belief is that socializing—children spending time with one another—begets socialization: the capacity for skillful and mature relating to other human beings. There is no evidence to support such an assumption, despite its popularity. If socializing with peers led to getting along and to becoming responsible members of society, the more time a child spent with her peers, the better the relating would tend to be. In actual fact, the more children spend time with one another, the less likely they are to get along and the less likely they are to fit into civil society. If we take the socialization assumption to the extreme—to orphanage children, street children, children involved in gangs—the flaw in thinking becomes obvious. If socializing were the key to socialization, gang members and street kids would be model citizens.

Dr. Urie Bronfenbrenner and his team of researchers at Cornell University in Ithaca, New York, compared children who gravitated to their peers in their free time to children who gravitated to their parents. Among these sixth graders the children who preferred spending time with their parents demonstrated many more of the characteristics of positive sociability. The kids who spend the most time with one another are the most likely to get into trouble.[10]

Such findings are not surprising. They are only what we may expect once we understand the natural order of human development. Attachment and individuation are necessary for maturation, and maturation is necessary for genuine socialization. Social integration means much more than simply fitting in or getting along; true social integration requires not only a mixing with others but a mixing without losing one's separateness or identity.

To be sure, socializing plays a part in rendering a child capable of true social integration, but only as a finishing touch. The child must first of all be able to hold on to herself when interacting with others and to perceive the others as separate beings. This is no easy task, even for adults. When a child knows her own mind and values the separateness of another's mind, then—and only then—is she ready to hold on to her sense of self, while respecting that of the other person. Once this developmental milestone is achieved, social interaction will hone the child's individuality and hone his relationship skills as well.

The real challenge is helping children to grow up to the point where they can benefit from their socializing experiences. Very little socializing is required to refine the raw material once it is at the state of readiness. It is the raw material that is precious and rare—an individuality robust enough to survive the grinding pressures of peer interaction. Mixing indiscriminately and prematurely, without adults being involved as the primary attachment figures, will lead either to conflict, as each child seeks to dominate the other or has to resist being dominated, or to cloning, as a child suppresses his sense of himself for the sake of acceptance by others. "We thought that playing with other kids was very important for our boys when they were very young," says Robert, the father of two sons, now both teenagers. "Frankie, our eldest, drove his playmates crazy with his demands that every game be done his way. He threw tantrums if they didn't follow his lead—it became difficult, finally, to arrange play dates for him. The younger one, Rickie, became a follower. He just copied whatever other kids initiated. He never learned how to be a leader or even to play on his own."

I can imagine that at this point many readers are wondering, "But what of the importance of learning how to get along?" I'm not disputing the advantages of getting along; what I am saying is that if we make it the priority, we're putting the cart before the horse. By placing getting along at the top of the agenda for immature beings, we are really pushing them into patterns of compliance, imitation, and conformity. If the child's attachment needs are strong and directed toward peers, she may diminish herself to make things work. She will lose her individuality. Many of us experience a similar risk even as adults when we are too desperate to make things work with someone else: losing ourselves with others, giving in much too quickly, backing away from conflict, avoiding any upset. Children have even greater difficulty holding on to themselves when interacting with others. What is praised as getting along in children would, in adult life, be called compromising oneself or selling oneself short or not being true to oneself.

If we were truly in harmony with the developmental blueprint, we would not be so concerned about children getting along with one another. We would place a higher value on children's becoming able to hold on to themselves when interacting with others. All the socializing in the world could never bring a child to this point. Only a viable relationship with nurturing adults can give birth to true independence and individuality, qualities that we all, as parents, would most want for our children. Only in that context can unfold the fully developed personality, a human being able to respect self and to value the personhood of others.

## IT IS NOT FRIENDS THAT CHILDREN NEED

But don't children have social needs? One of the most pressing concerns and questions of the parents and educators I meet has to do with the child's perceived need for friends. "Children must have friends" is perhaps the most common argument I hear on behalf of placing young kids in peer situations.

The very concept of friendship is meaningless when applied to immature people. As adults, we would not consider a person to be a true friend unless he treated us with consideration, acknowledged our boundaries, and respected us as individuals. A true friend supports our development and growth, regardless of how that would affect the relationship. This concept of friendship is based on a solid foundation of mutual respect and individuality. True friendship is not possible, therefore, until a certain level of maturity has been realized and a capacity for social integration has been achieved. Many children are not even remotely capable of such friendships.

Until children are capable of true friendship, they really do not need friends, just attachments. And the only attachments a child needs are with family and those who share responsibility for the child. What a child really needs is to become capable of true friendship, a fruit of maturation that develops only in a viable relationship with a caring adult. Our time is more wisely spent cultivating relationships with the adults in our child's life than obsessing about their relationships with one another.

Of course, it is self-fulfilling that when a child replaces parents with peers, friends become more important than family. We declare that this must be normal and then take the irrational leap of assuming that this must also be natural. We then go out of our way to make sure our children have "friends," putting at risk the relationships with the family. Peers displace parents ever further, and the downward spiral perpetuates itself.

One more word about friendship. Developmentally, children have a much greater need for a relationship with themselves than for relationships with peers. There has to emerge a separation between sense of self and inner experience (see Chapter 9). A person must gain the capacity to reflect on her thoughts and feelings, a capacity that, again, is a fruit of maturation. When someone has a relationship with herself, she can like her own company, agree and disagree with herself, approve and disapprove of herself, and so on. Often, relationships with others preempt a relationship with oneself or are attempts to fill in the vacuum where a solid relationship with the self should be. When a person isn't comfortable with his own company, he is more likely to seek the company of others—or to become attached to entertainment technology such as television or video games. Peer-oriented relationships, like too much TV watching, interfere with developing a relationship with oneself. Until the child manifests the existence of a relationship with himself, he is not ready to develop genuine

relationships with other kids. Much better for him to spend time interacting with nurturing adults or in creative play, on his own.

## PEERS ARE NOT THE ANSWER TO BOREDOM

In our peer-crazy world, peers have become almost a panacea for whatever
ails the child. They are often touted as the solution to boredom, to eccentricity, and to self-esteem problems. To parents who have an only child,
peers may also seem to function as a substitute for brothers and sisters.
Here, too, we are mining for fool's gold.

"I'm bored" or "This is boring" are all-too-familiar childhood refrains.
Many parents find themselves trying to alleviate their child's boredom by
facilitating peer interaction of one kind or another. The solution may work
temporarily, but it exacerbates the underlying dynamic, just as a hungry
infant given a pacifier will only become hungrier, or a drinker who tries to
drown his sorrows in alcohol will be, in the end, even more unhappy. And
the worst of it is that in using peers to soothe boredom, we are promoting
peer orientation.

What are the true causes of boredom? The void that is felt in boredom
is not a lack of stimulation or social activity, as is typically assumed. Children become bored when their attachment instincts are not sufficiently
engaged and when their sense of self does not emerge to fill this void. It is
like being in neutral, on hold, waiting for life to begin. Children who are
able to feel the shape of this hole are more likely to talk about feelings of
loneliness, missing, and separateness. Or alternatively, their words bespeak
the lack of emergence: "I can't think of anything to do," "Nothing interests
me right now," "I've run out of ideas," "I'm not feeling very creative." Children not aware of this void in a vulnerable way feel listless and disconnected and talk about being bored.

In other words, the hole that is usually experienced as boredom is the
result of a double void of attachment and of emergence: the child is not
with someone with whom he can attach and feel comfortable, and, on the
other hand, he lacks sufficient curiosity and imagination to spend time
creatively on his own. The child who, for example, is bored in the classroom is neither invested in making things work for the teacher nor interested in what is being presented. Both attachment to the teacher and the
emergence of self-motivated wonder and curiosity are missing. The child's
psychological defenses against vulnerability keep her from registering this
void for what it is, a sense of emptiness within herself. She believes that the

boredom arises outside herself and is a quality or attribute of her situation and circumstances. "School is so boring," or "I'm so bored, there's nothing to do," when she is at home.

Ideally, such a void comes to be filled with the child's emergent self: initiative, interests, creative solitude and play, original ideas, imagination, reflection, independent momentum. When this doesn't happen, there is an urgent impulse to fill this vacuum with something else. Boredom is what a child or adult feels who is unaware of the true causes of his emptiness. Because the void is felt so indirectly, the solution is correspondingly vague. Instead of looking to our inner resources, we want a fix from the outside—something to eat, something to distract, someone to engage with. This is usually where the child's brain seizes on stimulation or social activity as the answer. Television, electronic games, or outside stimulation can cover up the void temporarily but never fill it. As soon as the distracting activity ceases, the boredom returns.

This dynamic becomes particularly acute in early adolescence, especially if attachments to adults have not become deep enough and the emergent self is undeveloped. But whether the child is three years old or thirteen, it is into this void that we as parents tend to bring a child's peers. We may arrange a play-date for the younger ones or encourage them to pursue their peers. "Why don't you see if so-and-so can play?" we say. It is precisely when children are bored, however, that they are also the most susceptible to forming attachments that will compete with us. We are saying in effect, "Take your attachment hunger to your friends and see if they can help," or "If you can't endure your sense of aloneness, go to your peers to get an attachment fix," or "Why don't you see if someone else can substitute for the sense of self that you seem to be lacking." If we really understood the roots of boredom, it would be a sign for us that our children were not ready to interact with others. The more prone to boredom they are, the more they need us and the more of their own selves needs to emerge. The more bored they are, the less prepared they are for peer interaction. For such a child it is not peer interaction we should facilitate but connections with adults or time for herself.

Peer orientation actually exacerbates the problem of boredom. Children who are seriously attached to each other experience life as very dull when not with each other. Many children, after a time of being with each other for an extended period of time, like a sleepover or a camp, will, on their return, experience tremendous ennui and seek immediate reconnection to their peers. By arresting the maturing process and triggering the flight from vulnerability, peer orientation also blocks the emergence of the vital, curious, engaged self in the child. If parents have any control over the situation at all, a time of boredom is a time to rein in the child and to fill the attachment void with those whom the child truly needs to be attached to—ourselves.

## WHEN IS PEER CONTACT ACCEPTABLE AND HOW MUCH SHOULD WE ALLOW?

It's possible, despite my disclaimers earlier in this book, that some readers may have gained an impression that I'm against children playing with other kids or having friends, even if immature ones. That would hardly be possible and it would also be completely unnatural. Kids have always had playmates their age, in all societies throughout history, but in most of those societies there was no danger of peer contacts being transformed into peer orientation. Children's interactions occurred in the context of strong adult attachments. Today's parents also cannot be expected to isolate their children from peers, but they do have to be aware of the dangers.

When and under what circumstances should we encourage or allow children to be around one another? It is only to be expected that children will be around each other in day care, in kindergarten, on the playground, in school. But if we made sure that our children were deeply attached to us, we shouldn't have to fear them spending time together, although we do have to limit such times and we should make sure that a nurturing adult is close by and involved. The point is not that we ought to completely forbid peer interaction, but that we should have modest expectations: play time with other kids is fun, and that's it. After every play experience we should be sure to collect our kids. And certainly, when a child has spent most of the week and most of each day in peer company, we are courting the competition if we then arrange play dates for after school and on the weekend as well.

What type of childhood friendships are okay? Although, as I have explained, friendship in its true sense is hardly the word I would use to describe most childhood relationships, it's only natural that kids will want friends. The friendships we can welcome for our children are the ones that don't draw them away from us—ideally, they will be with other children whose parents share our values and also recognize the importance of adult attachments. Such children are less likely to become our unwitting competitors. And we can be active here—we can encourage our children's friends to have relationships with us. I will say more about this in our final chapter.

And what type of play? I would discourage reliance on technology when it comes to play, because it preempts originality and creativity. But we don't have to prescribe for our children how to play—children have always known how to play. We just have to make sure that their attachments to us are strong enough that their emergent, curious, motivated, imaginative selves are not shut down by peer orientation.

Finally, as I keep pointing out in this chapter, the problem in our society is not simply that our kids hang out together, but that we actually encourage extensive peer contact, looking to it as the answer to such problems as socialization or boredom or, as I will soon explain, self-esteem.

## PEERS ARE NOT THE ANSWER TO "ECCENTRICITY"

Peer interaction is routinely prescribed for yet another purpose: to take the rough edges off children who may be a bit too eccentric for our liking. We seem to have an obsession in North America with being "normal" and fitting in. Perhaps we as adults have become so peer-oriented ourselves that instead of seeking to express our own individuality, we take our cues for how to be and how to act from one another. Perhaps we remember from our own childhood the cruel intolerance of children toward those who are different and want to save our children from such a fate. Perhaps on some level we feel threatened by expressions of individuality and independence. Whatever the reason, individuality and eccentricity are out of favor. To be cool is to conform to an exceedingly narrow range of acceptable ways of looking and acting. By not standing out, we seek safety from shame, and it's not surprising that children should think this way, too. What is regrettable is that we as adults should dignify this homogenizing dynamic by honoring it and deferring to it.

The more a child depends on accepting adults, the more room there is for uniqueness and individuality to unfold and the greater the insulation against the intolerance of peers. By throwing our children to their peers, we cause them to lose the protective shield of adult attachments. They become all the more vulnerable to the intolerance of their peers. The more detached from us they become, the more they have to fit in with their peers; thus the more desperate they are to avoid being different. While they may lose their "eccentricity" in this manner, what to us looks like welcome developmental progress derives, in fact, from crippling insecurity.

## DON'T RELY ON PEERS TO
## SUSTAIN A CHILD'S SELF-ESTEEM

Another pervasive—and pernicious—myth is that peer interactions en-hance a child's self-esteem. We all want our kids to feel good about them-selves. Who among us would not want our children to have a sense of significance, to know that they matter, to believe they are wanted, to think that they are likable? The popular literature would have us believe that peers play a pivotal role in shaping a child's self-esteem. The central mes-sage seems to be that children need a circle of friends who like them in order to have a sense of self-worth. We are likewise informed that to be shunned or rejected by peers sentences a child to crippling self-doubt. There is no lack of media reports or popular journal articles to illustrate the damage inflicted on the lives of those children who have not been ac-cepted by their peers. One former textbook writer on developmental psy-chology concluded that a child's self-esteem has little to do with how a parent sees the child and everything to do with the child's status in her peer group.[11]

Given the importance of self-esteem and the supposed significance of peers in shaping it, it seems only right that we would do everything in our power to help our children cultivate friendships and to compete favorably with their peers, to make them as likable to one another as possible. Today's parents are gripped by a fear of their children being ostracized. Many par-ents find themselves buying the clothes, supporting the activities, and fa-cilitating the interaction that is believed necessary to enable their children to win friends and hold on to them. Such approaches seem only right, but they only *seem* to be right.

Peers do indeed play a pivotal role in the self-esteem of many children. That is exactly what it means to be peer-oriented. An important part of ori-entation in the world is to have a sense of one's own value and importance as a person. As peers replace parents, they become the ones who influence children's sense of what to value in oneself and in others. We shouldn't be surprised, therefore, to find that peers influence a child's self-esteem. This is not, however, how it always was, how it should be, or how it needs to be. Nor is the kind of self-esteem that is rooted in peer interaction even healthy.[12]

We are facing, first of all, a superficial understanding of the very con-cept of self-esteem. The ultimate issue in self-esteem is not how good one feels about oneself, but *the independence of self-evaluations from the judg-ments of others*. The challenge in self-esteem is to value one's existence when it's not valued by others, to believe in oneself when doubted by others, to accept oneself when judged by others. Self-esteem that is worth anything at all is the fruit of maturity: one has to have a relationship with oneself, be capable of mixed feelings, believe something to be true despite conflicting feelings. In fact, the core of healthy self-esteem is a sense of viability as a separate person. We can almost see the pride well up in a child when he is able to figure out something by himself, to stand up for himself, know he can handle something on his own. The real issues of self-esteem, therefore, involve conclusions about the validity and value of one's own existence. True self-esteem requires a psychological maturity that can only be incubated in warm, loving relationships with responsible adults.

Because peer-oriented children have difficulties growing up, they are far less likely to develop a sense of self-independence from the way others think of them. Their self-esteem will never become intrinsic, never rooted in a self-generated valuation. It will be conditional, contingent on the favor of others. Thus, it will be based on external and evanescent factors such as social achievement or looks or income. These are not measures of self-esteem. Genuine self-esteem does not say, I am worthwhile because I can do this, that, or the other. Rather, it proclaims, I am worthwhile whether or not I can do this, that, or the other.

If this view of self-esteem seems strange to some people, it's only because we live in a culture that indoctrinates an idea of self-esteem based on how we look to others. We all want to keep up with the Joneses, we all long to show off our new car or trophy boyfriend or girlfriend or spouse, and we all experience a rush of heady pride when others acknowledge or envy our achievements. But are we really esteeming the self? No, what we are esteeming is what others think of us. Is that the kind of self-esteem we want our children to develop?

The absence of an independent core to self-esteem creates a vacuum that must be filled from the outside. Trying to backfill this void of independent self-esteem with substitute material like affirmations and status and achievement is futile. No matter how positive the experiences, nothing ever sticks: the more praise one receives, the hungrier for praise one becomes; the more popular one gets, the more popular one strives to be; the more competitions one wins, the more competitive one becomes. We all know this intuitively. Our challenge is to use our influence with our children to break their dependence on popularity, appearance, grades, or achievement for the way they think and feel about themselves.

Only a self-esteem that is independent of these things is going to truly serve a child. For him to rely on his peers for something as important as his sense of significance could be disastrous. Built upon such shaky foundations, the higher a child's self-esteem, the more insecure and obsessed he will become. Kids are notoriously fickle in their relationships. They lack any sense of responsibility to temper their moods or any commitment to one another's well-being. To render a child dependent on such unpredictable evaluations is to sentence him to perpetual insecurity. Only the unconditional loving acceptance that adults can offer is able to free a child from obsessing over signs of liking and belonging.

Until children become capable of independent self-appraisal, our duty is to give them such powerful affirmation that they will not be driven to look elsewhere. Such affirmations go much deeper than positive phrases of love and praise—they must emanate from our very being and penetrate to the child's core, allowing her to know that she is loved, welcomed, enjoyed, celebrated for her very existence, regardless of whatever "good" or "bad" she may be presenting us with in any given moment. Under no circumstances is it in the child's best interests to focus on making him likable to his peers. The only way to get peers to matter less is for us to matter more.

## PEERS ARE NO SUBSTITUTES FOR SIBLINGS

One more perceived problem for which peers are thought to be the preferred solution is that of the only child. The myth has taken hold that children need to be around other children to turn out okay. Parents with one child are often quite distressed about their predicament and attempt to compensate for this presumed deprivation by becoming social conveners for their child, facilitating play dates and arranging get-togethers with other children. How can children possibly play without playmates or learn to get along without friends? they think.

We must understand, in the first place, that peers are not the same as siblings and that siblings are more than playmates. Siblings share the same working compass point. The unique attachment with the sibling is the natural offspring of the attachment with the parent. Although there are exceptions, attachments with siblings should coexist, without inherent conflict, with attachments to parents. Sibling relationships should be like the relationships of planets revolving around the same sun, secondary in nature to the relationship of each planet to the sun. More appropriate substitutes for siblings are cousins, not peers. If cousins are rare or inaccessible or a bad influence, it would be more appropriate to cultivate the kinds of family friendships in which other adults are willing to assume the role of surrogate uncle or aunt to each other's children. Relationships with adults should be the primary working attachments for the child.

To clarify once more, the trouble is not in children playing with one another, but in being left to one another when their basic attachment needs have not been met by the adults in charge. This is when our children are most at risk for forming attachments that compete with us. The more well-attached our children are to the adults who care for them, the less concerned we need to be about restricting their social play.

But don't children need to play with one another? We have to see the difference here between what children want and what they need. The play that children need for healthy development is emergent play, not social play. Emergent play (or creative solitude) does not involve interacting with others. For young children, the closeness and contact with the person attached to must be secure enough to be taken for granted. That sense of security allows the child to venture forth into a world of imagination or creativity. If playmates are involved, they stem from the child's imagination, like Hobbes for Calvin or Pooh and friends for Chistopher Robin. The parent is always the best bet for this kind of play, serving as an attachment anchor—although even the parent must not overdo it, lest the emergent play deteriorate into social play, which is far less beneficial. Children are not able to serve the function of an attachment anchor with one another, so their emergent play is almost always preempted by social interaction. Because of the strong emphasis on peer socialization, emergent play—play arising from the child's creativity, imagination, and curiosity about the world—has become endangered.

Again, I'm not saying that some social play will, by itself, harm a child's development, but it will not further it either. So, once more, it's not that children shouldn't spend time with one another, but we should not expect such play to meet their deepest needs. Only nurturing adults can do that. In our urgency for our children to socialize, we leave little time for our kids to be with us or to engage in the solitary, creative play I've called emergent play. We fill up their free time with play dates—or with videos, television, electronic games. We need to leave much more room for the self to emerge.

And that brings us back to the question of peers as sibling-substitutes. Children need adults much more than they need other children. Parents have no reason to feel bad about children who do not have siblings, nor should they feel compelled to fill the void with peers.

If we experienced the true legacy of peer orientation first—the increased counterwill, the loss of respect and regard for authority, the prolonged immaturity, the increase in aggression, the emotional hardening, the lack of receptiveness to being parented or taught—we would move quickly to address the problem. We would waste no time in working to restore our rightful place in our children's lives. But because the first fruits of peer orientation look so good, we have no inkling of what awaits us. We believe that peers are the answer to many of the problems child-rearing will throw our way. We will pay a heavy price. We must resist the temptation to welcome the Trojan Horse within our walls.

# RE-CREATE THE
# ATTACHMENT VILLAGE

$M$ANY ADULTS NOW in their forties or beyond recall childhoods in which the village of attachments was a reality. Neighbors knew one another and would visit one another's home. The parents of friends could act as surrogate parents to other children. Children played in the streets under the gaze of friendly, protective adults. There were local stores where one bought groceries or hardware or baked goods and many other items, and in these stores the merchants were more than faceless purveyors of mass-manufactured items in a chain-store setting. Much like Mr. Hooper on "Sesame Street," they were individuals one came to know and even cherish. The extended family—uncles, aunts, in-laws—would be in regular contact with one another and could also, if need be, spell the parents in the task of caring for children. Things were not ideal—they hardly ever have been in human existence—but there was a sense of rootedness, belonging, and connection that served as the invisible matrix in which children matured and gained their sense of the world. The attachment village was a place of adult orientation where culture and values were passed on vertically from one generation to the next and in which, for better or worse, children followed the lead of grown-ups.

For many of us, that attachment village no longer exists. The social and economic underpinnings that used to support traditional cultures have vanished. Gone are the cohesive communities, where extended families lived in close proximity, where children grew up among mentoring adults who did their work close to home, where cultural activities brought together generations. Most of us must share the task of raising our children with adults neither we nor our children have previously met. The majority of children in North America leave their homes almost every day to go to places where adults with whom they have no attachment connection assume responsibility for them. Keeping our children at home, for most of us, would be not be feasible. If we wish to reclaim our children from peer orientation or to prevent them from becoming peer-oriented, we have only one other option: to re-create functional villages of attachment within which to raise our child. We may not be able to put Humpty Dumpty together again, and we certainly cannot refashion obsolescent social and economic structures, but there is much that we *can* do to make things easier for ourselves and our children.

A house, as the saying·goes, is not a home. The problem with peer-oriented children is that they are still in our houses but no longer at home with us. They leave our houses to go "home" to be with one another. They use our phones to call "home." They go to school to be at "home" with their friends. They feel "homesick" when not in touch with one another. Their homing instincts have been skewed to bring them close to one another. Instead of preferring to be in the parents' houses, peer-oriented adolescents become like nomads, drifting together in groups or hanging out in malls. Home may be where they belong, but their sense of home is no longer with us.

Only in the context of an attachment village can we create homes for our children in the truest sense. Both home and the village are created by attachment. What makes the village a village is the connections among the people. Connections also make the home, whether they be to the home itself or to the people in it. We truly feel "at home" only with those we are attached to.

Only when a child is at home with those responsible for him can his developmental potential be fully realized. Helping children feel at home with the adults we entrust them to is one and the same task as creating a village of attachments for them to grow up in. In traditional attachment communities a child never had to leave home—he was at home wherever he went. Today children also shouldn't have to leave home, or at least the sense of being at home with the caring adults, until they are mature enough to be at home with their own true selves.

Attachment villages *can* be created, if we possess the vision and the drive. Like attachment itself, village building must become a conscious activity. We have no reason to pine over what no longer exists, but every reason to restore what is missing.

## DEVELOP A SUPPORTING CAST

We need to value our adult friends who exhibit an interest in our children and to find ways of fostering their relationships with them. We also need to put a high premium on creating customs and traditions that connect our children to extended family. Being related is not enough—genuine relationship is required. Unfortunately, many grandparents have also become too peer-oriented to assume their role in the attachment hierarchy. Many would rather be with their friends than their grandchildren, and in our mobile and fragmented society, many also live far away. If contact with our extended family is impossible or for some reason not in our child's best interests, we need to cultivate relationships with adults who are willing to fill in.

The way we socialize also needs to change. Socializing tends to be peer-oriented in North America, splitting along generational lines. Even when several generations are together, the activities seem to be peer-based: adults hang out with adults, children with children. To create villages of attachment, our socializing would need to cultivate hierarchical connections. During our stay in Provence, we saw that socializing almost always included the children. Meals were prepared, activities were selected, and outings were planned with this in mind. The adults took the lead in collecting the children. This kind of family socializing took us by surprise at first, but it made perfect sense from an attachment perspective. The greater the number of caring adults in a child's life, the more immune he or she will be to peer orientation. As much as possible, we should be participating with our children in villagelike activities that connect children to adults, whether through religious or ethnic centers, sports activities, cultural events, or in the community at large.

On a street around the corner from my coauthor's house the parents have organized themselves into what they call "the little block that can." Social relations are deliberately cultivated among the families living on this block. There are benches and picnic tables outside several of the homes where parents and kids of all ages gather. The children have learned to relate to all the adults on this street as attachment figures, surrogate aunts and uncles. Once a year the street is shut off to traffic for what, in effect, is a village festival. There are games, food is served, music is played from loudspeakers. The local fire department drives up with a red engine and children frolic in the spray of the fire hose.

Every parent needs a supporting cast, and the less one exists naturally, the more it needs to be cultivated by design. We all need someone to substitute for us from time to time, and most of us need to share our parenting responsibilities with others. Selecting these substitutes carefully and fostering our child's attachment to these adults should be our priority. It isn't enough that a nanny or babysitter is available, is trustworthy, and has passed the required courses. What makes it all work is for the child to accept the parental substitute as a working compass point and to feel at home with that person. This kind of relationship needs to be primed and cultivated. Including the potential candidate in some family activities and inviting him to a family meal may be just the kind of structure required to prime a connection.

Under today's conditions, in many families both parents need to work—to say nothing of the growing number of single-parent families. We cannot turn the clock back to some idealized past when one parent, usually the mother, stayed at home until the children were grown, or at least in school. Economically and culturally we have reached a different stage. But we do have to ensure that our kids form strong relationships with the adults we entrust to take our place—as I will explain in the next section.

My cowriter, Gabor, visited Mexico for the first time recently. He was impressed by the sheer happiness of the children he saw in the economically deprived Mayan villages along his route. "Joy shone from the faces of these kids," he says, "we observed none of the alienation and aggression one witnesses among kids in North America. There was a naive openness about them, an innocence, despite the harsh lives of their parents." The Mayans, like indigenous groups everywhere, practice "attachment parenting" without any consciousness of it. They carry their little ones about everywhere for the first few years and, in general, bring them up in traditional attachment villages. The idea of parents parting from infants or toddlers would strike them as strange. Similarly, according to a recent newspaper report, in Nairobi, Kenya, an entrepreneur who had opened a shop selling baby carriages to young mothers explained why business was slow. "Women here don't see why they would need a contraption in which to push their kids about," she said. "They just carry them wherever they go." And again, any visitor to Africa cannot help but notice the joyful spontaneity, the natural smiles, and freely loose bodily movements of the African child. That comes from close contact with loving adults in the attachment village. Alas, it's a culture now being devastated by war and famine in many places.

I bring up these examples not to blame our own culture, but to show what we have lost by way of instinctive, attachment-based parenting. We may not be able to return to such practices, but we have to compensate for their loss in any way we can. Hence my insistence that we do our very best to re-create the attachment village to the best of our abilities and to whatever extent our circumstances permit.

I am often asked at what age a child is ready to handle the separation of a parent's going back to work or, perhaps, leaving the child to go on a holiday. My answer is almost always a question about the nature of their supporting cast. Only attachment can create a substitute for a parent; hence, we need to cultivate those attachments. Our social culture is no longer doing that job. Along with bringing a baby into this world now comes the responsibility of creating our own supporting cast. If we became conscious of attachment and assumed this role, we might overhear conversations like this:

"How are you getting along with finding a good babysitter for Samantha?"

"We think we found someone who looks promising. Right now, they're in the kitchen together cooking up a storm. She seems to have Samantha's number. I want them to spend time together and for Samantha to be totally connected with her before I leave them on their own. After that, it should be a piece of cake."

Adult attachments are especially important in adolescence. When pushing away from parents, as maturing adolescents tend to do, having an alternative adult to turn to can keep the adolescent from turning to peers. If they are to serve this function, however, these relationships need to be cultivated long before the child reaches adolescence. If we are to be replaced, it would be much better with substitutes we had already handpicked.

## MATCHMAKE WITH THOSE RESPONSIBLE

In the traditional village, children's attachments were generated by the attachments of the parents. In most cases today we have little choice over the adults—for example, the teachers—to whom we must entrust our children. In these situations, the challenge is more to matchmake our children with those responsible for them. Matchmaking involves priming two persons in such a way that they are more likely to become attached to each other. We often matchmake quite instinctively to foster warm connections between siblings or, say, between our children and their grandparents. We need to employ this instinctive attachment dance in creating an attachment village.

Sometimes children attach spontaneously to those in charge: day-care workers, teachers, babysitters, grandparents. But if that is not the case, we needn't stand idly by. There is much we can do to facilitate a working relationship between the child and the one who is taking our place. Matchmakers usually have a number of tricks up their sleeves. Once the objective is clear to us, it's surprising how easily the rest will follow.

One of the most important tools is the introduction. An introduction is an opportunity to create friendly first impressions. It is also a natural way of giving our attachment blessing. We need to be seen by our child in friendly interaction with the person to whom we are about to pass the baton, whether that person is a preschool teacher, a day-care worker, a piano teacher, a ski instructor, the principal, or the classroom teacher. The trick is to seize the lead in becoming acquainted with the adult to whom we are entrusting our child and then to assume control of the introductions. It is a golden opportunity for matchmaking.

If we lived in a world in harmony with developmental design, parents and teachers would first establish friendly connections with each other, and then parents would assume their rightful role in making the introductions. School mixers, instead of bringing children together with their peers, would facilitate interaction among members of the adult attachment team. Structures would be in place to prepare passing our children smoothly from one adult to another. And yet what is the reality today? My coauthor and I were recently invited to lead a seminar for professionals in a British Columbia town. We learned to our surprise that the local high school was planning to hold a graduation ceremony without parents this year, on the grounds that enrollment had reached such numbers that no space was large enough to hold all the students and their relatives at the same time. Yet the town has several large facilities, including a hockey rink. Not lack of space but lack of awareness is the problem!

Another important instrument of matchmaking is to endear the unconnected parties to each other. Whether it is passing on compliments or interpreting signs of appreciation, the matchmaker's goal is to make it easy for the parties to like each other. Too often, we as parents skip this step and get on with discussing our concerns and the things that went wrong. Relationship is the context for working with the child and is, therefore, the priority. Relationship must be established first and foremost, before we deal with what does not work. As parents we must take the lead. All it takes is for us to become conscious of this objective and the rest should come quite naturally. For example, to the teacher we may find ourselves saying things like "You've made quite an impression on our daughter," "We can tell our son really likes you and is eager not to disappoint you," "Our son was asking about you when you were absent. He really missed you." To our child, we may say things like "Your teacher had some nice things to say about you," "He wouldn't take such an interest in you if you weren't important to him," "Your teacher said he missed you and hoped you'd get better soon." One can usually find something that can be interpreted in a positive way to prime a connection between one's child and the adult responsible for her.

All children need adult connections so they don't fall through the attachment cracks. When a child has enough adults to depend on as he moves from home to school to day care to playground, there is little danger of peer orientation taking root. Our job is to make sure the child is covered by a working attachment with an adult at all times and that we function as an attachment relay team. We need to make sure we have successfully passed the attachment baton before we let go. It's when we drop the baton that our children are in danger of getting collected by someone else.

There is no end to the kind of matchmaking that can be done. One school-based program, pioneered by Dr. Mel Shipman in the 1980s, began with matching senior citizens with elementary school children in Toronto's east side. The program involved only an hour of contact a week, but the positive impact of the cross-generational interactions had a ripple effect through the whole school. Many students considered these relationships to be life-changing, as did many of the participating elders. The success of the Riverdale Inter-Generational Project fueled a province-wide movement that now involves several hundred agencies in fostering caring connections between the generations.[1] This popular program has also spread to a number of states on the eastern seaboard. It is interesting that the instigators of this wonderful initiative, unaware of peer orientation, couldn't adequately explain their program's success. Once we factor in peer orientation, we can easily understand the beneficial effects of cross-generational contact. For both the young and the elderly, it satisfied a deep need.

A teacher who has formed a working relationship with a student has the power of matchmaker to facilitate relationships with other teachers and staff members responsible for the child—the librarian, the playground supervisor, the principal, the counselor, but especially next year's teacher. What a difference it would make if teachers would use their existing attachment power to create working relationships with other adults the student needs to depend on! My beloved Mrs. Ackerberg was the best thing that could have happened to me in the first grade, but had she played matchmaker with my second-grade teacher and passed the attachment baton, I might not have had to wait until fifth grade for an attachment with another teacher to take hold.

## DEFUSE THE COMPETITION

We live in a world rife with attachment competition. The potential for conflict exists every time our child forms a new attachment with someone we do not have a relationship with. Schools generate competing attachments. Divorce and remarriage generate competing attachments. Existing villages of attachment often disintegrate in the wake of competing attachments, rendering children much more susceptible to peer orientation. We must consciously defuse as much of this competition as possible, whether the competing attachments are with different adults in the child's life or between the parents and the peers.

Sometimes the competing attachment can be with another parent—a divorced parent, a stepparent, a foster parent. As much as it is possible to do so, it's important to convey to the child that closeness with one parent does not need to mean distance from the other. We need to turn what may seem to be either/or relationships into this-and-that relationships. We may do so by talking about the other parent in a friendly way and facilitating contact with the parent who is absent. Sometimes the competition will diminish for the child when she can perceive two of her parents interacting in a friendly way: sitting next to each other at a school function, cheering together at a child's baseball game, supporting the child at a music recital. Difficult as it may be for adults to rise above their differences, it is well worth the effort. Not only can the attachment village be preserved when closeness to one parent does not demand distance from another, it can even be expanded.

What is most often the case is that the competition, actual or potential, resides not with other adults but with the child's peers. There are hundreds of ways to defuse this divisiveness. Primarily, we can, ourselves, cultivate relationships with our child's friends, ensuring that we remain in the picture and that his connections also involve us. This may entail, for example, answering the phone and greeting your child's callers by name, even engaging in some conversation. Once children are sufficiently peer-oriented, they would often prefer to pretend we don't even exist. Our only hope to counter this is to insist on making ourselves present—in a friendly way, of course. The same thing is true for entering the house. Allowing our children's friends to enter by a back door or side door enables them to escape the normal attachment rituals of family greetings and introductions. Likewise, creating a separate area in the house where children can isolate themselves from us is the last thing we want to do. We want to get them into the common living areas where we can maintain connection and subvert the either/or mentality. When it comes to attachment, those who are not in relationship with us are likely to become our competition. What sometimes breaks the ice and brings them into relationship with us is serving them a meal in a family setting. I realize this kind of intervention isn't easy, but I speak from personal experience when I say that it's well worth the effort, as well as the awkwardness you may feel when you first try it.

When children reach adolescence, there is usually pressure on parents to facilitate peer get-togethers and parties. If peer orientation is in the air, the implicit or explicit message is for parents to make themselves scarce during this time. Again, it is important for parents to seize the lead, foil the polarization, and set a precedent. By the time Bria, our third daughter, arrived at this age, we were well practiced at this maneuver. When the inevitable request came along with the plea to make ourselves invisible, we took the initiative. Yes, of course she could have a party. No, of course we would not get lost. In fact, we would be very active hosts and put on a spread none of her friends could refuse. I decided to barbecue so I could ask each guest what they wanted and how they wanted it. Meanwhile, my unannounced agenda was to get into their face in a friendly way, make eye contact if possible, solicit a smile and a nod, get a name and try to remember it, and introduce myself as well. I enlisted Bria's little brothers as servers. The message would be clear—relating to Bria meant relating to her family. She was a package deal. When we presented our plan to be active and visible hosts, Bria's first reaction was to be mortified! She doubted it would ever work. She feared that none of her friends would come and that if they did would never talk to her again. Her fears were unfounded. I certainly was not able to make inroads with everyone, but I doubt the ones I failed with would have ever been inclined to show up again anyway. The kids it worked with were much more likely to seek the kind of relationship with our daughter that would not compete with us.

Yet another way of defusing potential competition is to cultivate relationships with the parents of our children's friends. In a preexisting village of attachment, we would already have a connection with the parents of the kids our children are interacting with. Not living in such a world, the only option we have is to build the village from the ground up—from our child's peers to their parents. If we fail to do this, the attachment world of our children remains splintered and fractured and full of inherent competition. We may not be able to control who our children's friends are, but if we can make friendly connections with the parents, we will bring some harmony and unity to their attachment world. Can we always succeed in doing this? Of course not. The differences may be too great to bridge. But we should, at least, try. The stakes are too high for us to ignore any opportunity.

My wife and I were fortunate in this regard with Bria. The parents of two of her close friends were most amenable to the idea of cultivating connections designed to bring the girls' worlds together. We had already developed a rapport with Bria's girlfriends, and the other parents had also done their homework. My agenda was to defuse the potential competition, creating a world where proximity with peers was not at the expense of proximity to parents. Village building worked better than I ever could have thought possible. The icing on the cake was Millennium New Year's Eve. Before the event, each one of us in the family had shared our fantasies about what we would like to happen on this special evening and what we wanted it to mean. Bria's fantasy was to be together with not only her best friends but her best friends' families, including their guests. We invited them all under our roof and spent the evening enjoying one another's company. We toasted the young women who inspired us to create a village from the bottom up, creating connections that otherwise would never have existed. The event was testimony to the fact that when peers and parents don't compete, our children can have both.

Only when their attachment world splinters do peers and parents live in different spheres. Our challenge is to create the kind of attachment relationships with our children, and the kind of attachment village for them to live in, where peers can be included without parents being displaced.

Because childhood is a function of immaturity, the duration of childhood is increasing in our society. At the same time, since true parenthood is a matter of relationship and exists only while the child is actively attaching to us, the duration of hands-on parenthood is rapidly decreasing. This is where peer orientation comes in: when attachments are skewed, we lose our parenthood. For parenthood to fade before the end of childhood is disastrous for both parent and child. When we are stripped of our parenthood, our children lose the positive aspects of childhood. They remain immature, but are deprived of the innocence, vulnerability, and childlike openness required for growth and for the unfettered enjoyment of what life has to offer. They are cheated of their full legacy as human beings.

Who is to raise our kids? The resounding answer, the only answer compatible with nature, is that we—the parents and other adults concerned with the care of children—must be their mentors, their guides, their nurturers, and their models. We need to hold on to our children until our work is done. We need to hold on not for selfish purposes but so they can venture forth, not to hold them back but so they can fulfill their developmental destinies. We need to hold on to them until they can hold on to themselves.

# GLOSSARY

**adapt/adaptation/adaptive process**
The adaptive process refers to that natural growth force by which a child is changed—develops emotionally or learns new realities—as a result of coming to terms with something that cannot be changed. This is the process by which children learn from their mistakes and benefit from failure. This is also the process by which adversity changes a child for the better.

**adolescence**
I am using the term *adolescence* to refer to the bridge between childhood and adulthood. It generally refers to that time from the onset of puberty to the assumption of adult roles in society.

**affair**
See *attachment affair*.

**alarm**
See *attachment alarm*.

**attachment**
In scientific terms, an attachment refers to the drive or relationship characterized by the pursuit and preservation of proximity. Proximity is Latin for "nearness." In its broadest definition, human attachment includes the movement toward nearness of every kind: physical, emotional, and psychological.

### attachment affair

Take away the sexual connotation and this analogy works for peer orientation. The essence of a marital affair is when an outside attachment competes with or takes away from contact and closeness with a spouse. It is when peer attachments draw a child away from parents that they damage development.

### attachment alarm

Human brains are programmed to alarm their hosts when facing separation from those to whom they are attached. The attachment alarm functions on many levels: instinct, emotion, behavior, chemistry, and feeling. If the alarm is felt, it can be experienced as fear, anxiety, conscience, nervousness, or apprehension and will generally move a child to caution. If this alarm is not felt consciously, it can manifest itself as tension or agitation.

### attachment brain

A term for the parts of the brain and nervous system that serve attachment. It does not refer to one particular location but rather a particular function of the brain shared by several brain regions. Many other creatures have this attachment functioning as part of their brain apparatus, but human beings alone have the capacity to become conscious of the attachment process.

### attachment conscience

Refers to the bad feelings that are triggered in a person—especially a child—when he is thinking, doing, or considering something that would evoke disapproval, distancing, or disappointment in those to whom he is attached. The attachment conscience helps to keep children close to their attachment figures—ideally, their parents. When a child becomes peer-oriented, the attachment conscience serves the peer relationship.

### attachment dance

See *collecting dance.*

### attachment dominance

To facilitate dependence, attachment automatically assigns a person into a dependent care-seeking position or a dominant caregiving position. This is especially true of immature creatures, such as children—or immature adults, for that matter. Children are meant to be in a dependent care-seeking position with the adults responsible for them.

### attachment frustration

The frustration that is evoked when attachments do not work: when contact is thwarted or when a sense of connection is lost.

**attachment incompatibility**
Attachments are incompatible when a child cannot preserve closeness or a sense of connection in two relationships simultaneously. Incompatibility is created when, for example, the child gets one set of cues for how to act and how to be from parents and a completely different set from peers. The more incompatible the working attachments, the more likely attachment will polarize.

**attachment reflex**
There are many primitive attachment reflexes designed to preserve proximity through the senses. The infant grasping the parent's finger pressed into her palm is one example.

**attachment village**
The network of attachments that provide the context within which to raise a child. In traditional societies, the attachment village corresponded to the actual village in which people lived and grew up. In our society, we have to create the attachment village.

**attachment void**
The absence of a sense of contact or connection with those one should be attached to.

**backing into attachments**
Establishing likeness or connection with someone through distancing and alienating others. Two children, for example, will draw close to each other by insulting or belittling a third.

**bipolar nature of attachment**
Like magnetism, attachment is polarized. Whenever proximity is pursued with one person or a group, contact and closeness with others is resisted. The child will especially resist those whom he perceives as competition to those with whom he is actively seeking attachment. When the child becomes peer-oriented, these others are the parents and other nurturing adults.

**collecting dance**
A term referring to the human courting instincts that are meant to get others attached to us. I have chosen the term *collecting* to get rid of the sexual connotations that are associated with courting and wooing. The "dance" refers to the interactive aspect of this process.

**compass point**
Used here to refer to the human point of reference that is created by attachment from which a child gets his bearings and takes his cues. Every child needs a human compass point.

**competing attachment**
See *attachment incompatibility*.

**counterwill**
This term refers to the human instinct to resist pressure and coercion. This instinct serves attachment in keeping children from being unduly influenced by those they are not attached to. Counterwill, unless magnified by peer orientation or other factors, also serves development in making way for the formation of a child's own will by fending off the will of others.

**defended against vulnerability**
The human brain is designed to protect against a sense of vulnerability that is too overwhelming. When these protective mechanisms are chronic and pervasive, it leads to a state of being defended against vulnerability. These protective mechanisms involve emotional and perceptual filters that screen out information that the person would find wounding and painful.

**defensive detachment**
See *detachment*.

**detachment**
This term refers to a resistance to proximity; such resistance is one defense against vulnerability. Most often, contact and closeness is resisted to avoid the wounding of separation. This instinctive reaction is a common defense mechanism but if it becomes stuck and pervasive, it destroys the context for parenting and for healthy development.

**differentiation**
Refers to the growth process of separating or individuating. If attachment with nurturing adults is the first phase of development, differentiation is the second. Entities or beings must first be sufficiently differentiated before they can be successfully integrated. For this reason, healthy differentiation must precede socialization, otherwise the person will not be able to experience togetherness without losing his sense of self.

**dominance**
See *attachment dominance*.

**emergent**
See *emergent process*.

**emergent energy**
See *emergent process*.

**emergent process**
That life process of differentiation whose goal is a child's viability as a separate being. It is characterized by a venturing-forth kind of energy that arises spontaneously from within the developing child. One sees it in toddlers. This process is spontaneous but not at all inevitable—it depends on a child's attachment needs being met. The emergent process gives rise to many of the attributes we find desirable in a child: sense of responsibility, accountability, curiosity, interest, boundaries, respect for others, individuality, personhood.

**emotion**
The term has two root meanings: "to be stirred up" and "to move." Emotion is what moves the child, at least until intentions have become strong enough to determine behavior. Any creature with a limbic system, the emotional part of the brain, has emotion, but only humans are capable of being conscious of their emotion. The conscious part we call feelings. Emotion has many aspects: chemical, physiological, and motivational. Emotions do not have to be felt to move us—often we are driven by unconscious emotions.

**emotional intimacy**
A sense of closeness and connection that is felt emotionally.

**flatlining of culture**
The loss of the traditional vertical transmission of culture in which customs and traditions are handed down from generation to generation. It is also a play on words that connotes the death of culture, as in the "flatlining" of brain waves.

**flight from vulnerability**
See *defended against vulnerability.*

**identification**
A form of attachment in which one becomes the same as the person or thing attached to. For example, to attach to a role is to identify with a role.

**immediacy principle**
The principle of learning theory that holds that to obtain a change in behavior, one must intervene immediately when a child is out of line. This principle was derived from studies with pigeons and rats.

**individualism**
This term is often confused with individuality and gives it a bad name. Individualism refers to the idea that the needs of the individual are paramount over the needs of the group or the community. This confusion often leads people to think that individuation is the opposite of community, as opposed to the prerequisite for true community.

**individuality**

That part of personality that is indivisible and is not shared by anyone else. Individuality is the fruit of the process of becoming a psychologically separate being that culminates in the full flowering of one's uniqueness. To be an individual is to have one's own meanings, one's own ideas and boundaries. It is to value one's own preferences, principles, intentions, perspectives, and goals. It is to stand in a place occupied by no other.

**individuation**

The process of becoming an individual, distinct and differentiated from others, and viable as a separate being. This concept is often confused with individualism, defined above.

**instinct**

By instinct is meant the deep urges or impulses to act that are common to all humans. Since attachment is the preeminent drive, most of our instincts serve attachment. The source of these impulses to act is deep within the limbic system of the human brain. Human instincts, however, like the instincts of other creatures, need the appropriate stimuli from the environment to be properly triggered. They are not necessarily automatic.

**integration process**

The natural growth force involving the mixing of separate entities. In this book, we use this phrase to refer to the developmental process that occurs as different elements of the personality come together to create a new whole — for example, hostile emotions can be integrated with feelings that would check them, such as compassion or anxiety. It is this mixing that produces perspective, balance, emotional maturity, and social maturity. The essence of integration, in the social realm, is mixing without blending, or togetherness without the loss of separateness. This requires sufficient prior differentiation.

**integrative mind**

When the integrative process is active, the mind collects the thought or feeling that would conflict with whatever is in focus. This brings balance and perspective.

**integrative functioning**

See *integration process.*

**intuition**

When I use this term, I am usually referring to knowledge that is sensed rather than known, unconscious as opposed to conscious. Our intuition will only be as good as our insight, however. The more accurate we are in our perceptions, the more we can trust our intuition.

### maturation

That process by which a child comes to realize his or her human potentials. Although psychological growth is spontaneous, it is not inevitable. If circumstances are not conducive, a child can age without ever truly growing up. The three primary processes by which children mature are emergence, adaptation, and integration.

### orient/orienting/orientation

To orient is to get one's bearings. As human beings, this involves not only getting a sense of where one is but also who one is and how much one matters. It also entails making meaning of one's surroundings. A significant part of orienting is to get one's cues for how to be and what to do, for what is important and what is expected. As long as children are not yet able to orient themselves, they orient by those they are attached to. Peer-oriented children look to their peers, not to adults, to get their bearings and for their cues on how to be, how to see themselves, on what values to pursue.

### orienting void (orientation void)

Because children orient by those they are attached to, they feel lost and disoriented when the sense of connection is gone. This void of cues and meanings is intolerable for children, usually forcing reattachment to someone or something—in our culture, most often this reattachment is to peers.

### parental impotence

I am using this term in the strictest meaning of the word: *lacking sufficient power.* Parents need to be empowered by their child's attachment to them to fulfill their parental responsibilities. The weaker this bond, the more impotent the parent becomes.

### parenthood

By parenthood I am referring to the office of parenting, in the way the ancient Romans used the word—a special duty, charge, or position conferred upon a person. For the Romans, this special work was conferred upon them by their government. For parents, this special service is something that can be conferred only by the attachment of a child. Being the biological parent, adoptive parent, or stepparent does not automatically mean parenthood in this sense—only through the attachment of the child is a parent inducted into office and equipped for service.

### power to parent

Many people confuse power with force. By power I mean not coercion or punishments but the natural authority that parents have when their children are actively connecting with them and look to them for their cues on how to be, how to behave, what values to pursue. In fact, the more power we have, the less we need to resort to force—and vice versa.

**preschooler syndrome**
I use this term to describe the set of traits and problems that results from a lack of
integrative functioning in children. Normal in preschoolers, I dub these traits and
problems the preschooler syndrome when they characterize children and adolescents who are no longer preschoolers but have not grown out of this developmental deficiency. In our culture, peer orientation is the most common cause of such
arrested development.

**psychological immaturity**
See *maturation.*

**psychological intimacy**
A feeling of closeness or connection that comes from being seen or heard in the
sense of being known or understood.

**scripting**
The scripting analogy is borrowed from the profession of acting where the behavior must be acted out because it does not originate in the actor. Such is the case
with maturity. Social situations demand a maturity that our children may not yet
have attained. We cannot make them grow up on command but we may be able
to get them to act mature in given situations by providing the cues for what to do
and how to do it. For a child to accept such direction, the adult must be in the position of cue-giver in the child's life, a fruit of the child's attachment to the parent.
Good scripting focuses on what to do instead of what not to do, and provides cues
that can be easily followed by the child.

**sense of agency**
The Latin roots of "agent" mean "to drive" as in *to drive a chariot.* To have a sense
of agency is to feel as if one is in the driver's seat of life—a place in which options
appear and choices exist. Children are not born with a sense of agency; it is a fruit
of the maturing process of emergence or individuation.

**socialization**
The process of becoming fit for society. This has been traditionally perceived as a
singular process, separate and distinct from the other two important developmental processes, attachment and individuation. Upon closer examination, however,
most socialization happens through attachment and the processes that serve it—
identification, emulation, quest for significance, the preservation of proximity. Attachment is the first of these three developmental processes, differentiation the
second. When these two are functioning well, true socialization can occur spontaneously.

**teachability**
To be teachable is to be receptive to being taught and motivated to learn. The

teachability factor refers to those aspects in the learning equation that are psychological, relational, and emotional in nature. Teachability is not the same as intelligence. A child can be very smart and completely unteachable and vice versa.

### tears of futility

It is a human reflex to cry when futility sinks in, especially if the frustration has been intense. The corresponding feelings are ones of sadness and disappointment. Futility is what we experience when something will not work or cannot work. When futility registers emotionally, signals are sent to the lacrimal glands resulting in the eyes watering. These tears are different from the tears of frustration. The experience of getting that something is futile and the accompanying feelings of sadness and letting go are important for a child's development. Peer-oriented kids are remarkably lacking in tears of futility.

### temper

I use the term in its root meaning which denotes a *mix*. Temperament is a *mix* of traits, temperature a *mix* of hot and cold, etc. The Romans used this term to describe the proper *mix* of ingredients to make potter's clay. The key to civilized behavior and self-control is mixed feelings. To lose one's temper would have meant, therefore, to lose the mix of conflicting impulses and feelings that would enable self-control.

### tempering element

The thoughts, feelings, or intentions that would arrest the impulses to act in inappropriate ways—for example, love would temper a desire to hurt, fear of consequences can temper an impulse to act in a destructive way, or the capacity to see another person's point of view tempers a tendency to be dogmatic. Such tempering brings balance to personality or perspective to perception.

### untempered

By untempered is meant unmixed or unmitigated or one-sided. To be untempered is to be lacking any sense of internal dialogue, conflict, or discord in consciousness. The primary sign of emotional and social immaturity is untempered experience and expression. The untempered person has no mixed feelings about anything. See also *temper*.

### vulnerable/vulnerability

To be vulnerable is to be capable of being wounded. As humans, not only can we feel our wounds but our vulnerability as well. The human brain is designed to protect against a sense of vulnerability that is too overwhelming. See also *defended against vulnerability*.

# NOTES

CHAPTER 1: WHY PARENTS MATTER MORE THAN EVER

1. Judith Harris, *The Nuture Assumption* (New York: Simon & Schuster, 1999).

2. Michael Rutter and David J. Smith, eds., *Psychosocial Disorders in Young People: Time Trends and Their Causes* (New York: John Wiley and Sons, Inc., 1995).

3. This was the conclusion of Professor David Shaffer, a leading researcher and text-book writer in developmental psychology, after reviewing the literature on peer influence. Commenting on the current research, he states ". . . it is fair to say that peers are the primary reference group for questions of the form 'Who am I?' " (David R. Shaffer, *Developmental Psychology: Childhood and Adolescence*, 2nd ed. [Pacific Grove, Calif.: Brooks/Cole Publishers, 1989], p. 65.)

4. The suicide statistics are from the National Center for Injury Prevention and Control in the United States and from the McCreary Centre Society in Canada. The statistics on suicide attempts are even more alarming. Urie Bronfenbrenner cites statistics that indicate that adolescent suicide attempts almost tripled in the twenty-year period between 1955 and 1975. (Urie Bronfenbrenner, "The Challenges of Social Change to Public Policy and Development Research." Paper presented at the biennial meeting of the Society for Research and Child Development, Denver, Colorado, April 1975).

5. *Harper's*, December 2003.

6. Professor James Coleman published his findings in a book entitled *The Adolescent Society* (New York: Free Press, 1961).

CHAPTER 3: WHY WE'VE COME UNDONE

1. John Bowlby, *Attachment*, 2nd ed. (New York: Basic Books, 1982), p. 46.

2. Robert Bly, *The Sibling Society* (New York: Vintage Books, 1977), p. 132.

3. These were the findings when two scholars examined the results of ninety-two studies involving thirteen thousand children. In addition to more school and behavior problems, they also suffered more negative self-concepts and had more trouble getting along with parents. Their findings were published in *Psychological Bulletin* 110 (1991): 26–46. The article is entitled "Parental Divorce and the Well-being of Children: A Meta-analysis." Indirectly related is a 1996 survey by Statistics Canada that found children of single parents much more likely to have repeated a grade, be diagnosed with conduct disorder, or to have problems with anxiety, depression, and aggression.

4. Research by the British psychiatrist Sir Michael Rutter brings home this point. He found that behavioral problems were even more likely in children living in intact but discordant marriages than in children of divorce who were living in homes relatively free of conflict. (Michael Rutter, "Parent-Child Separation: Psychological Effects on the Children," *Journal of Child Psychology and Psychiatry* 12 [1971]: 233–256.)

5. Bly, *The Sibling Society*, p. 36.

6. Erik Erikson, *Childhood and Society* (New York: W.W. Norton, 1985).

CHAPTER 5: FROM HELP TO HINDRANCE: WHEN ATTACHMENT WORKS AGAINST US

1. John Bowlby, *Attachment*, 2nd ed. (New York: Basic Books, 1982), p. 377.

CHAPTER 6: COUNTERWILL: WHY CHILDREN BECOME DISOBEDIENT

1. M. R. Lepper, D. Greene, and R. E. Nisbett, "Undermining Children's Intrinsic Interest with Extrinsic Rewards: A Test of the Over-justification Hypothesis," *Journal of Personality and Social Psychology* 28 (1973):129–137.

2. Edward Deci, *Why We Do What We Do: Understanding Self-Motivation* (New York: Penguin Books, 1995), pp. 18 and 25.

CHAPTER 7: THE FLATLINING OF CULTURE

1. Howard Gardner, *Developmental Psychology*, 2nd ed. (New York: Little, Brown & Company, 1982).

2. *The Globe and Mail*, April 12, 2004.

3. *Vancouver Sun*, August 30, 2003.

CHAPTER 8: THE DANGEROUS FLIGHT FROM FEELING

1. A sample of such studies would include:

- J. D. Coie and A. N. Gillessen, "Peer Rejection: Origins and Effects on Children's Development," *Current Directions in Psychological Science* 2 (1993):89–92.
- P. L. East, L. E. Hess, and R. M. Lerner, "Peer Social Support and Adjustment of Early Adolescent Peer Groups," *Journal of Early Adolescence* 7 (1987):153–163.
- K. A. Dodge, G. S. Pettit, C. L. McClaskey, and M. M. Brown, "Social Compe-

tence in Children," *Monographs of the Society for Research in Child Development* 51 (1986).

2. The most extensive study was the National Longitudinal Study of Adolescent Health in the United States, which involved some ninety thousand American teens. The study by psychologist Michael Resnick and a dozen of his colleagues was entitled "Protecting Adolescents from Harm: Findings from the National Longitudinal Study on Adolescent Health" and published in the *Journal of the American Medical Association* in September 1997. This is also the conclusion of the late Julius Segal, one of the pioneers of resilience research, as well as the authors of *Raising Resilient Children*, Robert Brooks and Sam Goldstein. (R. Brooks and S. Goldstein, *Raising Resilient Children* [New York: Contemporary Books, 2001].)

3. Segal is quoted by Robert Brooks, Ph.D., of Harvard Medical School in his article "Self-worth, Resilience and Hope: The Search for Islands of Competence." This article can be found in the electronic reading room of the Center for Development & Learning. The url address is www.cdl.org/resources/reading_room/self_worth.html.

4. John Bowlby, *Loss* (New York: Basic Books, 1980), p. 20.

CHAPTER 9: STUCK IN IMMATURITY

1. Robert Bly, *The Sibling Society* (New York:Vintage Books, 1977), p. vii.

2. For a full discussion on the physiological aspects of human brain development and their relationship to psychological growth, see Geraldine Dawson and Kurt W. Fischer, *Human Behavior and the Developing Brain* (New York: Guildford Press, 1994), especially chapter 10.

3. Carl Rogers, *On Becoming a Person* (New York: Houghton Mifflin, 1995), p. 283.

CHAPTER 10: A LEGACY OF AGGRESSION

1. This statistic was cited by Linda Clark of the New York City Board of Education, in an address to the 104th annual meeting of the American Psychological Association.

2. These statistics were cited by Michelle Borba, author of *Building Moral Intelligence*, in an address to a national conference on safe schools, held in Burnaby, British Columbia, February 19, 2001.

3. The report by Barbara Cottrell is called *Parent Abuse: The Abuse of Parents by Their Teenage Children*. It was published by Health Canada in 2001.

4. This survey was conducted by David Lyon and Kevin Douglas of Simon Fraser University in British Columbia and released in October of 1999.

5. The suicide statistics are from the National Center for Injury Prevention and Control in the United States and from the McCreary Centre Society in Canada.

6. W. Craig and D. Pepler, *Naturalistic Observations of Bullying and Victimization on the Playground* (1997), LaMarsh Centre for Research on Violence and Conflict Resolution, York University, quoted in Barbara Coloroso, *The Bully, the Bullied, and the Bystander* (Toronto: HarperCollins, 2002), p. 66.

7. According to U.S. government statistics, alcohol is involved in 68 percent of manslaughters, 62 percent of assaults, 54 percent of murders or attempted murders, 48 percent of robberies, 44 percent of burglaries, and 42 percent of rapes. An online reference for these government statistics is *www.health.org/govpubs/m1002*.

CHAPTER 11: THE MAKING OF BULLIES AND VICTIMS

1. Natalie Angier, "When Push Comes to Shove," *New York Times*, May 20, 2001.

2. S. H. Verhovek, "Can Bullying Be Outlawed," *New York Times*, March 11, 2001.

3. W. Craig and D. Pepler, *Naturalistic Observations of Bullying and Victimization on the Playground* (1997), LaMarsh Centre for Research on Violence and Conflict Resolution, York University, quoted in Barbara Coloroso, *The Bully, the Bullied, and the Bystander* (Toronto: HarperCollins, 2002), p. 66.

4. Stephen Suomi is a primatologist at the National Institute of Child Health and Human Development in Maryland. It is here that he studied the effects of rearing environments on the behavior of young rhesus macaques. His findings have been published in S. J. Suomie, "Early Determinants of Behaviour. Evidence from Primate Studies," *British Medical Bulletin* 53 (1997):170–184. His work is also reviewed by Karen Wright in "Babies, Bonds and Brains" in *Discover Magazine*, October 1997.

5. Natalie Armstrong, "Study Finds Boys Get Rewards for Poor Behaviour," *Vancouver Sun*, January 17, 2000.

6. Angier, "When Push Comes to Shove."

CHAPTER 12: A SEXUAL TURN

1. Study published in the *Canadian Journal of Human Sexuality*, reported in *Maclean's Magazine*, April 9, 2001.

2. *The Globe and Mail*, April 24, 2004, p. A6.

3. Barbara Kantrowitz and Pat Wingert, "The Truth About Tweens," *Newsweek*, October 18, 1999.

4. Our source for this is Dr. Helen Fisher's book *Anatomy of Love* (New York: Ballantine Books, 1992). Dr. Fisher is an anthropologist at the American Museum of Natural History and is the recipient of a number of prestigious awards in recognition of her work.

5. These were the conclusions reached by Dr. Alba DiCenso of McMaster University and her colleagues (G. Guyatt, A. Willan, and L. Griffith) when assimilating and reviewing the findings of twenty-six previous studies from 1970 to 2000. This substantial study was published in the *British Medical Journal* in June of 2002 (vol. 324) under the title "Intervention to Reduce Unintended Pregnancies Among Adolescents: Systematic Review of Randomized Controlled Trials."

CHAPTER 13: UNTEACHABLE STUDENTS

1. One example is the authors' home province of British Columbia, for example, where educators and school trustees were perplexed by a 2003 study that showed such a decline.

2. Fueling this peer-learning model in education circles is an unfortunate misunderstanding of the ideas of Jean Piaget, the great Swiss developmentalist, on cooperative learning. Piaget did indeed state that children learn best when interacting with one another. Not taken into account is the developmental perspective within which he was theorizing—the idea that a strong sense of self needs to emerge before peer interaction can facilitate true learning. According to Piaget, it was only as children came to know their own minds that interacting with one another would sharpen and deepen their understandings. He perceived authoritarian teachers as having a dampening effect on this process of cognitive individuation, at least in comparison with the more egalitarian relationship of peers. Piaget's theories were formulated forty years ago in continental Europe where students were highly adult-oriented and the educational system hierachical. In North America, Piaget's idea was taken out of developmental context and applied in a completely different social milieu. Completely severed from its original moorings in adult attachment, the peer learning model has become the rage among educational theoreticians.

There is nothing wrong with Piaget's idea in the proper setting: cooperative learning does stimulate thinking, but only with those children who have formed their own ideas about a subject in the first place and are capable of operating from two points of view simultaneously. Otherwise, the interaction serves to suppress budding individuality, discourage originality, and facilitate peer dependence.

CHAPTER 14: COLLECTING OUR CHILDREN

1. Allan Schore, *Affect Regulation and the Origin of the Self: The Neurobiology of Emotional Development* (Hillsdale, N.J.: Lawrence Erlbaum Associates, 1994), pp. 199–200.

2. Stanley Greenspan, *The Growth of the Mind* (Reading, Mass.: Addison-Wesley, 1996).

CHAPTER 17: DON'T COURT THE COMPETITION

1. This has been a consistent finding across numerous studies. An example of such a study is R. E. Marcon, "Moving Up the Grades: Relationship Between Preschool Model and Later School Success," *Early Childhood Research & Practice* vol. 4, No. 1 (Spring 2002).

2. This according to a special *Time* article (August 27, 2001) on home education. There is good reason for this apparently, as students educated at home achieve the highest grades on standarized tests and outperform other students on college entrance exams, including the Scholastic Aptitude Test (SAT).

3. Jon Reider was quoted in G. A. Clowes, "Home-Educated Students Rack Up Honours," *School Reform News*, July 2000.

4. Bureau of Labor Statistics, U.S. Department of Labor, Washington, D.C., 2000.

5. Sarah E. Watamura, Bonny Donzella, Jan Alwin, Megan R. Gunnar, "Morning-to-Afternoon Increases in Cortisol Concentrations for Infants and Toddlers at Child Care: Age Differences and Behavioural Correlates," *Child Development* 74 (2003): 1006–1021.

6. Carol Lynn Martin and Richard A. Fabes, "The Stability and Consequences of Young Children's Same-Sex Peer Interactions," *Developmental Psychology* 37 (2001): 431–446.

7. Early Child Care Research Network, National Institute of Child Health and Human Development, "Does Amount of Time Spent in Child Care Predict Socio-emotional Adjustment During the Transition of Kindergarten?" *Child Development* 74 (2003):976–1005.

8. Stanley I. Greenspan, "Child Care Research: A Clinical Perspective," *Child Development* 74 (2003):1064–1068.

9. Eleanor Maccoby, emerita professor of developmental psychology at Stanford University, was interviewed by Susan Gilbert of the *New York Times* for her article "Turning a Mass of Data on Child Care into Advice for Parents," published July 22, 2003.

10. This study is discussed in Cornell University professor Urie Bronfenbrenner's book *Two Worlds of Childhood* (New York: Russel Sage Foundation, 1970).

11. The former textbook writer is Judith Harris and she makes this claim repeatedly in her book *The Nuture Assumption* (New York: Simon & Schuster, 1999).

12. The first literature on self-esteem was unequivocal regarding the role of the parent. Carl Rogers and Dorothy Briggs—among many others—held that a parent's view of the child was the most important influence on how a child came to think of him- or herself. Unfortunately, parents have been replaced as the mirrors in which children now seek a reflection of themselves.

Contemporary literature and research reflect only what *is*, not what *should be* or what *could be*. In our attempts to find out about children, researchers ask questions about where they get their sense of significance and about who matters most to them. The more peer-oriented children become, the more they indicate their peers as the ones that count. When this research is published, the results obtained from peer-oriented young subjects are presented as normal, without any attempt to place them into some kind of historical or developmental context. To further complicate the issue, self-esteem tests are constructed using questions that focus on peer relationships, closing the circle of illogic. Thus, psychologists are led astray by the skewed instincts of the children they are studying. The conclusions and recommendations derived from such research are tainted by the peer orientation dynamic that created the very problems the hapless researchers were trying to address!

CHAPTER 18: RE-CREATE THE ATTACHMENT VILLAGE

1. The Historical Chronology of Intergeneration Programming in Ontario is published on the Internet by United Generations.

# INDEX

GORDON NEUFELD, PH.D., a clinical psychologist in private practice in Vancouver, British Columbia, has spent much of his professional life creating coherent theories for understanding child development. He is nationally recognized for his work on aggression and violence among children and youth and appears regularly on radio and television, both in Vancouver and nationally. More information about his work can be found on his website: www. GordonNeufeld.com.

GABOR MATÉ, M.D., is a Canadian physician and author. His most recent book, *When the Body Says No: Understanding the Stress-Disease Connection*, was a best-seller in Canada and has been published in many languages. He currently works for a clinic for street people and is writing a book on addiction. Dr. Maté lives in Vancouver, British Columbia. Visit his website at www.drgabormate.com.

ABOUT THE TYPE

This book was set in Electra, a typeface designed for Linotype by W. A. Dwiggins, the renowned type designer (1880–1956). Electra is a fluid typeface, avoiding the contrasts of thick and thin strokes that are prevalent in most modern typefaces.